A VERY DIFFERENT STORY

Studies on the Fiction of Charlotte Perkins Gilman

Liverpool Science Fiction Texts and Studies
General Editor DAVID SEED

Series Advisers

I. F. Clarke, Edward James, Patrick Parrinder and Brian Stableford

1. Robert Crossley *Olaf Stapledon: Speaking for the Future*
ISBN 0-85323-388-8 (hardback)

2. David Seed (ed.) *Anticipations: Essays on Early Science Fiction and its Precursors*
ISBN 0-85323-348-9 (hardback), ISBN 0-85323-418-3 (paperback)

3. Jane L. Donawerth and Carol A. Kolmerten (eds) *Utopian and Science Fiction by Women: Worlds of Difference*
ISBN 0-85323-269-5 (hardback), ISBN 0-85323-279-2 (paperback)

4. Brian W. Aldiss *The Detached Retina: Aspects of SF and Fantasy*
ISBN 0-85323-289-X (hardback), ISBN 0-85323-299-7 (paperback)

5. Carol Farley Kessler *Charlotte Perkins Gilman: Her Progress Toward Utopia, with Selected Writings*
ISBN 0-85323-489-2 (hardback), ISBN 0-85323-499-X (paperback)

6. Patrick Parrinder *Shadows of the Future: H. G. Wells, Science Fiction and Prophecy*
ISBN 0-85323-439-6 (hardback), ISBN 0-85323-449-3 (paperback)

7. I. F. Clarke (ed.) *The Tale of the Next Great War, 1871–1914: Fictions of Future Warfare and of Battles Still-to-come*
ISBN 0-85323-269-5 (hardback), ISBN 0-85323-279-2 (paperback)

8. Joseph Conrad and Ford Madox Ford (Foreword by George Hay, Introduction by David Seed) *The Inheritors*
ISBN 0-85323-560-0 (hardback)

9. Qingyun Wu *Female Rule in Chinese and English Literary Utopias*
ISBN 0-85323-570-8 (hardback), ISBN 0-85323-449-3 (paperback)

10. John Clute *Look at the Evidence: Essays and Reviews*
ISBN 0-85323-820-0 (hardback), ISBN 0-85323-830-8 (paperback)

11. Roger Luckhurst *'The Angle Between Two Walls': The Fiction of J. G. Ballard*
ISBN 0-85323-821-9 (hardback), ISBN 0-85323-831-6 (paperback)

12. I. F. Clarke (ed.) *The Great War with Germany, 1890–1914: Fictions and Fantasies of the War-to-come*
ISBN 0-85323-632-1 (hardback), ISBN 0-85323-642-9 (paperback)

13. Franz Rottensteiner (ed.) *View from Another Shore: European Science Fiction*
ISBN 0-85323-932-0 (hardback), ISBN 0-85323-942-8 (paperback)

14. Val Gough and Jill Rudd (eds) *A Very Different Story: Studies in the Fiction of Charlotte Perkins Gilman*
ISBN 0-85323-591-0 (hardback), ISBN 0-85323-601-1 (paperback)

15. Gary Westfahl *The Mechanics of Wonder: the Creation of the Idea of Science Fiction*
ISBN 0-85323-563-5 (hardback), ISBN 0-85323-573-2 (paperback)

A VERY DIFFERENT STORY

Studies on the Fiction of Charlotte Perkins Gilman

Edited by
Val Gough and Jill Rudd

LIVERPOOL UNIVERSITY PRESS

First published 1998 by
LIVERPOOL UNIVERSITY PRESS
Liverpool L69 3BX

All the essays in this volume appear in print for the first time except for 'Utopian Fictions and Political Theories' by Ruth Levitas which is based in part upon her earlier essay 'Who Holds the Hose: Domestic Labour in Bellamy, Gilman and Morris', which appeared in *Utopian Studies*.

British Library Cataloguing-in-Publication Data
A British Library CIP record is available

ISBN 0-85323-591-0 (hardback)
ISBN 0-85323-601-1 (paperback)

Typeset in 10/12.5pt Meridien by
XL Publishing Services, Lurley, Tiverton

Printed and bound in Great Britain by
Marston Lindsay Ross International Ltd,
Oxfordshire

Contents

Abbreviations

H	Charlotte Perkins Gilman, *Herland* (1st pub. 1915), intro. by Ann J. Lane (London: Women's Press, 1979)
L	Charlotte Perkins Gilman, *The Living of Charlotte Perkins Gilman: An Autobiography*, intro. by Ann J. Lane (Madison: University of Wisconsin Press, 1991)
OW	Charlotte Perkins Stetson, *In This Our World* (Boston: Small, Maynard & Co., 1899)
R	Charlotte Perkins Gilman, *The Charlotte Perkins Gilman Reader*, ed. Ann J. Lane (London: Women's Press, 1981)
SS	Charlotte Perkins Gilman, *'The Yellow Wallpaper' and Selected Stories*, ed. Denise D. Knight (Newark: Delaware Press, 1994)
YW	Charlotte Perkins Gilman, *The Yellow Wallpaper* (1st pub. 1892), afterword by Elaine R. Hedges (London: Virago Press, 1981 or New York: The Feminist Press, 1973)

Acknowledgements

The editors would like to thank the British Academy for their generous support of the international conference on Charlotte Perkins Gilman which took place at Liverpool University in June 1995. Opus Technology also acted as sponsors of that event. There are many who contributed to the organization of the conference, but we are particularly grateful to Professor Miriam Allott who provided invaluable support and advice at all stages of the process. Thanks are also due to the Department of English at the University of Liverpool. Without the meticulous help of Rachel Connor in the preparation of the manuscript, our role as editors would have been a much more arduous one. Finally, we are grateful to Robin Bloxsidge at Liverpool University Press, who gave invaluable support to the project from its inception.

Contributors

Janet Beer is Professor and Head of English at Manchester Metropolitan University. Her teaching and research interests are in nineteenth- and early twentieth-century American women's writing and contemporary women's writing in Canada. Her most recent book, *Kate Chopin, Charlotte Perkins Gilman and Edith Wharton: Studies in Short Fiction*, was published in 1997 by Macmillan.

Bridget Bennett is a lecturer in the Department of English and Comparative Literary Studies at the University of Warwick. Her books include an edited collection of women's short stories from the turn of the century entitled *Ripples of Dissent* (London: Dent,1996), *The Damnation of Harold Frederic* (Syracuse University Press, 1997), and a collection of essays, edited with Jeremy Treglown, *Grub Street to the Ivory Tower* (Oxford: Oxford University Press, 1998). She is currently working on a monograph on nineteenth-century American spiritualism and, with Dominic Montserrat, a collection of nineteenth-century short fiction about Egypt.

Anne Cranny-Francis is Associate Professor in English and Cultural Studies at Macquarie University, Sydney, Australia. She has published on feminist cultural production, popular fiction (science fiction, fantasy, utopian fiction and detective fiction), film, television, popular music, nineteenth-century fiction, and English as a discipline. Her books include: *Feminist Fiction: Feminist Uses of Generic Fiction* (Cambridge: Polity Press; NY: St Martin's Press, 1990); *Engendered Fiction: Analyzing Gender in the Production and Reception of Texts* (NSW University Press, 1992); *Engendered Fiction: Analysing gender in the production and reception of texts* (NSW University Press, 1992), *Popular Culture* (Deakin University Press, 1994) and *The Body in the Text* (Melbourne University Press, 1995).

Chris Ferns teaches English at Mount Saint Vincent University, in Halifax, Nova Scotia. His research interests include utopian literature, gender theory, and historical fiction. His work on Gilman forms part of a larger study of gender, *Narrating Utopia: Ideology, Gender, Form in Utopian Literature*, which has now been accepted for publication. His publications include *Aldous Huxley: Novelist* (London: Athlone, 1980), and numerous articles on utopian literature and historical fiction.

Val Gough is lecturer in English at the University of Liverpool. She has published on Virginia Woolf, Charlotte Perkins Gilman and language and gender, and she is currently working on two books: *Hélène Cixous: Feminist Mystic* and *Looking at Language and Gender in Literature*. She co-organized the first international conference on Gilman at University of Liverpool, July 1995.

Amanda Graham is a graduate teaching assistant at the University of Hull, currently working on Luce Irigaray and the fiction of Edna O'Brien.

Mary A. Hill is a Presidential Professor of History at Bucknell University, Lewisburg, Pennsylvania. She has published widely on Gilman, including: *Charlotte Perkins Gilman: The Emergence of a Radical Feminist 1860–1896* (Philadelphia: Temple University Press, 1980); *Endure: The Diaries of Charles Walter Stetson* (Philadelphia: Temple University Press, 1985); and *Charlotte Perkins Gilman: The Journey From Within* (Lewisburg: Bucknell University Press, 1995).

Ruth Levitas is Senior Lecturer in Sociology at the University of Bristol. She has written widely on utopianism and political ideologies, and she is particularly interested in the history of socialism and feminism. Her pulbications include *The Concept of Utopia* (1990), *The Ideology of the New Right* (ed.) (1986) and *The Inclusive Society? Social Exclusion and New Labour* (1998).

Jill Rudd is a lecturer in English at the University of Liverpool. She works on Women's Writing and also on Late Medieval English Literature. She has written articles on Margaret Atwood's *The Handmaid's Tale*, violent women in mainstream films (*Thelma and Louise*, *Dirty Weekend* and *Drowning By Numbers*) and has published on *Piers Plowman*. She co-organized the first international conference on Gilman held in July 1995 in Liverpool.

Alex Shishin is currently an Associate Professor in the Department of Literature, Kobe Women's University, Japan. He has recently completed a utopian work of fiction entitled *Real Time: A Japanese Utopian Romance* as part of his dissertation for a PhD in English from the Union Institute. A political journalist, creative writer and photographer, as well as a scholar, he has published primarily in Japan in such journals as *Asahi Evening News*, *Mainichi Daily News*, *Kyoto Journal*, *Abiko Quarterly*, *Sunday Afternoon*, *Edge* and *The Language Teacher*. A study of *Herland's* industry and utopian socialism appeared in *New Perspective*, Winter 1995. Shishin's interests in utopian and dystopian literature have led to scholarly work on writers including George Orwell and Nathaniel Hawthorne.

Anne Tanski teaches English at the Allegheny Campus of the Community College of Allegheny County in Pittsburgh. Her passion has always been the English Renaissance, and her current research interests lie in examining the histories of Queen Elizabeth I and Queen Victoria, comparing the literature written during their reigns and examining both queens' personal literary endeavours. Tanski is particularly interested in Gilman's *The Yellow Wallpaper* and her lesser known stories.

Introduction

VAL GOUGH AND JILL RUDD

In 1890, a poem called 'Similar Cases' by Charlotte Perkins Gilman appeared in *The Nationalist*. In it, Gilman propounded the overarching theme that was to concern her until she died in 1935: that humankind and the world *can* be changed for the better. The poem earned her much praise in Nationalist circles and marked the beginning of a reformist career which was to last some forty-five years.[1] During that time, Gilman established a national reputation as a speaker on women's issues and socialism: she published *Women and Economics* (1898)—for which she was most well-known while she was alive—followed by five more books, namely *Concerning Children* (1900), *The Home: Its Work and Influence* (1903), *Human Work* (1904), *The Man-Made World; or, Our Androcentric Culture* (1911) and *His Religion and Hers* (1923), and she continued to write poetry, short stories and novels. In 1909 she began to produce her own monthly magazine, *The Forerunner*, with each volume typically containing one or more short stories, a chapter of a serialized novel, poetry, articles and book reviews. No less than eight serialized novels appeared in the journal over the seven years of its publication: *What Diantha Did* (1910), *The Crux* (1911), *Moving the Mountain* (1911), *Mag-Marjorie* (1912), *Won Over* (1913), *Begnina Machiavelli* (1914), *Herland* (1915) and *With Her in Ourland* (1916). Yet of all her work, only the darkly tragic short story *The Yellow Wallpaper* (1892)—ironically her most well-known work today—does not assert optimistically the possibility for utopian change. It is this utopianism—as it is found in Gilman's fiction—which is the focus for this collection.

Gilman's best-known and critically addressed novel is the utopian *Herland*, which several of the essays in this collection revisit in order to deepen our understanding of the complexity of her utopian vision. *Herland* was first printed in book form in 1979 by The Women's Press (London) and Pantheon Books (New York) with an introduction by Ann J. Lane, and has since been recognized as a feminist classic which employs—and subverts—the traditional utopian form. The lesser-known *Moving the*

Mountain is deserving of more attention than it has so far received, and one full chapter in this volume is devoted to it. The utopia which Gilman depicts in *Moving the Mountain* is the United States in the 1940s, the people having chosen socialism just twenty years before. The sceptical visitor to this world, through whose eyes we see the utopia, is John Robertson, a man who has been lost in Tibet for thirty years. Gilman uses John's conversations with various inhabitants of her fictional utopia to introduce the reader to all the utopian ideas she held most dear: social organization based not on profit (and hence involving waste) but on social good; the professionalization of domestic labour and child-care; technology used sensibly and ecologically; education employed as the mechanism to create and improve utopia; motherhood as a collective institution; and religion as a form of utopian thought. Her short stories explore similar possibilities, and several of the essays in the collection examine what—through reprints—are becoming increasingly accessible works.[2]

Gilman wrote in her autobiography: 'I have never made any pretense of being literary. As far as I had any method in mind, it was to express the idea with clearness and vivacity, so that it might be apprehended with ease and pleasure' (L pp. 284–85). Yet as several critics have argued, Gilman's own statements about her lack of literary skill cannot be accepted at face value.[3] She was, in fact, acutely aware of the constitutive function of literature, and she sought to exploit its performative function (what Judith Butler describes as the 'reiterative and citational practice by which discourse produces the effects that it names'[4]). Through art, Gilman believed, we know the past, govern the present, and influence the future. Hence she viewed literature, as Carol Farley Kessler has argued, as 'cultural work', as potentially effecting utopian change.[5]

Gilman delineated her vision of the social function of literature in *The Man-Made World; or, Our Androcentric Culture*, where she wrote that 'The makers of books are the makers of thoughts and feelings for people in general. Fiction is the most popular form in which this world-food is taken.'[6] Yet it is precisely because Gilman saw literature as 'world-food'—nourishing the mind and encouraging utopian growth—that her fiction presents particular challenges for scholars, who must confront the complex relationship between artistry and didacticism in her work. Indeed, that very dichotomy must be dismantled if the full achievement of Gilman's fiction is to be appreciated. It is now clear that in its didactic politics of writing, Gilman's literary work forces reassessment of conventional evaluative criteria, in line with her own call for '... not only new achievements to measure but new standards of measurement'.[7] Rachel Blau DuPlessis has usefully reminded us that women writers, particularly of utopian and science fiction, have written 'teaching stories contain[ing] embedded elements from "assertive discourse"—genres like sermon, manifesto, tract, fable— ... in which elements like character and plot function mainly as the bearers of philosophical propositions or moral arguments'.[8] Gilman's skilful manipulation of genre conventions in the service of her utopian vision is only now fully becoming apparent.

Not all the essays in this volume deal directly with Gilman's novels and short stories, but all contribute a valuable context in which to study her fiction. Mary Hill's essay concentrates on Gilman's letters to her second husband, Houghton Gilman, during the four years prior to their marriage, 1897–1900. Hill shows how the personal discourse Gilman created in her letters to Houghton paralleled, but also noticeably diverged from, the public discourse she created in her fiction and non-fiction. Significant portions of Gilman's personal struggle, particularly against self-loathing and internalized patriarchal expectations, are presented as surmountable problems in her fiction, yet remain as painful ongoing battles in her letters. This 'darker side' provides a salutary counter-discourse to the mythologizing of Gilman as an unalloyed feminist heroine, which, says Hill, it is all too tempting to indulge in. The letters demonstrate Gilman's private struggle with the complexities and contradictions of her situation as a radical feminist thinker contemplating marriage. Marilyn Frye has argued that 'to uncompromisingly embody and enact a radical feminism ... you ... cannot be heterosexual in the standard meaning of the word—you cannot be any version of a patriarchal wife ... to embody and enact a consistent and all-the-way feminism you have to be a heretic, a deviant, an undomesticated female, an impossible being'.[9] Frye's terms echo Gilman's own self-descriptions in her letters to Houghton. They remind us that Gilman's private battle against conventional heterosexual norms provides an invaluable dimension to our understanding of her public treatment of this issue in her short stories and particularly her utopian novel *Herland*, which in its depiction of Ellador and Van's marriage, fictionally offers us a potential, but never actualized model of radicalized heterosexuality.[10]

The novel *Herland* provides the focus for Chris Ferns' examination of the ideological implications of utopia as a narrative form. Ferns' essay contributes valuably to the ongoing critical conversation about what happens when a feminist writer such as Gilman seeks to rewrite utopian narrative in the service of a gender ideology very different from that which such narrative typically encodes. Ferns shows that Gilman dances through the 'ideological minefield' of utopian generic conventions with mixed success: *Herland* returns a sense of genuine dialogue to the proceedings and encourages an active critical participation on the part of the reader (features largely suppressed by traditional utopian narrative forms), yet remains conventional in its depiction of the Herlanders as domesticated women, and fails to avoid the stasis characteristic of conventional fictional utopias. Again, then, we see evidence of the current trend in Gilman scholarship to acknowledge and explore, rather than suppress, the inconsistencies and contradictions of her work.[11]

The adventurousness of Gilman's narrative techniques is well demonstrated in the next two essays in the volume. Through a close reading of *Herland,* Bridget Bennett follows the errant adventures of Gilman's metaphors and shows how she redefined and regendered domestic, ideological and textual spaces. Ambivalence, textual indeterminacy and playfulness characterize *Herland's* textual effects and show that *The Yellow Wallpaper* is not the only text by Gilman to manifest modernist elements. Bennett takes a leaf from Gilman's book and allows a degree of playfulness in her own critical approach, matching Gilman's own witty ingenuity in an examination of the way Gilman exploited the literal and metaphorical resources which pockets offered. Finally, Bennett argues that Herland as fictional space can be seen as a lesbian 'pocket' of woman-identified women.[12]

Janet Beer similarly demonstrates Gilman's literary versatility in an analysis of her use of a variety of genres including the detective story, fantasy, fable, romance, and parable, as well, of course, as utopian fiction. Beer shows how generic resources are exploited and surpassed in a range of texts including the unpublished detective story entitled *Unpunished* (1929); short stories like 'The Vintage' (1916), 'Wild Oats and Tame Wheat' (1913), and 'The Unnatural Mother' (1916); Gilman's serialized novel *The Crux* (1910) and her utopian novel *Herland.* Metaphors of infection and sickness permeate these texts and others, conveying Gilman's message that conventional marriage debilitates women and that a body politic that is sick produces physically and psychologically diseased and disabled individuals. Again, the 'dark side' of Gilman's personal struggle against depression functions as the hidden subtext of such narratives, for while in her fiction Gilman depicted ways of healing sickness, in her autobiography she wrote of 'the long limitation'—the long-term debility—which she felt she had suffered as a result of her own breakdown (induced by her first marriage and the birth of her daughter, Katherine).

The way that the themes of role conflict, female isolation and biological sin interrelate in complex and radical ways in 'Making a Change' (1911) and *The Crux* (1910) is examined by Anne E. Tanski, who demonstrates Gilman's audacity in treating the taboo of sexually transmitted diseases, and shows that Gilman's ideas are as relevant today as ever by drawing parallels with contemporary issues surrounding HIV infection. These stories by Gilman manifest the optimism so characteristic of her utopian imagination, in their conviction that solutions can be found to the most apparently intractable of problems.[13]

That Gilman's fiction was very much a vehicle for her utopian theories is also demonstrated by Ruth Levitas' essay, which examines the theoretical framework regarding domestic labour which underpins many of Gilman's utopian stories, particularly 'Aunt Mary's Pie Plant' (1908), *What Diantha Did* (1909-10), 'The Cottagette' (1910), 'Making a Change' (1911) and *Moving the Mountain* (1911). Levitas places these stories in the context of turn-of-the-century socialist debates about labour and domestic labour, comparing her work to that of Edward Bellamy and William Morris, and relating her ideas to those of François Fourier, August Bebel and Emile Durkheim. Again the radicalism but also the limitations of Gilman's thinking come under scrutiny: Levitas shows how, and why, the sexual division of labour remains intact in Gilman's thinking, just as it does in that of Bellamy and Morris.

Continuing this contextualization of Gilman's fiction, Alex Shishin turns back to *Herland* and examines some of the political and economic theories which underpin the novel and its depiction of an all-female utopia. Shishin detects an ambivalence towards technology in the novel, and notes teasing gaps and absences in the narrative regarding precise methods of production. Gilman conveys her theories of production indirectly, by exploiting the literal and metaphorical meanings of forestry, which, says Shishin, is an industry which suits her political and economic vision. Current ecofeminist thinking has been described as an 'enchanted forest' which resists the 'technological desert' of modern methods, and Amanda Graham argues that *Herland* anticipated elements of modern social ecofeminism (non-essentialist) *and* cultural ecofeminism (essentialist) in complex and contradictory ways. That *Herland* includes the struggle between the 'forest' and the 'desert' *within* its utopian vision is, says Graham, one of its particular strengths.

Val Gough's essay shifts the focus to Gilman's critically neglected utopian novel, *Moving the Mountain* (1911) which, she argues, presents a particular problem for modern critics. Gough joins Chris Ferns in examining the ideological implications of utopian narrative form, arguing that *Moving the Mountain* has been neglected precisely because (unlike *Herland*) it *does* present its utopia as a blueprint. The novel uses conventional utopian devices uncongenial to modern critics used to privileging 'critical utopias' which avoid or deconstruct programmatic modes of thought. Calling for a revaluation of the novel, Gough shows how Gilman's choice of narrative form in *Moving the Mountain* is neither coincidental nor due to a failure to think through the ideological implications of narrative form, but, rather, deliberately mirrors Gilman's theories about religion, social evolution and the nature of utopian change. Thus, for example, forms of social control depicted thematically in the novel parallel the narrative control enacted formally in the text. What critics have been reluctant to acknowledge (perhaps, as Mary Hill says, in the desire to produce a one-dimensional feminist heroine) is that Gilman's conception of the nature of utopian thought *did not* exclude the suppression of dissent or the foreclosure of dialogue.

The way that Gilman negotiated the uneasy tensions between narrative control and hermeneutic indeterminacy is studied by Jill Rudd in her analysis of a number of Gilman's animal fables and animal poems, including 'Two Storks' (1910), 'When I Was a Witch' (1910), and 'The Lady Oyster' (1912). Proud of her ethics of obedience and duty (which she saw as essential to utopian behaviour) yet equally drawn into resistance and rebellion by her radical ideas, Gilman, Rudd shows, struggled for narrative control over texts where the slippage between the literal and the metaphorical, and the proliferation of multiple, sometimes contradictory meanings, complicated and occasionally undermined her didactic message. The clear implication of this and many other essays in the volume is that Gilman's relationship to generic forms was a complex one deserving further critical attention.

The final essay, by Anne Cranny-Francis, continues this generic analysis by examining how, in *The Forerunner* (1909-16), Gilman exploited the resources of an amazing range of genres in order to construct her feminist utopian polemic. Gilman's theoretical message was disseminated via poems, articles, short stories, sermons, serialized novels, book reviews, commentaries, advertisements and 'problem pages' which all appeared in the journal, and Cranny-Francis shows that Gilman deliberately exploited the intertextual and intergeneric resonances set up by her juxtaposition of such a variety of genres. As Cranny-Francis says, and as this volume demonstrates, Gilman had a materialist understanding of contemporary social practice *along with* a sophisticated metatextual grasp of contemporary discursive practice.

Notes

1 See Larry Ceplair (ed.), *Charlotte Perkins Gilman: A Nonfiction Reader* (New York: Columbia University Press, 1991), pp. 25–44, for a discussion of the influence of Nationalist thought on Gilman.

2 See Ann J. Lane (ed.), *The Charlotte Perkins Gilman Reader* (London: Women's Press, 1981); Barbara H. Solomon (ed.), *Herland and Selected Stories by Charlotte Perkins Gilman* (New York: Signet, 1992); Lynne Sharon Schwartz (ed.), *The Yellow Wallpaper and Other Writings by Charlotte Perkins Gilman* (New

York: Bantam, 1989).

3 See, for example, Carol Farley Kessler, *Charlotte Perkins Gilman: Her Progress Toward Utopia with Selected Writings* (Liverpool: Liverpool University Press, 1995), p. 268.

4 Judith Butler, *Bodies that Matter* (London: Routledge, 1993), p. 2.

5 Carol Farley Kessler, *Charlotte Perkins Gilman*, pp. 1–12.

6 Charlotte Perkins Gilman, 'The Man-Made World' (1911), in Lynne Sharon Schwartz (ed.), *The Yellow Wallpaper and Other Writings by Charlotte Perkins Gilman*, p. 222.

7 Charlotte Perkins Gilman, 'Our Brains and What Ails Them' (1912), in Larry Ceplair (ed.), *Charlotte Perkins Gilman: A Nonfiction Reader*, p. 231; for discussion of how didacticism functions as a part of feminist utopian writing, see Jane L. Donawerth and Carol A. Kolmerten (eds), *Utopian and Science Fiction by Women* (Liverpool: Liverpool University Press, 1994), p.3.

8 Rachel Blau DuPlessis, 'The Feminist Apologues of Lessing, Piercy, and Russ', *Frontiers*, 4 (Spring 1979), pp. 1–8.

9 Marilyn Frye, *Willfull Virgin: Essays in Feminism* (Freedom, CA: Crossing Press, 1992), p. 136.

10 See Val Gough, 'Lesbians and Virgins: The New Motherhood in *Herland*' in David Seed, ed., *Anticipations: Essays on Early Science Fiction and its Precursors* (Liverpool: Liverpool University Press, 1995), pp. 195–215.

11 Thomas L. Erskine and Connie L. Richards provide a useful delineation of the changing nature of criticism on *The Yellow Wallpaper* (1892), and the way that current studies refuse to ignore the 'unheard of contradictions' which earlier analyses suppressed (Charlotte Perkins Gilman, *The Yellow Wallpaper*, ed. Thomas L. Erskine and Connie L. Richards [New Brunswick: Rutgers University Press, 1993], pp. 3–23).

12 Along similar lines, Val Gough has argued that Herland can be seen as a lesbian narrative space (Val Gough, 'Lesbians and Virgins').

13 The title of the 1995 conference on Gilman at Liverpool University was 'Charlotte Perkins Gilman: Optimist Reformer', echoing an epithet given Gilman by William Dean Howells.

Charlotte Perkins Gilman and the Journey from Within

MARY A. HILL

Once upon a time, three beautiful young women, living with their mother in a peaceful, quiet little town, were visited by a young prince who delighted them with his knowledge, charm and beauty. He had a beautiful castle with a huge library and even a theater for poetry readings, operas, and plays. After several months of courting and entertaining all three sisters, the prince asked the eldest for her hand in marriage. 'Yes, he is handsome and resourceful', she told her sisters, 'but his beard looks far too blue. I cannot marry him'. The prince then asked for the second sister's hand in marriage, but she too was concerned: 'Yes, he's handsome; and especially I like his books, and concerts and plays. But his beard bothers me as well; the color is too blue'. So the prince asked the youngest sister for her hand in marriage, and this time was successful. She was delighted to move into his lavish castle, and to enjoy his concerts, operas, and plays. One day, however, the prince explained that he must leave for several days. The Princess could enjoy all the pleasures of the castle, he told her. She could use his set of keys for all the rooms. But there was one small exception; one key, the smallest key must not be used. When the prince departed, the Princess and her sisters enjoyed roaming around the castle, but after a while, of course, they could not resist using the smallest key. With screams of horror, they opened the door to Bluebeard's cellar and saw his piles and piles of women's bones. They slammed the door. They tried to hide the key. But gradually it started dripping Blood. When Bluebeard returned, therefore, he knew that the sisters had seen his secret cellar and must be destroyed [there are, of course, several possible endings for this story, but in the context of a celebration of Gilman's utopian and reformist writing…]. *The youngest princess was only momentarily terrorized by Bluebeard's*

> *cruelty and power, however, and quickly organized a formidable resistance, saved herself from burial in Bluebeard's castle, and devoted the remainder of her life to saving the lives of countless of her sisters.*

I've been intrigued lately by the Bluebeard story, by the question of why and how Gilman managed to resist her Bluebeard, and also by the question of why and how, as a woman's movement leader, she kept essential portions of her struggle secret. It is almost as though she sensed what academics often sense as well, that there are certain issues we should refrain from openly approaching, certain small keys that, if wise, we should not use. At conferences on poverty, for example, or even on homelessness (often scheduled, ironically, at Sheraton or Hilton Hotels) as academics we should approach our work 'objectively'. Don't be too emotional (especially if untenured). Be logical. Be rational. Be cool. Or we will be pushed into Bluebeard's cellar ourselves.

When we claim our heroines in women's history, therefore, and likewise when we think about our lives, we learn early that there are certain questions we should think about; and certain ways they should be discussed. Most often we learn to emphasize our rational, positive achievements, our public record, our clearly reasoned understandings. It is much harder—and much less wise—to talk about our darker side, about underlying problems, about what some might call psychological confusions, or anger, or rage. We do not want to expose our *own* dilemmas. And understandably, if we are admiring, we are reluctant to expose the dilemmas of our sisters of the past as well, particularly if our work might hurt them, or if their words will be taken out of context, or trivialized and not revered. To paraphrase one academic colleague's comment: Let's not put Gilman into that already overpopulated gallery of neurotic women. Let's focus instead on her rational achievement, her public record, her theoretical and intellectual success.

Gilman's published legacy—equivalent to some 22 books—was a substantive and brilliant challenge to prevailing androcentric ideology, and in a multiplicity of fields: history, anthropology, economics, psychology, literature, literary criticism. So let's *not* focus on the 'mad woman in the attic', some historians would argue. Let's *not* look at Gilman terrified by the yellow bulbous creatures her wallpaper encaptures. And likewise let's *not* focus on the cunning strategies of her escape: '*Ha Ha—I've got out, in spite of you.*'[1] Let's focus instead on her clean cut dignity, the charismatic woman's movement leader, rational and calmly understanding.

But we know—and a lot of us resent the fact—that writers have been tampering with our stories for years. They have laundered our ancient fairy tales, for instance, taking out or enfeebling the witches, undermining our connection with the lustful sexy Baubo, or with Baba Yaga and her love of human bones. They have revised and censored slave narratives as well, making them palatable to Victorian audiences and readers, choosing distancing words like 'miscegenation' instead of realistic words like 'rape'. Very few have screamed about the bones piled up in Bluebeard's cellar, about the pain in their own and other women's lives. As Audre Lorde puts it:

> In this disastrous time, when little girls are still being stitched shut between their legs... when 12-year-old Black boys are shot down in the street at random by uniformed men who are cleared of any wrong-doing, when ancient and honorable citizens scavenge for food in garbage pails, and the growing answer to all this is media hype or surgical lobotomy; when daily gruesome murders of women from coast to coast no longer warrant mention in *The New York Times*, when grants to teach retarded children are cut in favor of billion-dollar airplanes... what depraved monster could possibly be always happy?[2]

Audre Lorde cried about injustice, about the cancer in the body politic, about the cancer consuming her own body as well. Likewise, Toni Morrison took us to the Bluebeard cellar. She insisted, in *Beloved* (1987), that we look not only at the white-washed sections of his castle, but in his dungeon rooms as well, and ask questions of the skeletons: Why, black mother, did you kill your baby daughter? Why, when threatened by enslavement, did you slit your daughter's throat?

Let's call it like it is, say Toni Morrison and Leslie Silko.[3] Let's end the silence. Let's retrieve our stories, find our voices, scream our message if need be. Likewise Gilman cried about injustice, about child labour, poverty, and pollution of the earth. And while publicly she certainly expressed radical perspectives—many would argue that she was more radical than most—we now know that she wrote secretly as well, and on some crucially important questions. Her published works show many of her significant conclusions, her logical strategies, her rational analyses. But her private letters show another side: her journey of resistance, her *experience* of Bluebeard's cave, her need, as James Joyce might have put it, for exile, silence, and cunning. Her letters show her full-scale battle, her struggle with insanity, like Audre Lorde's with cancer, her struggle with the death not of the body but of the spirit, with the death of the wild woman, with the death of the best part of ourselves: if we learn self-loathing as women, as blacks, or as those with little power.

The focus of this chapter is Gilman's letters to her second husband, Houghton Gilman, during the four years prior to their marriage,

1897–1900. Twenty- to thirty-page letters she wrote him on an almost daily basis, love letters some might call them, passionate, revealing, intensely private, and very different from the published writings for which she has justifiably received national, even international acclaim. Publicly she was a brilliant theorist for the woman's movement. But privately she left a prolific record also, a story of the underlying battles with almost every women's issue she publicly discussed.[4] In *Women and Economics* she theoretically analysed and exposed the destructive effects of sex-based inequalities. And in her private letters she acknowledged that many of her perceptions had emerged from agonizing gender conflicts in herself. As she explained in *Women and Economics*, 'We ourselves, by maintaining this artificial diversity between the sexes... have preserved in our own characters the confusion and contradiction which is our greatest difficulty in life.'[5] And to Houghton she described an enigmatic conflict in herself: 'To prove that a woman can love and work too. To resist this dragging weight of the old swollen woman-heart, and force it into place—the world's Life first—my own life next. Work first—love next. Perhaps this is simply the burden of our common womanhood which is weighing on me so.'[6]

By 1897, the year the letters begin, Gilman had secured modest economic independence. She had successfully challenged the commonly accepted roles of womanhood—the dutiful daughter, the loving wife, the 'natural' mother. And professionally as well as personally she was securing greater freedom for herself. And yet the correspondence was none the less traumatic. During the same years she was writing *Women and Economics* and countless other articles and lectures, she was also writing to Houghton almost daily—exposing her insecurities, trusting her passions, and exploring what some might call a 'different way of knowing',[7] including Bluebeard's dungeon, what she called her 'catacombs'.

By 1897, both Charlotte and Houghton were fairly well established, she as a speaker and writer travelling cross-country on her lecture tours, and he as a Wall Street lawyer, a relatively successful, if not a particularly ambitious man. In fact, in some respects Houghton was an androgynous kind of character. Gentle, kind, and sensitively responsive to other people's needs, he was patient enough to endure her contradictions, and confident enough to support her public work. The 'personal impression you make on me is of intense Beauty', she wrote to him. 'The harmony—simplicity—restraint—the clear Greek quality of being the thing you are, perfectly... it is Beautiful.' Besides, she continued in another letter, 'You seem very near somehow', 'a kind of background to most of my thinking when I'm not at work'. Or again, 'It is astonishing how many times a day I incline to write to you.'[8] And write she did—more than enough to equal several of her books.

In important ways, Charlotte's conflict with Houghton differed from the one with Walter Stetson. Whereas Walter had imposed the standard female expectations—the dutiful mother, the ideal wife—these letters show the toughness of her struggle not to impose them on herself. Despite her theories, and despite a supportive easy-going Houghton, she had still to battle against the destructive lessons her culture had imposed.

Take the issue of women's need for work and economic independence, for example. On the one hand, Gilman was determined to continue lecturing and writing, to act according to her theory. She argued that meaningful work is not only essential to human life; it *is* human life. It is a basic impulse, a social passion as natural as breathing. Obviously women should not content themselves only with domestic service. Women need, or rather people need, professionalized housekeeping, and kitchenless houses, and satisfying work commitments, which for the most part she insisted on having for herself. 'I wish you could have heard me last Sunday night', she wrote after one particularly successful lecture. 'I never spoke better in my life. A full church. A big platform all to myself. And it *came!* It just poured out in a great swelling river and all those people sat and took it in.' 'What a wonderful life it is—to go everywhere—to meet everyone—to eat and drink so largely of human life.'[9]

So on the one hand Gilman enthusiastically continued with her lecturing and writing. But since she also valued a nurturing, satisfying love relationship, she struggled with the social definitions which said that femininity and creativity were mutually exclusive, which said that while for men, professional work was positive and self-affirming, for loving women it was a mark of aggressiveness and selfishness instead. She thus wrote apologetically to Houghton:

> Don't you see dear how much at a disadvantage I am beside you? Try and feel like a woman for a moment—put yourself in their place. You know what a woman wants to bring a man—a boundless wholesouled love, absolutely and primarily his own.
> I haven't that...
> A long beautiful service and devotion, given wholly to his interests.
> I haven't that...
> I can only give you a divided love—I love God—the world—my work as well as I love you...
> O my dear—do you not see what poignant grief and shame it is to a woman to have no woman's gifts to give![10]

Or again, in a somewhat later letter, 'I'm sorry that I can't add my life to yours—woman fashion... the usual style of immersion of the wife in the husband'. But '[I need to] work out such a plan of living as shall leave me free to move as move I must... *I must not* focus on "home duties". Remember it is not an external problem with me—a mere matter of material labor and time... it is practical enough to be a question of life or death with me.'[11]

Although Gilman was determined to continue working, she could do so only reluctantly, apologetically, and with enormous guilt about the 'feminine' responsibilities society had always claimed were hers. It was almost as though she sometimes felt compelled to use typical 'feminine' disclaimers, deceptions some might call them, playing coy, or emphasizing her child-like weakness to protect Houghton's sense of strength. By elaborating on her fears and limitations, occasionally she would try deflecting his attention from her professional successes, and thereby manage to disguise her power. Sometimes she dealt with Houghton's more laid-back personality by pushing him to be assertive: 'It is a woman's business to wait, not a man's. It is for a woman to be patient and still—not a man. If you are truly lover and husband—show it. If not—God bless you and Good-bye.'[12] But if she occasionally tried to quell her fears by pushing Houghton to adhere to standard gender expectations, more frequently she struggled with the tendency to impose them on herself. As she would later put it in her published writing, that while '*men, man, manly, manhood*' meant the 'world and all its activities', 'when we say *Women*, we think *Female*, the sex' (H p. 56). Or as she wrote privately to Houghton, 'I suppose all this flamboyance of mine makes it seem as if you weren't getting on so fast by contrast. But Bless you! Mine is all talk—a mountain in labor. You have seen the mice I bring forth.' And this disclaimer after *Women and Economics* had been published and nationally acclaimed. Or again, 'You talk about being "overshadowed" by your wife—I suppose there will be some people who will think so—but if they only could know how I *feel*! Why when I think of you I feel like a thin forlorn hungry cold little kitten... that you had taken in and done for.' Or as she also put it, she wanted to be treated as the 'dear foolish tired little girl' who needed to come into his 'arms and rest'.[13]

What we have in Gilman's letters are contrasts that are repeatedly disturbing. The strong public advocate of woman's full equality felt a 'compelling desire... to complain and explain—to whimper... and seek for sympathy which don't do me any good if I get it'.[14] She was looking for, and hoping for, a 'right relation', as Carter Heywood calls it, an intimate, centring, 'love' relationship in which she could express her needs and passions and fully be herself.[15] But repeatedly she floundered. She wanted satisfying work, but apologized for needing it. She wanted a passionate intimate relationship, but for that she felt a 'tidal wave of shame'. 'I feel wicked', she wrote to Houghton, 'shamelessly wicked—as if some one had caught me eating an angel—or plucking the poor thing in preparation for the feast.' 'My love for you drags me, tears me, pulls me toward you. My reason stands up like a rock, when the waves drop back—and always says the same thing—... *You are not fit to marry him.*' 'I cannot fully harmonize you with the rest of it. I suppose it is only the essential pain of the woman nature forced out into world service.'[16] Or as she put it another letter:

> I wish I could make a picture of the thing [herself] as I see it—sulky, frightened, discouraged, 'rattled' to a degree; one foot forward and the other back, ready to rush forward in tumultuous devotion one minute, and run away shrieking in the next—fingers in ears![17]

'Unreasonable', 'disagreeable', 'absurd'—repeatedly Gilman viewed herself as a 'vacillating wretch' swinging back and forth between painfully conflicting needs. 'I don't wholly like to be held—and yet I do!' 'Makes me kind of angry too. Seems a weakness. To be so tangled up in another person.' She described herself as a broken goblet 'that everything spills out of—I can't *keep* any feeling—they flow over and through me, and you never can be sure of what you are going to find'. 'O Houghton—I am so *tired* of all this restless doubt and hope and fear and flickering joy... I've got to the place I wanted. I can write what I please and say what I please and the world is ready to listen. And here I am floundering helplessly among my own affairs—doing no work at all. It is shameful—shameful.'[18]

For years I struggled with Gilman's letters. I found myself frustrated and disappointed by her contradictions and confusions, and by the 'feminine' self-hatred that she disguised beneath her firm, impressive public stance. At first I argued that she could understand causes of women's victim status, but not succeed in overcoming them. Publicly she would call for women to be strong and independent; but with Houghton—as though unable to sustain the courage of her own convictions—she would become the 'forlorn' and squalid 'little kitten', the 'babblesome and childish' little girl.[19] As is so often the case in women's history, we thus confront a disturbing pattern. Taught from childhood to accept 'feminine' self-abnegation, to 'love' in dependent and self-denying ways, women find it hard to respect themselves, much less to recognize, accept, and respect authenticity and purpose in their work. Like so many professional women even today, Gilman was unable consistently to feel the self-respect she publicly projected. Impressive though she clearly was, she could not free herself completely of the 'burden of our common womanhood' that through her published works she helped us understand.

When I first studied Gilman's letters, I thus argued sympathetically (and rather condescendingly) that she was a victim of destructive patriarchal norms, that publicly she launched a persuasive rational attack on the forces that restricted women, yet privately waged war against herself, and far more brutally, more emotionally and passionately. And yet gradually I have come to read these letters differently: as a reflection of her pain and struggle, but not of her capitulation; as an exploration of her labyrinth of fears and insecurities, but as a demonstration also of her absolute determination to resist. In fact, in some respects Gilman's letters are more radical even than many of her published writings, more powerful and also more courageous. For while her published works stand as important statements of resistance in the more abstract, theoretical arena, her private letters expose the underlying 'feminine' realities of war. Struggling for self-respect and professional commitment in the context of a 'love' relationship, she had to fight against the fear that she was too forceful and ambitious, or too emotional and passionate, or too strong and confident, or too 'rebellious' and thus 'unfeminine'. In any case, like so many women, she occasionally absorbed the social message and momentarily believed that she deserved the worst of punishments. Or to use the metaphors more frequent in her letters, she was a 'monster' threatening to swallow or destroy her lover, and thus needed to be crushed, shattered, or drowned.[20]

In my view, Gilman's letters are powerfully important in women's studies not in spite of her depressions—but perhaps in part because of them: because she documented them so well; because she faced them head on—her madness, her catacombs; because she did not dodge or cower; because she refused to be a victim, and undertook a journey of resistance, herself as warrior woman fighting to stay whole. The violence of Gilman's metaphors is striking—as is her courage, her determination to resist conventional heterosexual norms. As she put it in one letter, she was like the 'old campaigner'—sometimes 'crippled' by the battle, but also proud to have survived the war. 'I *feel* most like a soldier in a seventy year's war. Sometimes bitterly depressed, often defeated, long imprisoned, scarred and wounded beyond recognition but not crippled past all usefulness.'[21] It was almost as though, like Persephone, she was willing, in fact she was uncompromisingly determined, to explore the dark side, to travel to the underworld, to take Houghton to her 'catacombs'.[22] 'Blind' and 'creeping', she still kept moving forward, still kept turning up old 'gravestones' or 'trap-door-stones', and finding 'all these buried things, dead and alive'. She would experience an 'awful landslide', severing her 'way down to the bones', 'all the flesh and blood' removed. Yet even then she still continued. Terrified of 'madness', of what she called a 'gray fog darkness'—at 'its long worst it meant pitch blackness—unillumined and unilluminable'—it was almost as though she were using 'illness' as a spur, 'gravestones', or 'trap-door' stones serving to intensify her search.[23] 'The sensations of bad dreams are nearest', the 'clinging weight', the 'overmastering dread... Well—there is a waking after bad dreams. They pass with the night... Perhaps this will pass. But I fear me it will not till life passes.'[24]

Most of Gilman's letters say a lot about her day-time 'terrors', but most say far less about her dreams at night. But there is one recorded though undated dream—never published as far as I know—with imagery that is absolutely striking. She felt an 'irresistible impulse' to enter the 'dark frowning mouth of a huge cavern', she wrote, even though its 'dark passages' were completely covered with 'sticky slime' and 'sluggish water'. I quote the dream in its entirety:

> I had a dream, and I thought that I was wandering alone in a forest, the extent of which I did not know. The moon though at its full gave but little light, for it was repeatedly obscured by huge black clouds which drove rapidly across its face. It was late in the autumn, and the chill damp wind which moaned and sobbed in the trees cast showers of dead leaves at my feet.
>
> I had not the least idea of how I came here, or where I was going, but with a feeling common to dreams this did not at all disturb me. So I pressed on pushing my way through damp underbrush, and sometimes sinking to my knees in some hidden pool of stagnant water. Strange noises and rustlings were heard on every side, and presently the clouds overhead having united in one black canopy it began to rain; not fiercely, nor gently, but heavily with a dull whispering sound as if the elfish inhabitants of these trees and swamps were talking of me in muffled voices.
>
> Suddenly and without any warning, I found myself directly in front of the dark frowning mouth of a huge cavern. Impelled by a[n] irresistible impulse I entered it and pursued my journey. The floor of this cavern was covered with loose stones, long stalactites depended[?] from the roof, and dark passages opening on every side ran from the gloomy twilight which filled this part of the cave to regions of still greater blackness. The floor and sides of this cavern were covered with sticky slime from little streamlets of sluggish water that oozed slowly from crevices in the roof of the cavern, and trickled down the walls or dripped directly from above. As troops of bats left their places in the top of the cave where their dusky forms could hardly be distinguished from the rocks on which they hung; and circled noislesly [*sic*] about my head. Toads and lizards hopped and crawled about my feet, fat black spiders with long hairy legs ran up and down the walls, and in the shadow of the boulders I sometimes caught sight of the coiled form and gleaming eye of some foul serpent.

As I proceeded deeper into the darkness of the cave, shadowy forms of the most fantastic and horrible shape emerged from the gloom of the side passages, and followed me with stealthy steps. Suddenly I was seized with a most intense thirst. I saw a deep black pool lying at one side of me, fed by a small stream that oozed sluggishly from behind a rock, and so far overcame my repugnance as to stoop to its brink; but I recoiled with a scream of horror. It Was Blood!

The Things that followed me seemed to feel a horrid joy at my disgust, and leaped about over the rocks and stones, clapping thier [*sic*] hands and seeming to laugh and gibber with delight, but all was silent as the grave. Suddenly the comparatively narrow gallery in which I was walking opened into a lofty hall the roof of which I could but just discern, while the ends strecthed [*sic*] away into unfathomable darkness. While I was gazing into this great void of blackness, I perceived a faint glow approaching from one end of this hall. It came nearer and nearer, a ghostly band began to play on their respective instruments, but without making the least noise, and I perceived a long procession of stately forms, attended by servants bearing torches of phosphorous, and proceeded by the silent band. The first figure which I distinguished among the throng was a tall & stately one. That haughty brow, the eagle eye, that bloody toga wrapped so proudly over the deadly wounds beneath, could belon[g] to no one but that great Roman soldier, aid, statesman who fell by the murderous hand of Brutus. After him came a long train of personages all famous in history. After this stately cavalcade had passed I attempted to cross the hall, but my path was interrupted by a river, or some body of water, the farther side of which I could not see, and the depth of which I had no means of measuring. I stopped in despair at the thought of being lost in this awfull region of darkness and horror, but my sight was suddenly gladdened by perceiving what I supposed to be an old decayed log gently rising and falling with the motion of the sable waters. I decided to risk my fate on this fragile support, rather than stay [where] I was; so I seated myself on the old log and pushed of[f] from the shore with my feet. Imagine my horror and dismay at feeling this supposed log move under me with an undulating motion that told me but too plainly that I had trusted myself on the back of a gigantic sea-serpent. This fearfull creature was like nothing on this earth, for its head, which it raised from the waters turned about to gaze on me in horrid derision, had the semblance of humanity, though so frightfully grinning and distorted, that it resembled Medusa's in its hideousness. Seated then on the back of this horrible monster, I was traversing at a frightfull speed

> an unknown waste of waters, and picture my feelings when with a horrible snort the creature began to sink in the waters. I cried for help till my cries were smothered in the water. I tried to keep my hold on the monster[']s slippery back; but in vain, the water surged in my ears, a humming noise sounded in my brain, and I knew no more.[25]

Some seventy-five years later, French feminist writer Hélène Cixous also writes about travelling to the underworld and seeing the laugh of the Medusa: 'You only have to look at the Medusa straight on to see her', she writes, 'she's not deadly. She's beautiful and she's laughing', and her 'Dark Continent is neither dark nor unexplorable'.[26] Understandably we've been taught to fear her. As women we have been taught *to be afraid*, to avoid and fear the Bluebeard cellar, to be ashamed of the strength, the curiosity, the determination that would take us there. In fact, Cixous asks, where is the woman who has not been ashamed of her strength, her beauty, her intellectual and sexual vitality? Where is the vivacious, infinite woman who, driven to self-disdain, has not accused herself of being a monster—sick, neurotic, self-absorbed? Of course woman are 'sick'. But their shameful sickness is in *refusing* death, in making trouble, in recording their struggles, in hearing one another into speech.[27] At first of course we travel to the dark side fearfully: Inanna stripped of her accomplishments, her attributes, her identity; Persephone likewise painfully exposed to the underworld. But the more we hear one another's stories, the more we find the hidden passageways and possibilities, the more our writing changes. It becomes subversive, volcanic, outrageous, finally breaking up the patriarchal truths with laughter and delight.[28]

Hélène Cixous, Marion Woodman, and countless other women writers see the journey to the dark side as a creative and necessary process, as an inevitable part of the Life/Death/Life cycle, night into day, light into dark, spiralling toward wholeness, whole-making and therefore holy: to face the shadow and thereby learn to touch the soul; to confront the dark side; to avoid projecting hates and fears on others; to expose the death-dealing forces in our culture; to exorcise the outside monsters; to confront the monsters in ourselves. One has to lose oneself to find oneself. It takes a death to find the gold inside ourselves.

So returning once again to Gilman's letters, I would argue that she travelled to the dark side, that she explored Bluebeard's pile of women's bones. Perhaps what we should note, therefore, is *not* that Gilman sometimes was depressed, but rather that she was willing to explore 'dangerous' and 'threatening' emotions. For in the process she was learning to respect them, to disarm them, to trust her feelings, and thus to tap important sources of her energy within herself. In fact, she often used her letters as her 'morning prayers', she wrote to Houghton. Confronting and working through the 'monster' feelings, she began to move from metaphors of violence to images of birthing, of spiritual awakening, of re-affirming her own power. It 'doesn't feel like quicksand anymore', but like rowing on the 'open ocean...—the oars dipping or not dipping as the waves may rise—... and withal the tremendous elation of that very power beneath—the vast rise and swell'. Or again, it is as if 'some system of irrigation were gradually spreading in a desert country, reclaiming more ground daily, and making the wilderness to blossom as the rose'. 'I feel as if I had been only playing—before—that *this* is life and I am but just born!'

Proudly but surreptitiously, Gilman used her letters as a source of healing, of empowering, a bridge back and forth between equally important human needs. Enthusiastically and passionately she could describe the satisfactions of her work commitments: the sense of 'uniting power', of 'constructive power', 'rich and sweet with the response of hungry hearts'. And increasingly she could delight also in her relationship with Houghton. He was inspiring a 'mended strengthened re-born feeling', she wrote to him, a sense of 'heavenly wonder, so utterly unknown, undreamed of in my life'.[29]

> ... surely you can read it in my eyes—hear it in my voice, feel it in my arms about your neck—taste it on my lips that lean to you. You make me so happy—so happy my darling! I love you—love you—love you![30]

Or even more passionately:

> Sweetheart! You shall kiss me anywhere you want to and all you want to as soon as ever there is a chance. I will wait till you are exhausted and begin operations on my own account.[31]

With Houghton standing as her lover, friend and witness, and with correspondence serving as her 'morning prayers', Gilman began to move toward an affirmation of the 'wild woman' forces, the erotic, the 'goddess' energies which so often she had effectively disguised. For a time, Gilman had internalized an anti-woman image. And in sheer self-protection, she often would continue to sustain it in her public life. But privately—since the relationship with Houghton was 'the secretest secret I ever had'—she was trusting and enjoying energizing sensual and spiritual dimensions within herself. 'Ceaselessly hungry' for life, she was a 'voracious comet', she wrote to Houghton, a 'wild floating soul', a 'flouncing kite', a 'cold queer rebellious unnatural sex-failure' that is 'well, is not bad to take!'[32]

> ... well, sometimes I feel like 'a heathen goddess come again'—a wonderful struggling mixed feeling, half shame, half pride, of being—to most people's knowledge a stern cold thinker, a calm pleasant friend of men, dearly loved by women, the favorite of children—a widow—a celibate, a solitary—and inside—Ashtoreth![33]

Ashtoreth, the fertility goddess: in ancient cultures she was worshipped as the Queen of Heaven. In Palestine she dates back to the time of earliest Semitic occupation. Solomon built a shrine to her near Jerusalem. In Babylon and Assyria her name was Ishtar. But if Ashtoreth was powerful to Gilman, she was not so pleasing to many of her contemporary writers. To Biblical scholar and professor George Barton, for instance, writing in 1891, Ashtoreth was a goddess who, 'measured by our standards', would be considered a 'demon of impurity'. To the prophets of Israel, Ashtoreth and her 'impure cults' were a threat to 'the very basis of family life and social purity'. Her behaviour was 'in some details [so] disgustingly obscene', that as cultures became more 'civilized' they necessarily had to 'root out' her 'excessive impurity' and impress 'a higher moral standard upon the people as a whole, which in subsequent centuries wrought out its beneficent results'. After all, this Biblical scholar continues, Israel's prophetic leaders wanted 'obedience to Yahweh; and Yahweh required a life of moral purity, of mercy towards the poor, and a service of himself as absolute and whole-hearted as a wife should render her husband'. This conflict with heathenism, with Ashtoreth and her allied cults, must finally be replaced by moral purity and religious truth.[34]

No wonder Gilman loved her. No wonder she was excited about retrieving this rebel woman archetype, worshipped by thousands as a goddess. I'm excited, and obviously others are as well, with the research findings of contemporary scholars: Marija Gimbutas, for example, providing us with rich archaeological evidence for the prepatriarchal women who were so often revered and honoured; Gerda Lerner exploring some of the origins of patriarchy; China Galland following the path of the ancient Tara from continent to continent—from Tibet, to Poland, to Mexico—where often, as the 'Black Madonna', Tara was viewed as the protector of the most impoverished, the most oppressed; Carol Christ teaching us about 'Diving Deep and Surfacing'; Mary Daly calling for intergalactic travel, 'Outercourse', she calls it; or Clarissa Pinkoka Estes asking us to 'Dance with the Wolves'; or Ntozake Shange stating simply, 'I found god in myself / and I loved her fiercely'.[35]

So many women's stories, so many fairy tales, so many journey myths, suggest a gruelling challenge: Persephone in Hades, Inanna's descent into the underworld, Medusa, terrifying with her serpent hair. It is almost as though Gilman's day- and night-time images, her dream images as well as metaphors in letters, anticipate later understandings: that Medusa *had* been laughing as she took her to the underworld, that Medusa was beautiful as well as ugly, the serpent goddess in ancient Libya, her head surrounded by serpent hair, the revered symbol of divine female wisdom.

Ashtoreth, the fertility goddess, Medusa the life-giving and death-giving goddess with the magic moon blood—these archetypal images served ancient peoples. They served Gilman's generation. And they also serve our own. For not only do they help us to resist destructive patriarchal images, but also to celebrate women's creativity and power. Gilman recognized, as we do, the need for myth as well as reason. But more importantly, she recognized the need to see patriarchy itself as myth, and to allow Cassandra, silenced for centuries, finally to be heard.

In conclusion I would like to give Gilman a very heart-felt word of thanks. I have worked on her writings for years—her published works, and more importantly her private writings, and I would like warmly and publicly to thank her for several very special gifts:

First, for using her intellect to probe the intellectual complexity and depth of women's issues.

Second, for taking bold interdisciplinary perspectives; for having the chutzpah to probe the fields of biology, history, anthropology, economics, sociology, psychology—and as a consequence to roam out through galactic space, to use Mary Daly's words.

Third, for maintaining a healthy distance from academia. Because even though Gilman wished that she were more 'credentialed', and even though she teased from time to time about her lack of abc or xyz degrees, the result, I think, was that she kept her creativity intact. Unshackled by the sacred canon, she focused on her own priorities, and on the realities of her own and other women's lives.

Fourth, I want to thank her for plunging down into the underworld—depressing, painful and debilitating as that clearly was—and saving the record of that journey. Never yielding to the monsters of addiction that could have sapped her strength and offered cheap solutions, she confronted the Medusa she had been taught to fear and the Ashtoreth whom she grew to find and love within herself.

Fifth, for returning from the journey to the underworld—*The Journey From Within*—and then describing what she had learned. Joseph Campbell makes an important distinction between the hero and the celebrity. The celebrity, he suggests, seeks fame and recognition; the hero returns as messenger, as healer, or, in Gilman's case, as woman-empowering-woman.[36]

That is not to say that I admire everything about this woman's movement leader. Like most people, she had her limitations, her dark side, her racism, her ethnocentricity, her homophobia—all of which we must openly acknowledge. But she none the less was an impressive mentor, a delightful humorist, a spiritual leader, a radical critic of patriarchal history, an imaginative writer guiding us to prepatriarchal history, and a proud, lusty lady who urged us lustily to find the goddess in ourselves.

Notes

1 A paraphrasing of the conclusion of *The Yellow Wallpaper* (R p. 19).

2 Audre Lorde, 'Breast Cancer: Power vs. Prosthesis' in Pat C. Hoy II, Esther H. Schor and Robert DiYanni, eds, *Women's Voices: Visions and Perspectives* (New York: McGraw-Hill, 1990), p. 165.

3 See Leslie Silko, *Almanac of the Dead* (New York: Simon & Schuster, 1991); *Ceremony* (New York: Viking, 1971).

4 For an extensive treatment of these private letters see Mary A. Hill, ed., *A Journey From Within: The Love Letters of Charlotte Gilman, 1896–1900* (Lewisburg: Bucknell University Press, 1995).

5 Charlotte Perkins Gilman, *Women and Economics* (New York: Harper Torchbooks, 1966), p. 331.

6 Charlotte Perkins Stetson (CPS) to George Houghton Gilman (GHG), 26 July 1899, Arthur and Elizabeth Schlesinger Library of Radcliffe College (AESL).

7 Mary Field Belenky et al., *Women's Ways of Knowing: The Development of Self, Voice, and Mind* (New York: Basic Books, 1986).

8 CPS to GHG, undated letter, April 1897; 4 June 1897; 2 September 1897, 5 September 1897, AESL.

9 CPS to GHG, 5 June l897, 28 November 1899, AESL.

10 CPS to GHG, 14 November 1899, AESL.

11 CPS to GHG, 14 March 1900, 16 September 1898, AESL.

12 CPS to GHG, 25 January 1899, AESL.

13 CPS to GHG, 6 November 1898, 5 December 1898, AESL.

14 CPS to GHG, 3 November 1897, AESL.

15 See Carter Heyward, *Touching Our Strength: The Erotic as Power and the Love of God* (San Francisco: Harper & Row, 1989).

16 CPS to GHG, 20 January 1899, 5 May 1898, 15 March 1899, 14 March 1899, AESL.

17 CPS to GHG, 7 November 1897, AESL.

18 CPS to GHG, 16 May 1899, 6 November 1899, 28 July 1899, 26 July 1899, AESL.

19 CPS to GHG, 5 December 1898, 16 June 1897, AESL.

20 According to conventional narratives, white middle-class women were expected to experience the 'erotic impulse'. But if they also experienced the 'impulse to power', almost always they 'suffered individual guilt, each supposing herself a monster when she did not fit the acceptable narrative of a

female life'; Carolyn Heilbrun, *Writing a Woman's Life* (New York: W. W. Norton, 1988), p. 45.

21 CPS to GHG, 1 October 1897, AESL.

22 CPS to GHG, 8 November 1897, AESL. Although the traditional myth suggests that Persephone was raped by Hades and then was taken forcefully to the underworld, a more feminist version of the story envisions her as travelling voluntarily, purposefully, and autonomously. See, for example, Charlene Spretnak, 'The Myth of Demeter and Persephone' in Judith Plaskow and Carol Christ, eds. *Weaving the Visions: New Patterns in Feminist Spirituality* (San Francisco: Harper & Row, 1989), pp. 72–74.

23 CPS to GHG, 10 March 1899, 3 November 1897, 14 March 1899, 7 June 1897, AESL.

24 CPS to GHG, 22 September 1898, AESL.

25 CPG, undated document, AESL.

26 Hélène Cixous, 'The Laugh of the Medusa' in Pat C. Hoy II, Esther H. Schor and Robert DiYanni, eds, *Women's Voices: Visions and Perspectives* (New York: McGraw-Hil, 1990), p. 489.

27 Nelle Morton, *The Journey is Home* (Boston: Beacon Press, 1985).

28 Hélène Cixous, 'The Laugh of the Medusa', pp. 481–95.

29 CPS to GHG, 5 October 1898, 8 May 1898, 21 May 1898, 20 February 1898, AESL.

30 CPS to GHG, 20 February 1898, AESL.

31 CPS to GHG, 6 May 1898, AESL.

32 CPS to GHG, 29 November 1898, 4 May 1897, 28 December 1898, 2 April 1898, 12 March 1899, 18 December 1898, AESL.

33 CPS to GHG, 18 December 1898, AESL. In Greek mythology, Ashtoreth was a ruler of the universe, a Charioteer trying to live her life with authority, with self-mastery, trying to keep her balance while moving at high speeds.

34 George A. Barton, 'Ashtoreth and her Influence in the Old Testament', *Journal of Biblical Literature*, Tenth Year, 1891, Part II, pp. 73–91.

35 See Marija Gimbutas, *The Goddesses and Gods of Old Europe, 6500–3500 B.C.: Myth and Cult Images* (London, Thames and Hudson, 1982); Gerda Lerner, *The Creation of Patriarchy* (New York: Oxford University Press, 1986); China Galland, *Longing for Darkness: Tara and the Black Madonna, A Ten-Year Journey* (New York: Viking Press, 1990); Carol Christ, *Diving Deep and Surfacing: Women Writers on a Spiritual Quest* (Boston: Beacon Press, 1980); Mary Daly, *Outercourse: The Be-Dazzling Voyage* (San Francisco: Harper, 1992); Clarissa Pinkola Estes, *Women Who Run with the Wolves: Myths and Stories of the Wild Woman Archetype* (New York: Ballantine Books, 1992); Ntozake Shange, *For Colored Girls Who have Considered Suicide When the Rainbow is Enough* (New York: Bantam, 1982), p. 67.

36 Joseph Campbell, *The Power of Myth* with Bill Moyers, Betty Sue Flowers, eds (New York: Anchor Doubleday, 1988), pp. 151–52.

Rewriting Male Myths: *Herland* and the Utopian Tradition

CHRIS FERNS

When *Herland* first appeared in the pages of *The Forerunner*, almost exactly four hundred years had elapsed since the publication of Thomas More's *Utopia* in 1516—a period during which utopian narrative was a genre overwhelmingly dominated by men. Not only were the vast majority of utopias written by men, but utopian narrative itself may be seen to embody a distinctively male fantasy: one which reinscribes or even reinforces the patriarchal values of the society to which utopia proposes otherwise radical alternatives. The purpose of this chapter is to investigate the extent to which this reflects the ideological implications of the narrative form itself, and to examine the problems that arise when a writer —such as Charlotte Perkins Gilman—seeks to rewrite utopian narrative in the service of a gender ideology very different from that which such narrative normally encodes.

In More's original formulation, utopian narrative is a hybrid, derived from two quite disparate narrative models: the classical dialogue on the one hand, and what Ernst Bloch terms 'the sailor's yarn'—the contemporary discovery narrative—on the other. It is, even in More's hands, a somewhat awkward combination—yet at the same time one which makes a certain amount of sense in a Renaissance context. Where the opening up of the New World and the resurgence of interest in classical learning were two of the most powerful incentives to intellectual change, such a combination might be seen as peculiarly appropriate for the articulation of visions of new and different social structures—and certainly the enthusiastic adoption of More's narrative model by later writers such as Tomasso Campanella and Francis Bacon would seem to attest to this. Rather more puzzling, however, is its continuing influence long after the age of discovery had come to an end, and in the face of the emergence of other, more flexible narrative models. For, despite the importation of such novelistic or romance elements as a love interest or some form of intrigue, the basic pattern of utopian narrative remains largely unchanged until the 1970s, and the radical reworkings not only of utopian ideas, but also of their accompanying narrative structures, by writers such as Monique Wittig, Ursula Le Guin, Marge Piercy, and Sally Miller Gearhart. Gilman, by contrast, works very much within the constraints of the traditional narrative paradigm, with its guided tour of uncharted territory, supplemented by copious discussion of the wonders of utopian society, although it must be said that her modifications are of considerably greater narrative interest than, say, Edward Bellamy's inclusion of the mawkish courtship between Edith Leete and Julian West in *Looking Backward* (1888), or H. G. Wells's desperate attempt to enliven the utopian vision of *Men Like Gods* (1923), which features a full-blown insurrection against utopia led by a fictional representation of Winston Churchill.

To argue that utopian narrative embodies a distinctively male fantasy is, of course, hardly new.[1] However, in order to establish a context for a discussion of Gilman's rewriting of the traditional paradigm, a number of its aspects are worth examining. To begin with, it is clear that both the narrative models from which it derives carry their own ideological freight. And, for all their formal disparity, both classical dialogue and discovery narrative do share one thing in common: both are forms that effectively mask their ideological intent. Thus, while the dialogue ostensibly offers an interplay of voices from whose conflicting, subjective viewpoints a single, objective truth emerges, it is in fact, as Mikhail Bakhtin observes, a vehicle all too readily 'transformed into a simple form for expounding already found, ready-made irrefutable truth;'[2] a didactic tool which represents the very antithesis of Bakhtinian dialogic. While More's *Utopia* does preserve an element of genuine debate, his successors' use of the format almost invariably results in a scenario where one of the interlocutors becomes a passive audience for the authoritative utterance of the other. Some critics have attempted to present this in a more positive light, suggesting that the effect is to 'position readers to see their own society differently',[3] yet a less charitable reader response might be to complain that the debate has been blatantly rigged.

Discovery narratives, in both their original and utopian forms, prove similarly deceptive. Ostensibly offering a record of the discovery of the new and unknown, they all too often transform themselves into reinscriptions of the old. Columbus's accounts of naming the newly charted territories to the greater glory of God and the King of Spain are less celebrations of the wonders of the unknown, than of the opening up of new space into which the existing order can be re-projected. And if that space should happen to be already inhabited, so much the worse for the inhabitants. In many cases, the discovery narrative is essentially merely a prelude to the process of conquest and colonization—which is, surprisingly, very much the form it takes in its utopian reworking. Although More seems at first sight appealingly open to the example of the Other, in that his utopia is at one level an extrapolation from accounts of South American societies where money and private property were unknown, it is also a narrative of conquest. More's Utopia did not evolve into the state of perfection recorded by his narrator; rather, it was imposed on the indigenous population by a conquering king, who then proceeded to transform society in their best interests, although where he got his ideas of civic harmony from remains unclear. And this is a pattern which recurs, again and again. More's Utopians, for instance—while fighting only in self-defence—have succeeded in so dominating their neighbours that many 'have made a practice of asking for Utopians to rule over them', with the result that Utopian administrators are sent out to serve rotating terms, for all the world like colonial governors.[4] In Campanella's *The City of the Sun* (1623), likewise, the Solarians are constantly at war with their neighbours (although again, only in self-defence), and invariably win, following which conquered cities 'receive Solarian officials and a garrison from the City of the Sun and proceed to model their institutions after those of that city'.[5] Even in later, more pacific utopias there are echoes of this pattern, with a recurrent emphasis not so much on the construction of the new order, as on the erasure of what was already there. While Bellamy's future Boston retains its familiar geographical features, there is no vestige of the human structures that once accompanied them; in William Morris's *News From Nowhere* (1890), one of the principal utopian activities is the demolition of the ugly evidences of the old order; and in Wells's *In the Days of the Comet* (1906), the transition to utopia is accompanied by a 'vast exultant dust of house-breaking' as the world's cities are summarily levelled prior to the work of utopian reconstruction.[6] The fate of Edinburgh, Philadelphia and Chicago is precisely similar to that of the great City of Mexico at the hands of the conquistadores. And in this regard, Gilman could hardly be more traditional: the prelude to the establishment of her utopia is, after all, a war of extermination, in which the women of Herland slaughter the revolting slaves, although again, only in self-defence.

Dialogues where only one voice has authority; dreams of a rational new order beneath which lurk fantasies of conquest and destruction: one might argue that the masculine character of the utopian dream already begins to become apparent. Yet there is a deeper level at which both the utopian and the discovery narrative may be seen as embodiments of masculine desire. Ernst Bloch suggests that the dream of discovery is itself utopian—that underlying such overt motivations as the desire for commercial profit or new territory there is present a utopian ambition 'much too fantastic to manifest itself... openly': a fantasy of 'nothing less [than]... *the finding of the earthly paradise itself*'.[7] Which is quite literally true: Columbus himself was convinced that Eden was located somewhere upriver from the mouth of the Orinoco, and in his account of his third voyage, he even proposed that the earth, far from being spherical, was actually pear-shaped, or 'como un teta de muger en una pelota redonda'—like a woman's nipple on a round ball.[8] And on this nipple-like elevation, from which streamed the life-giving waters of paradise, he believed Eden was located (although he doubted it could be reached by conventional navigation).

This association of paradise with the female body was, again, hardly new. Nearly two thousand years before Freud, the gnostic heretic, Simon Magus, suggested that the Garden of Eden was merely an allegory of the womb, where the individual was innocent, happy, idle, and plentifully supplied with nourishment.[9] Nor was Columbus alone in such fantasies: as Annette Kolodny has shown, the representation of the New World as passive and female, awaiting conquest and penetration by the male discoverer, is disturbingly common.[10] Yet if this is a recurrent feature of discovery narratives, it is still more glaringly apparent in utopias. From More's crescent-shaped island, with its horns enclosing a large, placid bay, accessible only through a single narrow channel, to Aldous Huxley's *Island* (1962), where entrance is gained via 'a kind of headlong ravine where a little stream came down in a succession of filmy waterfalls',[11] utopias abound in images of womb-like enclosures entered by narrow passageways; while the recurrent utopian programme, with its reduced working hours, guaranteed food supply, security, and freedom from sexual guilt, suggests that utopia is essentially another dream of paradise, only put on a more rational basis.

What is clear, however, is that utopian bliss is to be attained only through the imposition of a distinctively male hierarchy. As has often been pointed out, for all its radical departures from existing social practice (the abolition of money and private property, for example), the one feature of existing society that remains fundamental to More's Utopia is the patriarchal family; while in Bacon's *New Atlantis* (1627) patriarchy is, if anything, raised to a higher power. There, the main social ritual described is the feast which celebrates any patriarch who has more than thirty living descendants. While the feast is described in loving detail, there proves to be one notable absentee: the wife who actually bore the children, who is shut up in a small closet with a grille in the gallery above, from which she may view the proceedings, though without being seen herself.

Of greater relevance to Gilman's use of the form, however, is its apparent capacity to undermine the efforts of writers to challenge or subvert its patriarchal norms. Campanella, for instance, proposes radical social changes, including the abolition of the family, and declares that in his City of the Sun 'both sexes are trained in all pursuits' (including warfare), and that men and women do exactly the same work 'whether of a mental or mechanical nature'.[12] Yet as soon as he comes to amplify this radical assertion of equality—surely astonishing for the early seventeenth century—he seems to draw back, adding the telling phrase 'con questa distinzione'[13] (with this distinction) which is followed by a long list of disabling qualifications whose effect is to reinstate virtually all the inequalities previously denied. In Bellamy's *Looking Backward*, likewise, while we learn that 'the independence of women' has finally been achieved, his portrayal of the actual role of women scarcely supports this assertion. While there is compulsory employment for both sexes until the age of forty-five, the main female character, Edith Leete, leads a life of apparent idleness, relieved only by the joys of courtship and frequent shopping expeditions. Moreover, although Bellamy makes much of the fact that economic considerations no longer dictate a woman's choice of marital partner, it soon transpires that this has a decidedly utilitarian aspect. Besides 'tending to race-purification', the resultant 'untrammeled sexual selection' is also a major incentive to industrial efficiency.[14] No longer tempted by wealth and rank, women now tend 'naturally' to love the most dedicated workers, with the result that sexual, rather than economic incentives fuel the utopian system of production:

> ... not all the encouragements and incentives of every sort which we have provided to develop industry, talent, genius, excellence of whatever kind, are comparable in their effect on our young men with the fact that our women sit aloft as judges of the race and reserve themselves to reward the winner. Of all the whips, and spurs, and baits, and prizes, there is none like the thought of the radiant faces which the laggards will find averted.[15]

Men, in other words, do the *real* work; women constitute the reward for its successful performance.

One could multiply examples: Wells's *A Modern Utopia* (1905), for instance, sets out to represent a utopia where the equality of women and men is a reality, yet contains one of the most blatant assertions of the sexual double standard ever written. No matter how honourable the intentions, it would seem, utopian narrative repeatedly reinscribes a fantasy of male control, of subordinating the 'natural' qualities of woman to the demands of a rational, hierarchical, and male-dominated order. What Anne Cranny-Francis refers to as the capacity of narrative convention to encode gender discourses which 'may subvert the oppositional gender discourse also coded into the text', and to exercise a 'conservative and conservatizing function... the gender ideology of which is patriarchal' is nowhere more apparent than in utopian narrative.[16] In choosing to work within its conventions, then, Gilman might be seen as entering something of an ideological minefield.

At first sight, Gilman's utopian narrative could scarcely be more conventional, in fact: whereas such immediate predecessors as Bellamy, Morris, and Wells had at least acknowledged the implications of the end of the age of discovery by either projecting their utopias into the future, or positing such science fictional scenarios as the existence of parallel universes, Gilman adheres to the time-honoured convention of the geographical utopia, still undiscovered, lying in some unspecified southland, and apparently inaccessible. While its actual configuration might suggest a somewhat different locus of desire—'This piece of geography', we are told, 'stands up like a basalt column' (H p. 38)—we are elsewhere informed that Herland is entirely walled in by mountains, following a volcanic outburst which resulted in 'the complete filling up of the pass—their only outlet' (H p. 54) to the world beyond. It is a familiar enough scenario, yet it is here that a first crucial difference becomes apparent. Whereas in the conventional utopia access to the forbidden territory is very much under male control,[17] Gilman's maternal landscape is represented as firmly in the possession of women.

This in turn lends a very different character to the otherwise standard narrative device of the visit to utopia. In most utopias, it would seem that the main problem faced by the visitor is getting in (although re-emerging from it can also prove traumatic); yet once this ordeal is past, the visitor's existence is largely problem-free: welcomed with open arms, fed, and spoken to in a language he understands, he enjoys an almost infantile freedom from care and responsibility (Huxley's *Island* provides perhaps the most extreme example: there the visitor's first experience is to be put to bed by a kindly doctor, and then lulled to sleep by the voice of a maternal young woman). In *Herland*, however, such infantilization proves rather less seductive. In a marked departure from conventional utopian practice, Gilman's visitors experience little difficulty in reaching utopia: they simply fly there (although it is noteworthy that their arrival is nevertheless accompanied by an obscure sense of transgression). It is only after they get there that their problems begin. Far from being welcomed with open arms, the narrator reports:

> Each of us was seized by five women, each holding arm or leg or head; we were lifted like children, straddling helpless children, and borne onward, wriggling indeed, but most ineffectually. (H p. 23)

'Struggling manfully, but held secure most womanfully' (H p. 23), they are carried inside, anaesthetized, undressed, washed, and put to bed, as one explorer ruefully acknowledges, 'like so many yearling babies' (H p. 25). What starts out with all the trappings of a tale of conventional male derring-do, in the tradition of Rider Haggard's *King Solomon's Mines* (1885), or Conan Doyle's *The Lost World* (1912), soon leaves its intrepid explorers feeling 'like small boys, very small boys, caught doing mischief in some gracious lady's house' (H p. 19).

In effect, Gilman transforms the standard device of the visit to utopia from the conventional (and in narrative terms, stultifying) guided tour into a satiric vehicle which, far more explicitly than most utopias, focuses attention on the shortcomings of the reader's own world. In this sense, in fact, Gilman might be seen as closer to the original example of More, who devotes nearly half of *Utopia* to an attack on the abuses and corruption of his own society, than to that of his successors, for whom the blueprint of the ideal society often overshadows consideration of the social problems that presumably render utopia desirable in the first place. While other writers provide the odd satiric flash—Bellamy's celebrated parable of the coach in *Looking Backward*, for example, or Morris's fantasy of making the Houses of Parliament literally, rather than merely figuratively, a storehouse for horse manure—few utopias offer so sustained a satire on existing society. Elizabeth Keyser, indeed, sees *Herland* as more in the tradition of *Gulliver's Travels* (1726) than of the conventional utopia—and certainly Gilman's utopians, like Swift's Houhyhnhms or the King of Brobdingnag, prove astute readers between the lines of their visitors' utterance. Despite what Van, the narrator, describes as 'a tacit endeavour to conceal much of the social status at home' (H p. 80), Herland's women prove singularly adept at drawing deductions not only from what they are told, but also from 'the things we palpably avoided saying' (H p. 80).

The effect of this is to return a sense of *genuine* dialogue to the proceedings: while Gilman's intent is no less didactic than that of earlier utopian writers, there are far fewer of the ponderous, one-sided set pieces that characterize so many utopian narratives. While her visitors may often make fools of themselves, what they say actually *matters*, in a way that is rarely the case in narratives where the visitor's main function is merely to assent to and be persuaded by what he is told. Gilman, in fact, devotes far less space than usual to direct disquisitions on the wonders of utopia, and far more to the reactions of the visitors to what they are experiencing, while at the same time exploiting the difference in gender to sharpen the contrast between their perspective and that of the inhabitants. As a result, although the dynamic of the relations between visitors and utopians remains in keeping with the traditional paradigm, the effect could hardly be more dissimilar. In *Herland* it is women who have the knowledge and power, the men who have to adjust to the values and expectations of the society in which they find themselves; and by enacting this reversal of conventional gender roles, Gilman calls attention to the situation of the visitor in a way that most utopian fictions do not. In place of the uncritical transmission of information which the visitor normally provides, as if his sole purpose were to provide the reader with the most faithful and unmediated account possible of utopia's merits, Gilman's visitors respond to their situation in a manner which is often confused, reluctant, or even frankly hostile. Rather than trying to close the gap in perception between the utopians and their visitor(s) as fast as possible, Gilman stresses its existence, at the same time encouraging the reader to judge the judgements of the visitors. *Herland*, in other words, encourages what most utopian fictions prior to it seek to suppress: an active critical participation on the part of the reader.

One side-effect of this is that the actual *character* of the visitor takes on a significance seldom encountered in the traditional utopia, where the visitor is often little more than a medium for the transmission of the utopian message. Whereas the sheer passivity of most visitors to utopia renders them virtually interchangeable—one feels that it would make very little difference to the actual narrative if it were Huxley's Will Farnaby who arrived in Bellamy's future Boston, or Bellamy's Julian West who landed in Huxley's Pala—in *Herland* the differing characters of Gilman's visitors matter, representing as they do radically different possible interactions between the values of utopia and those of the outside world. Thus, while the narrator, Van, may be seen as conforming fairly closely to the traditional norm, inasmuch as he is soon persuaded of the superiority of the utopian way, he is flanked by two companions whose long-held assumptions seem less susceptible to alteration by exposure to the utopian ideal.

The more immediately striking example is Terry, the ultramasculine leader of the expedition, whose only real interest in women is as objects of sexual desire. His initial vision, when informed of the existence of an exclusively female society, is 'of a sort of sublimated summer resort—just Girls and Girls and Girls' (H p. 7)—and he talks, only half-jokingly, of becoming a latter-day King Solomon. When the reality proves to be conspicuously different from his anticipations, it is he who leads an unsuccessful escape bid, who shows the clearest frustration with the constraints imposed on them, and who is most consistently critical of utopian society. Yet here again Gilman's focus is less on the perfections of utopia, than on the glaring inadequacies of the visitor's response. Brave, resourceful, charismatic, 'a man's man' (H p. 9), Terry seems at first sight the archetypal heroic explorer of (male-authored) romance. Yet in the context of Herland's value system his 'manliness' often seems indistinguishable from childish petulance. His evident resentment of women who do not conform to his expectations regarding appropriate female behaviour expresses itself in schoolboyish humour: he makes digs at the 'Colonels' or 'Grandmas', as he characterizes his captors, and contrives extremely forced puns on the names of the tutors he and his companions are assigned. Unable to get his own way, his frustration at the 'old-maid impudence' (H p. 33) that prevents him mixing with 'real girls', together with his conviction that '[t]here never was a woman yet that did not enjoy being *mastered*' (H p. 131), culminate in an attempted rape. Despite the example of an entire society of women controlling their own destiny and being happy doing so, he clings to his fixed belief that what a woman really wants is to be forced to submit to the 'superior' power of the man. Not even the dismal failure of his attempt at a practical demonstration seems to move him. While the response of his intended victim (a powerful kick in the testicles) would seem to constitute a convincing refutation of his thesis, he remains unpersuaded: '"I'd give a year of my life to have her alone again", he said slowly, his hands clenched till the knuckles were white' (H p. 143).

By itself, this might seem perilously close to caricature—which is not to say that a good deal of conventional male behaviour might not also be described in the same terms—but Terry's crude attempts at asserting male superiority are only one aspect of Gilman's representation of male responses to the threatening reversal of gender expectations which Herland represents. As well as Terry and the narrator, the party has a third member: Jeff, the doctor, who 'idealized women in the best Southern style. He was full of chivalry and sentiment, and all that. And he was a good boy; he lived up to his ideals' (H p. 9). As a result, it is Jeff who is by far the most enthusiastic about the matriarchal society they encounter—to the extent that his companions begin to regard him as 'something of a traitor—he so often flopped over and took their side of things' (H p. 51). Yet while Jeff displays none of the closed-minded opposition which Terry exhibits, neither does he seem in any way *changed* by his experiences, as the narrator is. Of the three, it is Jeff who most closely resembles the passive, uncritical observer of the traditional utopia. Having always idealized women, and seen them as other than they are (the narrator complains of his tendency to put 'rose-colored halos' [H p. 9] on them), his attitude on encountering women who differ markedly from those he is used to remains virtually unchanged: the irony that in Herland women's superiority is practical rather than theoretical appears to escape him. Like so many visitors to utopia, Jeff, while uncritically approving of its superiority, seems oddly immune to any sense of its otherness. Utopia is better; but it is not *strange*.

While Terry and the narrator, each in his own way, exhibit an acute awareness of the difference of the world in which they find themselves, Jeff far more closely resembles the traditional visitor, in that he seems already to have accepted the premises of utopia before even arriving there.

Yet while Gilman's focus on the problematic nature of the visitors' responses lends to her narrative a genuinely dialogic character that distinguishes it from utopias where the dialogue format merely serves to mask the unidirectional and monologic transmission of information, in other respects she is less successful at escaping the constraints imposed by her narrative model.[18] Thus, while at first sight her matriarchal society of 'ultra-women' could hardly be further removed from the patriarchal norms of utopian tradition, this reversal of one of utopian narrative's major premises in fact leaves many of its dynamics unaffected. As Susan Gubar points out, 'Gilman's strategy of reversal [often] threatens to invalidate her feminism by defining it in precisely the terms set up by the misogynists it would repudiate'.[19] While the feminine values which *Herland* endorses offer a positive alternative to the abuses of the patriarchal society of the three explorers, they nevertheless reflect a concept of femininity which is very much the creation of precisely that male-dominated society whose values Gilman rejects. As has often been pointed out, *Herland* is a utopia in which woman's sphere remains the home; the only difference is that here the home has expanded to embrace the entire community. When Terry sneers that '[t]here isn't a home in the whole pitiful place', Jeff retorts that '[t]here isn't anything else, and you know it' (H p. 98). Herland is a country which has been entirely domesticated: there are no wild areas—even the forests are groomed and cultivated to be useful as well as merely beautiful; the entire land has been purged of pests and mess-creating animals; and overall, we learn, 'their country was as neat as a Dutch kitchen' (H p. 53).

Yet while this would seem accurately to reflect the concept of domestic virtues prevalent at the time, it is also wholly in keeping with the visions of utopia offered by earlier, male writers. From More's *Utopia*, where even the cities are both identical and equidistant, to Wells's *Men Like Gods*, which shares Gilman's passion for cleanliness to the point of eliminating not only all pavement-fouling animals, but even 'the untidier sorts of small birds',[20] utopian narratives recurrently represent worlds where everything is in its place, known and accounted for. As in the best-run homes, utopia provides an environment where nothing ever goes wrong, indeed, where nothing ever *happens*. As Wells complains, in *A Modern Utopia*, the difficulty with most utopias is that they are 'static', rather than 'kinetic': process and change—anything that is liable to disturb order—are normally conspicuous in utopia only by their absence.

Herland is no exception in this regard. As in so many utopias, the account of its history is vague and in places even contradictory: from a developmental level described as being equivalent to 'that of Ancient Egypt or Greece' (H p. 67) at the time of its traumatic severing from the rest of the world, Herland has apparently advanced to the point where electric cars travel along modern highways, yet very little appears to have *happened* in the interim. The utopians, we are told, are 'agreed on most of the basic principles of their life; and not only agreed in principle, but accustomed for these sixty-odd generations to act on those principles' (H p. 122). Yet despite this continuity, the inhabitants of Herland, like those of so many other utopias, exhibit singularly little interest in the past. When the narrator asks his bride-to-be: 'Have you no respect for the past? For what was thought and believed by your foremothers?', she replies simply: 'Why, no... Why should we? They are all gone. They knew less than we do.' The women of Herland, he reflects, 'had ignored their past and built daringly for the future' (H p. 111). And this vagueness concerning history has its counterpart, at the narrative level, in a consistent vagueness with regard to the passage of time: 'the weeks ran into months' (H p. 33) is a typical formulation, and while we learn at the end that the visitors' stay has lasted 'more than a year' (H p. 137), there is virtually no specific indication as to when anything takes place during that period. Given the book's opening words—'This is written from memory, unfortunately' (H p. 1)—it would appear that this is a deliberate narrative strategy.

Yet what is perhaps most problematic in *Herland* is not so much the lack of action as (as a number of critics have pointed out) the absence of *desire*, which has apparently vanished along with the elimination of sexual difference. Herland's citizens are women whose 'great life-view had no shady places; they had a high sense of personal decorum, but no shame—no knowledge of anything to be ashamed of' (H p. 101). As the narrator later remarks: 'No wonder this whole nation of women was peaceful and sweet in expression—they had no horrible ideas' (H p. 111). Free from even such 'pleasant vices' (H p. 98) as drinking and smoking, it is a world which in the more acid words of Terry, is 'like a perpetual Sunday school' (H p. 99). Yet this, too, however much it might reflect contemporary stereotypes of 'feminine' virtues, is very much in keeping with utopian tradition. *Herland* shares with its predecessors the characteristic utopian impulse towards simplification: problems are not so much resolved, as avoided by the elimination of their source. As in More's *Utopia*, it is difficult to get into trouble, primarily because there is so little trouble to get into. A central aspect of More's utopian programme is the restoration of sexual innocence, largely through the control of, or elimination of sexual desire, and in this he is followed by the majority of his successors. From

Campanella's City of the Sun, where intercourse is supervised by a team of gymnasium instructors, doctors, and astrologers, or Bacon's New Atlantis, which is described as 'the Virgin of the world', down to Wells's Modern Utopia, where celibacy is one of the prerequisites for leadership, the same dream is evident: of a return to the innocence of childhood, or even infancy. When Gilman compares the awkward questions posed by her women to those of 'a clear-eyed, intelligent, perfectly honest, and well-meaning child' (H p. 62), she may be seen as echoing four hundred years of utopian tradition.

The problem with this, however, is that in doing so Gilman ends up reinstating the infantilization of the visitor which she began by satirizing. Whereas the reduction of the intrepid explorers on their arrival to the state of helpless children, undressed, washed, and put to bed, effectively satirizes the customary passivity of the traditional visitor to utopia, it is harder to discern any complicating irony in Gilman's later discussion of the 'marriages' contracted between the explorers and three of the inhabitants. Part of Gilman's purpose, of course, in putting forward the notion of marriages which include neither cohabitation nor sexual relations, is to focus attention on the assumptions of the male explorers, whose horror at the absence of what they have taken for granted is dealt with in some detail. (Or rather, to be more precise, the horror of two of the explorers: the idealistic Jeff does not appear to notice that there is anything unusual about the arrangements.) Yet when it comes to representing Herland's unconventional marital arrangements as desirable, Gilman resorts to some curiously revealing analogies. Trying to rationalize his wife's refusal to accept sexual relations as a 'natural' part of marriage, for instance, the narrator attempts to imagine:

> ... a devoted and impassioned man trying to set up housekeeping with a lady angel, a real wings-and-harp-and-halo angel, accustomed to fulfilling divine missions all over interstellar space. This angel might love the man with an affection quite beyond his power of return or even of appreciation, but her ideas of service and duty would be on a very different scale from his. (H p. 123)

Later still, having finally acknowledged the superiority of his wife's judgement, he continues:

> After I got over the jar to my pride... I found that loving 'up' was a very good sensation after all. It gave me a queer feeling, way down deep, as of the stirring of some ancient prehistoric consciousness, a feeling that they were right somehow—that this was the way to feel. It was like—coming home to mother. (H pp. 141–42)

Here the process of infantilization—which is elsewhere reinforced by his wife's use of such epithets as 'you blessed child' (H p. 110)—is represented in an entirely positive light. While the power relations envisaged in *Herland* are very different from those of the traditional male utopian fantasy, inasmuch as what is imagined is not the male recovery of prenatal security, but rather the restoration of the lost world of prehistoric matriarchy, the regressive character of the utopian dream remains very much in evidence.

One of *Herland's* most puzzling features, however, involves what would seem to be a clear departure from the utopian norm. Given that utopia so often represents a state of perfection or near-perfection, it follows that any change is likely to be for the worse, and the majority of male-authored utopias include provisions to prevent such an eventuality, whether it be the maintenance of well-trained and formidably equipped armies (although, of course, only for purposes of self-defence), keeping its whereabouts concealed, or extending its compass to include the entire world, thereby eliminating external enemies. In Herland, however, despite its inhabitants' evident satisfaction with things as they are, and in the face of all they have been able to deduce regarding the evils of the world outside, Gilman's women seem surprisingly open to the possibilities of renewed relations with men.[21] This does, of course, open the way for a sequel, duly provided in *With Her in Ourland* (1916), in which the narrator and his wife undertake a tour of his world, yet one of the oddest features of the decidedly abrupt conclusion which paves the way for this sequel is the women's apparent readiness to rely on their visitors' word of honour as gentlemen not to divulge Herland's whereabouts. Terry, angry and humiliated following his unsuccessful rape attempt, immediately protests that '[t]he first thing I'll do is to get an expedition fixed up to force an entrance into Ma-land' (H p. 146). Yet despite all they have witnessed regarding Terry's capacity for violence, the entirely alien concept of a gentleman's word apparently suffices, to the extent that a mere six lines later his promise has been accepted, and their departure ensues. Still more curious, though, is that it is also Terry, of all people, who gives the country its name. 'Herland' is represented as his invention, not that of the inhabitants. In more ways than one, Gilman's utopia is reliant on the word of a gentleman.[22]

Notes

1 See, for example, David Bleich, *Utopia: The Psychology of a Cultural Fantasy* (Ann Arbor: UMI Research Press, 1968).

2 Mikhail Bakhtin, *Problems of Dostoevsky's Poetics,* trans. and ed. Caryl Emerson (Minneapolis: University of Minnesota Press, 1984), p. 110.

3 Anne Cranny-Francis, *Feminist Fiction: Feminist Uses of Generic Fiction* (New York: St Martin's Press, 1990), p. 116.

4 Sir Thomas More, *Utopia*, trans. Robert M. Adams (New York: Norton, 1992), p. 69.

5 Tomasso Campanella, *The City of the Sun: A Poetical Dialogue*, trans. Daniel J. Donno (Berkeley: University of California Press, 1981), p. 77.

6 H. G. Wells, *In the Days of the Comet* (London: Macmillan, 1906), p. 200.

7 Ernst Bloch, *The Principle of Hope*, trans. Neville Plaice, Stephen Plaice and Paul Knight (Oxford: Blackwell, 1985), p. 751.

8 Christopher Columbus, *The Four Voyages of Christopher Columbus*, trans. Cecil Jane (New York: Dover, 1988), p. 131.

9 Frank P. Manuel and Fritzie Manuel, *Utopian Thought in the Western World* (Oxford: Blackwell, 1979), p. 43.

10 Annette Kolodny, *The Lay of the Land: Metaphor as Experience and History in American Life and Letters* (Chapel Hill: University of North Carolina Press, 1975).

11 Aldous Huxley, *Island* (Harmondsworth: Penguin, 1981), p. 6.

12 Tomasso Campanella, *The City of the Sun*, p. 49.

13 Ibid., p. 48.

14 Edward Bellamy, *Looking Backward 2000–1887* (Harmondsworth: Penguin, 1982), pp. 148–49.

15 Ibid., p. 149.

16 Anne Cranny-Francis, *Feminist Fiction*, p. 12.

17 Examples could be multiplied, but More provides as glaring an instance as any. In the narrow channel that offers the sole access to Utopia's womb-like bay, 'there is one rock that rises above the water, and so presents no dangers in itself; on top of it a tower has been built, and there is a garrison kept...' (*Utopia*, p. 34). Upon the clitoral rock, no obstacle in itself, More imposes the phallic image of the tower full of armed men.

18 While my purpose is to argue that the narrative paradigm is the root of some of the problematic features of Gilman's narrative, other critics see these as having specific ideological causes. Mary Hill, for example, sees some of *Herland*'s shortcomings stemming in part from the influence of Bellamy's Nationalist movement: 'like most Nationalists... [Gilman] was more effective in describing conditions which deprive human life of dignity and meaning than she was in projecting viable solutions'. Mary Hill, *Charlotte Perkins Gilman: The Making of a Radical Feminist* (Philadelphia: Temple University Press, 1980), p. 173.

19 Susan Gubar, '*She* in *Herland*: Feminism as Fantasy' in Sheryl L. Mayering, ed., *Charlotte Perkins Gilman: The Woman and her Work* (Ann Arbor: UMI Research Press, 1989), p. 198.

20 H.G. Wells, *Men Like Gods* (Harmondsworth: Penguin, 1987).

21 For perhaps a more logical, if disturbing, exploration of the implications of this scenario, see James Tiptree, 'Houston, Houston, Do You Read?' in Susan Anderson and Vonda McIntyre, eds, *Aurora: Beyond Equality* (New York: Fawcett, 1976).

22 In attaching such importance to a gentleman's word of honour, Gilman seems to be following Bellamy. In *Looking Backward*, the utopian Dr Leete says that 'the world has outgrown lying' (*Looking Backward*, p. 153); when the latter expresses astonishment, Dr Leete makes the astounding claim that: 'Falsehood, even in your day, was not common between gentlemen and ladies, social equals... Because we are now social equals... the contempt of falsehood is so universal that it is rarely that even a criminal in other respects will be found willing to lie' (ibid., p. 153).

Pockets of Resistance: Some Notes Towards an Exploration of Gender and Genre Boundaries in *Herland*

BRIDGET BENNETT

Charlotte Perkins Gilman was a writer for whom boundaries had little sanctity. For her they were to be challenged, explored, and circumnavigated. The restrictive boundaries of patriarchal institutions and of enclosed spaces are continually interrogated within and through her writing, either directly, by overt and political confrontation, or through metaphors and other formal devices. Her interest in debating the limitations of personal freedom for women led her to explore a great diversity of domestic spaces and limits, as well as to question the ways in which women function outside or beyond them. She was fascinated by issues of interiority, by arenas outside the public domain, and she extended her investigations into surprising minutiae. Her explorations range from the mind of a woman suffering from post-natal depression to the possibilities of the private sites which clothing offers: her advocacy of rational dress, for example. She was a keen upholder of the possibilities offered by pockets, which she saw as gendered spaces. In the late nineteenth and early twentieth century women's clothing tended not to have many (if any) substantial pockets, a fact which, arguably, suggests the boundaries or constraints which operated upon women. Men's clothes had pockets within which they might carry a range of useful objects and by this could extend the body's personal space and challenge the distinction between public and private. Pockets, though themselves dependent upon boundaries, also challenge them. They open on to the outside of clothes yet offer access to a private area within or beneath the exterior. So pockets exist at the intersections between public and private, external and internal, functioning both as the median between the two spheres but also belonging simultaneously to both and to neither.

The pocket is a marginal space. Its opening marks the boundary between surface and interior and enables it to partake of both worlds simultaneously, blurring distinctions. The hand reaches into the dark interior and disappears for a moment before depositing an object which is then lost to view or reappearing with one which then becomes part of an exterior domain. In this way the mystery of the pocket may open itself up to public scrutiny yet, due to its hidden nature, it still retains some elements of its enigma. The pocket is not instantly knowable but it *can* be known. Gilman recognized that women of her era had only limited access to these substantial pockets, mending them, for example (in other words maintaining them for men), or searching through them to find evidence of a male companion's misdeeds, a trope which is something of a commonplace in nineteenth-century fiction. She was a keen campaigner for dress reform throughout her career. On 23 October 1886 an article by her entitled 'Why Women Do Not Reform Their Dress' appeared in the *Woman's Journal.* On 5 February 1897 she notes in her diary that she lectured on 'The Body, The Dress and the House' and on 10 June 1896 on 'The Philosophy of Dress'[1] In 1923 she wrote triumphantly:

> The women of today are able to wear comfortable, beautiful and hygienic clothing, if they knew enough. There is far more latitude of choices, more freedom from narrow comment, and a clear improvement in a certain standardization of styles, as in the 'street suit', the business suit, and, best of all, the meeting of real athletic needs by the knickerbocker and riding suit.[2]

For Gilman the fantasy was partially of possession: of having pockets of one's own. In her fanciful 1914 story 'If I Were a Man' the protagonist, who is described as 'pretty little Mollie Matthewson', transforms into her husband for an unspecified period, and discovers what it is like to have this additional dimension to her, or rather his, personal space:

> Behind her newspaper she let her consciousness, that odd mingled consciousness, rove from pocket to pocket, realizing the armored assurance of having all these things at hand, instantly get-at-able, ready to meet emergencies. The cigar case gave her a warm feeling of comfort—it was full; the firmly held fountain pen, safe unless she stood on her head; the keys, pencils, letters, documents, notebook, checkbook, bill folder—all at once, with a deep rushing sense of power and pride, she felt what she had never felt before in all her life—the possession of money, of her own earned money—hers to give or withhold, not to beg for, tease for, wheedle for—hers. (R pp. 33–34)

Though the passage opens with a reflection on the pleasures of private spaces it quickly moves towards the thrill of being a property owner, and the potential of being a consumer. These are surprisingly full pockets: Mollie must bulge alarmingly. It is significant too that the pockets that Gilman, via Mollie, wants to have access to are those of a middle-class professional. Gilman also nicely reverses stereotypes: here a man is not investigating a woman's interior spaces, but instead it is the other way around. As I will argue later, this is what she does in *Herland* (1915). She combines a rhetoric of dimension ('rove'; 'full'; 'deep') with one of power ('assurance'; 'comfort'; 'possession') which connotes masculinity as well as class. To Gilman, pockets also signified the economic independence she battled for throughout her life. Reclaiming the pocket was, for her, a significant political concern. It is hardly surprising that in her utopian novel *Herland* the androgynous clothes have quantities of capacious and useful pockets. Though there is no need for the women of this novel to carry either keys or money, there are other possibilities for pockets and the desire for them, the fantasy of the pocket—of possessing and filling it, of having constant access to it—remains.

Just as Gilman's interest in pockets articulates her challenge to the boundaries of dress codes, so her diverse writing interventions in the world and her appropriation of many forms of writing, such as the romance, the quest narrative, the myth, as Janet Beer argues in her chapter in this volume, suggests her resistance to the constraints of writing boundaries. The difficulty of finding established and appropriate writing models (as well as pockets) and the boundaries of convention which her female protagonists can encounter as they try to express themselves are persistent themes in her writing: she wanted to communicate to other women and adopted numerous techniques (lectures, journalism, essays and fiction) in order best to do it. It is significant that the women of Herland who are continually producing written accounts of what their male visitors tell them are never without their notebooks and writing implements, presumably carried in their pockets. Although the women admit that it has been difficult to learn how to produce written narratives, they carry with them at least the possibility of being able to write, for they can carry their writing tools with them (Zava says: 'It took us a long time to learn how to write history' [H p. 47]). With their private apartments (two rooms of their own from childhood), their freedom from both financial necessity and domestic chores, the Herlanders seem to be able to control their interventions in the private and public spheres with ease.

Within Gilman's writing, the limits of women's personal space and freedom are often examined through the actual or imagined boundaries of, say, propriety or custom; age; sexuality and reproduction; and economics and the relation of women (primarily white, heterosexual, and middle-class) to the workplace and to domestic labour. Though she advocated an ethic of liberation from artificially manufactured boundaries, her interest was restricted, as I have suggested, to particular categories of women which makes some of her views unpalatable today. Her happy endings can ring false too. If it is frustrating for readers to be confronted with the plot manipulation necessary to produce women who free themselves from seemingly insuperably limiting circumstances, as her protagonists often do by the interventions of magic or of convenient and understanding mothers, these outcomes are at least consistent with the system of beliefs which made her want to be a dynamic forerunner, to borrow her own term.[3] If her protagonists often escape gender boundaries which threaten to confine them by unconvincing twists in their circumstances, it is partly because her writing resists being constrained into narrow literary forms. Her writing, though often realistic, is not strictly realist. It is often fantastical, frequently reads like a fairy tale complete, in several cases, with magic. These fluctuations between models, these appropriations of styles, this flexibility, are all highly characteristic of her refusal to be constrained. The fluidity (in one sense) of her writing identity suggests her reluctance to fix for herself or to appropriate a particular style. She seems unwilling to restrict herself to a single mode of expression, has a resistance towards possessing a consistent and predictable writing voice, and refuses to be put into a single explicatory category or pocket, so to speak. Her writing can be read partially as a sort of pastiche, or even a series of tableaux parodies, created for didactic purposes. Gilman may well be a more interesting and creative writer than she has been given credit for. Her imitative impulse might be considered in terms of her inability to find writing models which suited her purposes, might even be connected to a previously unsuspected sense of humour, however slight.[4] To start with, then, I want to look at the ways in which the narrative of *Herland* is constructed out of a patchwork of re-written patriarchal myths and idealized feminist fantasies.

In *Herland* Gilman constructs a paradigmatic female utopia through deconstructions and reworkings of ideologies which were coming under attack with increasing regularity in the latter part of the nineteenth century and early twentieth century. The publication of *The Women's Bible* (1895), for example, marked a significant challenge to Biblical authority.[5] *Herland* is a witty and ironic send-up of Judeo-Christian, American and patriarchal myths. The myth of the 'discovery' and settlement of America is mapped against the Genesis myth and against the background of the 1914–18 war so that the Genesis myth is also read by Gilman as an imperialist text which is itself about America. Further, the novel also works as a re-writing of myths of conquest and masculine endeavour and adventurism which were being celebrated in contemporary literature and journalism.[6] In the utopian world of *Herland*, the dystopian world of contemporary North America works as an invoked absent counterpart to the space of the novel. North America is outside the boundaries of this novel; it was to be explored more fully in *With Her in Ourland* (1916). The enclosed space of *Herland* (both nation and novel), a pocket of civilization in a vast dark continent, can be read against the theme of space which has so preoccupied commentators on North American culture and identity. This private world of woman's space, a kind of pocket in which all frontiers (geographical, sexual, economic, political) have been dramatically and enablingly shifted, operates as a liberating counterpart to the forced private world of *The Yellow Wallpaper* (1892).

At the start of *Herland* one of the male protagonists, an indolent wealthy young man, has turned to a life of exploration despite his complaint that 'there was nothing left to explore now, only patchwork and filling in' (H p. 2). Men have done it all—nothing remains but to piece together oddments (patchwork) and complement them with decorative ornamentation (filling in). The frontier has closed, boundaries are shrinking, space is disappearing, the would-be explorer has had to watch his potential terrain gradually reduce itself to disappointing dimensions. What is left for him to explore except the myth of origin itself? One question which the novel leaves unasked is what the three male explorers are looking for at the start of the novel. Are they in fact searching for an utopia? The question of what they are seeking, and of what they hope to see, is crucial to the novel, as is the technology which enables their voyage which marks it as a peculiarly modern method of colonization. For 1915, the year in which the novel appeared in *The Forerunner*, was also the year of the San Francisco Panama-Pacific Exposition, an event which included as its centrepiece a mechanized reproduction of the Panama Canal which had cost $500,000.[7] The exposition celebrated the elaborate and highly technical excavation and construction which had taken place over a decade and which marked the culmination of a colonial project which can be traced back to the sixteenth century.[8] The poster advertising the event was Perham Nahl's 'The Thirteenth Labor of Hercules' in which a vast and powerful superhuman male figure produces the channel for the canal by gigantic force. The looming figure, fantastically muscled, suggests both the dominance of white masculinity and the triumph of machine technology. The event celebrates the achievements of the past and looks towards the present and future, hinging upon the joint possibilities of imperialism and technology. It has interesting repercussions for *Herland*. The model of the Panama Canal was one which drew upon developments in aerial technology and presented the visitor to the exposition with what appeared to be an aerial view of the real canal rather than a reproduction. The effect of this was to challenge the categories of what is real and what is reproduced (in a further twist, the canal itself is an artificially constructed landmark). As one journalist noted, 'one can almost imagine he is taking an aeroplane trip over the Isthmus of Panama'. The effect of the display, as Bill Brown argues, is to make the 'real' canal redundant in a prefiguring of the implication which aerial cinematography was to have for the understanding of reality. Furthermore it offers a new method of reading reality which heralds an emergent Modernism: 'it could, like any miniature, present a transcendence that erases history and causality; and it could establish the proper power relation between spectator and spectacle, with the commodified image mimicking the commodified territorial possession that the Canal Zone itself had become'.[9]

The exhibit also offered a way of re-reading the possibilities of the aeroplane. As Paul Virilo has argued, the simultaneous advent of cinema and of aviation meant that the two had mediatory effects upon each other: 'By 1914 aviation was ceasing to be strictly a means of flying and breaking records... [I]t was becoming one way, or perhaps even the ultimate way of *seeing*.'[10] If the view of the Panama Canal celebrates the possession of land and of a land- and water-based colonial dominance, it implicitly extends that to the air itself. The poster confirms the mythic status of the creation of the canal and provides a male figure to stand against the 'colossal women' who symbolize the USA, Liberty, Columbia and the Republic.[11] The classical figure of Hercules will represent the power of the technological achievement, though interestingly it also sets up an iconic challenge to the technology which has enabled the event which it celebrates.[12] In a profoundly acute understanding of the significance of the aeroplane Gilman was, in 1915, already using this new technology as a way of 'seeing' in her writing, and she was also using the symbolism of the aeroplane to suggest a set of masculine and imperial values which she associates with the appropriation of technology by and for patriarchy. The aeroplane becomes the vehicle of the exploration of a body politic of women, the way in which the men (and the readers of the novel) first see the women of Herland. Yet further, what the men see initially is the gigantic sexualized body of a woman, as Herland is mapped out as the body of a colossal woman, in a parody of masculine adventure stories and a direct appropriation and subversion of colonial myths and myth-making. What Gilman is recognizing, it seems to me, is that the aeroplane also offers distinctive possibilities to women, not just to men. Though she undermines the association between men and machinery, she is also aware of the possibilities offered to women by the aeroplane, in the air. In *The Female*

Grotesque (1994) Mary Russo argues that the bodies of women flyers in the early decades of the twentieth century such as Amelia Earhart came to represent not just 'a thrilling and emancipatory icon, an instance of the gendered sublime, of progress, of modernity, and freedom', but also unencumbrance for they 'left behind the marks of the old models of womanhood and of course, all signs of non-Anglo-Saxon ethnicity'.[13] Russo includes in her chapter a 1921 photograph titled 'The Goddess of Flight'. A slender, athletic Caucasian woman with thick bobbed hair stands on tiptoes on a globe on which the Americas are represented. In her hands and along her outstretched arms she supports an aeroplane. Her body, from breasts to upper thigh, is wrapped in a sheet of sheer material which emphasizes her slim muscled form. The ends of this material sweep out behind her (they appear to be pinned up to a backdrop) so that they seem to be elegantly pointed wings, like those of a swallow. This still, sleek, though potentially active figure is, as Russo points out, literally on top of the world. She seems ready to soar off at a moment's notice, out of the picture, into the air, on her own just like the three women whom the explorers of Herland first meet, up a tree (like brightly plumaged birds). These three women seem to fly out of the tree and they disappear impossibly swiftly and athletically, leaving the three men behind them bewildered and furious.

Gilman ironically captures the frustration of would-be explorers' thwarted desires, sending up the moment at which the men discover traces of the mysterious woman land whose myth keeps confronting and evading them. The questing trinity of males whose investigation into an exclusively female land forms the basis of the plot, begin their project after the discovery of a piece of finely woven cloth at the foot of a waterfall emerging from an unclimbable sheer cliff (which turns out to be part of a huge phallic column), which has washed down out of Herland into a large area of land which may well be in South America (it is most probably Amazonia). The material becomes proof—material evidence one might say—for the existence of a group of women whose land had previously been doubted by the men (H p. 13). Since there was no rational or scientific evidence for the existence of the country, and it seemed to be a folk myth, believed in only by local people, the men have dismissed the possibility of the land from their minds. It was outside the boundary of the believable. The discovery, then, immediately establishes a doubt over their judgement, one which will be sustained throughout the novel. In using sewing to indicate civilization rather than machine technology, Gilman also challenges the terms in which civilization is evaluated. She takes the metaphor of sewing further, deliberately juxtaposing masculine endeavour and colonial expansion with domestic husbandry (eventually the women will sew up the men's aeroplane in a large bag to prevent them from escaping and will try to domesticate them, turning them into more or less celibate husbands). The material which the guide finds is a patch or fragment of an advanced female civilization which is, to the men, a blank space waiting to be filled in, or pocket waiting to be filled,[14] a land of others whose identity has been constructed by the indigenous dwellers of the lands around Herland, 'a strange and terrible Woman Land in the far distance' (H p. 2). It is this land that the three explorers plan to visit and to fill in by patient teaching of the ways of patriarchal civilization, by a mixed process of taming and teaching, and finally through procreation to fill it with copies of themselves. Having filled in those empty spaces of Herland, the men will report on their discovery to the 'cocky old professors' (the adjectives here are crucial—the professors are certainly male) and by laying claim to their discovery (H p. 5). Having 'discovered' the fragments of cloth, the men believe that the trajectory of their explorations will follow a pattern already established by other male explorers, one which has a very familiar written history. The novel charts the extent to which their expectations are challenged by their ensuing 'discoveries'.

It is appropriate that Terry the would-be explorer of Herland is known as 'the Old Nick' (H p. 1) with, as the narrator ominously reveals, 'good reason', and soon reasons are made amply clear: Terry is alarmingly predatory and devilishly handsome.[15] The punning possibilities of Terry's name and the significance of the woven cloth are quickly revealed. 'Woman have always been spinsters', Terry argues (H p. 8), punning on weaving and singleness, as a way of suggesting that a land of single women is one indeed worthy of exploration. He seems to hope that, like a collective group of sleeping beauties, these spinning women will be awakened by his kiss. Might it not be the case that Old Nick has a secondary interest: the man who is so keen to penetrate the dark forest and travel to the heart of an unknown female land is drawn by both the sexual possibilities of a land of single women and by the aberrant possibilities of a group living outside, on the edges of patriarchal civilization? His desire for distinctively unholy dalliances with the women of Herland and his ambition to enter Herland after men have not lived there for two thousand years suggests a neat Christian symmetry: Old Nick returns to the Garden after his long expulsion and exile and tries to tempt the descendants of Eve, climbing a tree and offering the first three women he meets the bait of a glittering necklace, his duplicitous words suggested by the fork of the trunk which he so precariously balances upon, his serpentine nature by the long stretch of his arm along a bough and his readiness to spring and catch the women: 'I did not like the look in his eyes—it was like a creature about to spring. I could already see it happen—the dropped necklace, the sudden clutching hand, the girl's sharp cry as he seized her and drew her in' (H p. 16). The sexual implications here are obvious, too obvious perhaps, but part of the pleasure Gilman has in *Herland* is in setting up the obvious in order to probe and subvert it. It is Terry who loses the necklace and learns a hard lesson of new knowledge, and the three women are able to examine and then reject what he offers them without being punished for transgressive behaviour. At the end of the novel Old Nick is once again expelled from the Garden, destined to keep his newly-gained knowledge a secret and not to reveal the whereabouts of Herland to those of his land.

As the three men approach Herland they become progressively excited by the prospect in store for them and the process of discovery becomes one of arousal and sexual self-discovery. Early in the novel the narrator complicates the terms of the plot by explaining that the discovery narrative is not the primary narrative, 'this story is not about that expedition. That was only the merest starter for ours' (H p. 2). So at the start of the novel the exploration has already shifted from an external exploration of an unknown terrain to one of the mind. The exploration is of the minds of the men of America and the women of Herland. The ambivalence of 'ours' suggests both that the exploration is theirs (by them) and that it is of them. This precisely articulates the double analysis which is carried out throughout *Herland*, through the surprising reversal of observation in which the women of Herland chart the men.

This ambivalence and textual indeterminacy allows for a range of readings. The suggestiveness of the text hints at a playfulness which will be carried on throughout Gilman's analysis. The description of the lake which the men travel to before they reach Herland is couched in terms of a spoofy send-up of masculine adventure novels:

> When we reached that and slid out onto its broad glistening bosom, with that high gray promontory running out towards us, and the straight white fall clearly visible, it began to be really exciting. (H p. 9)

The tremulousness in this passage comes both from the excitement at the prospect of discovery, and from the implied sexual nature of the encounter. As the men approach the mysterious country they are drawn towards a landscape which is both motherly and sexual. The breast cleverly anticipates the Edenic mother-oriented country (a land of milk and honey) but the 'straight white fall' of a giant cleavage, invites the eye downward and suggests the sexually charged nature of the adventure and of the men's imaginings. As they make their aerial investigation of the land they follow a triangular flight path to penetrate the unknown women's territory, travelling from the bosom of the lake up the swell of the edge of the land to the dark triangle, eagerly awaiting the prospects it holds in store for them. As they fly over the land the women hear 'our whirring screw' (H p. 11) and rush out to watch them. If Herland is here figured as the gigantic body of a woman, fertile, nurturing and unknown and thrilling—as the land is in the writing of Frank Norris's novel of California, *The Octopus* (1901)—it should be read as the antithesis to Hercules whose image dominated the San Francisco Panama-Pacific Exposition.[16] Yet just as Hercules displaces the actual labour which produces the Panama Canal, the vast female body which the men fly over, a giant projection of their fantasies, both displaces and represents the women that inhabit Herland who rely on force of numbers rather than superhuman individual strength. As the men travel across the country looking down from the air, they realize that the land that they have come to explore is not quite the virgin territory they envisaged; it was 'an enormous garden' (H p. 11), indeed it is a womb-like kindergarten, a gigantic and fertile place filled with women and female children who make a cult of maternity and celebrate motherhood.[17] The women have manufactured a nation which resembles a huge domestic space in a transformation which anticipates the blurring between the public and private which takes place in this utopia, and which, as I have argued, is also the nature of the pocket.

Throughout the novel, as is consistent with utopian writing, the difference between worlds is continually addressed, most strikingly through discussions of two worlds of women, the imagined world of Herland which only exists as a series of male fantasies, and the land of women that the men visit. Herland is a site of conflicting discourses. Even the name of the land/novel itself is a fantasy, as critics have noted.[18] The name of the place that the men have found remains elusive. The name that they impose upon it is, in its use of the possessive pronoun, allusive, for it continues the practices and systems of private property and of possession which is what the men, sons of capitalism, have come to expect. The women's name for the land which they have created for themselves resists the men and remains unknown, possibly unknowable, like the women themselves (unlike other feminist writers, Gilman does not attempt to transcribe a version of what this women's language might be). It may even be that the land does not have a name, and that for the women of Herland to name it would be an act of colonization which they are keen to resist. To some extent the men are forced to create a fantasy of Herland from the loose ends of narrative which they are able to unravel from the people who live in the land which surrounds Herland. If Gilman explores two versions of Herland, she also examines two North Americas, the North America that the men proffer for the consumption of the women of Herland, and the North America that the women infer from the gaps in the narrative that they are presented with; the patchiness, as it were, of the patchwork.[19] The third world of this novel, and the world which is clearly being invoked at least implicitly by Gilman, is one which is outside the boundaries of the novel, but which is always contained within and by the boundaries of her continued interests, the world of women's experience, of sexuality, of maternity, and of work.

In order to keep these three worlds interacting, Gilman continually reflects upon the ways in which information gets disseminated, and myths constructed. It is interesting to speculate about the self-consciousness of her project in this respect. She is acutely interested in an analysis of the processes of creating and transcribing history for public consumption. The novel continually questions the ways in which narratives of discovery get written—who writes them? Why? And for what sort of a readership? The novel resists the men's desires (they never write their account of discovery) while itself providing an account of Herland through its own pages (actually the narrative is more complex than this but this will do for the purposes of this account). What is eventually written is a reverse form of a discovery narrative in which the explorers become the explored. The women of Herland write down everything that the men say, making note of omissions, pinpointing silences, and putting it all together to form a chart of their responses. Their carefully constructed account, which takes note of absence as well as presence, the given as well as the resisted, is never revealed within the text of *Herland*, for in a sense it does not have to be. The alert contemporary reader is already familiar with the information which the women want to elicit from their male visitors and so has privileged access to the resisting text. The men themselves are the uncharted territory which gets mapped and plotted: in this novel the colonizers are colonized, the explorers explored (H p. 145). It is the ironic process of discovery and filling, the parodic moment of American colonial history, which the novel itself 'fills in' for its readers, and the readers fill in for the novel. Part of the novel's didactic purpose then is to challenge the boundaries between what is given and what is withheld in order to allow the reader to be active in the construction of the women's texts, which remain of the novel, part of its range, but not *within* the novel, not part of its text.

One of the meetings which is being parodied at the moment the men meet the women of Herland is that between colonial explorers and an unknown, possibly 'savage' people. The North American men come from the sky, they are white men, hairy men, who get hairier as the novel progresses. At their first meeting with the women of Herland they find that the women are in trees, like apes, though the women are not hairy, as the men (who are university educated, and probably readers of Lombroso) have expected. The narrator suggests 'grimly', 'Inhabitants evidently arboreal... Civilized and still arboreal—peculiar people' (H p. 17). One significant distinction between the women of Herland and the fantasies of the North American invaders is the lack of the women's facial hair. The men had envisaged that they would be hag-like; elderly, misshapen, and hairy, like witches perhaps, or some other form of female grotesque. This expectation is introduced early in the novel where issues of hairiness are used to denote masculinity or an absence of femininity. Gilman was to draw upon such suggestions elsewhere. In 'The Girl in the Pink Hat' which was published the following year, a false moustache proves the undoing of a man who plans to seduce a naive young woman. 'There he is', she says as he waits for her at the railway station, 'But how funny! He's got another hat—and another coat—how funny! But I'd know his moustache anywhere!' (R p. 46).[20] In *Herland* the men's beards are accorded a striking degree of prominence, for they are the markers of otherness, of masculinity, when clothing does not distinguish between the sexes. In a land which has been without men for two thousand years, the familiar semiotic and symbolic codes which distinguish North American women from men are unnecessary.[21] Terry, the most masculine of the men, has a 'most impressive mustache' at the start of the novel which marks his masculinity. Soon, though, all three men have beards, and since their beards are the only external distinguishing feature between themselves and the women, they are used explicitly to make this distinction (H p. 45).[22] They carry a heavy metonymic load. It is the hirsute outsiders with their flowing locks and ever-growing unstoppable beards who are spectacular and excessive, not the women. The men expect wilderness or wildness both of the women and of their land, and they encounter civilization, a land like a garden, its crops carefully tended and controlled and women who are healthy, athletic and disease-free. The men hope for sexual deprivation and a highly developed sexuality and instead they encounter parthenogenesis. They imagine that their expectations will be mapped out on the bodies of the Herlanders and so anticipate mutant growths of luxuriant facial hair such as those which crones or witches have been accorded within the popular imagination. They believe that single women (spinsters), living outside known society, might resemble the aberrant women or their own society; witches or hags. Despite debunking this belief abruptly, Gilman nevertheless draws upon it for some humour aimed against the three men. The women have bred supercats to live amongst them; a new breed which are mute and do not have destructive impulses (they do not chase birds) but are esteemed companions, familiars perhaps. She skilfully draws upon the discourses of riotous excess (instead of midnight orgies the women hold dignified, even dull ceremonials and yet the older women form a pentagonal bodyguard around the men) and those of sexual invitation (the young women are often described as being bewitching, and even explicitly called witches).[23] Like witches, the women live in an area outside patriarchy, on boundaries, on the edge, in a woman-centred pocket of civilization in which men have been redundant for two thousand years. It is this aspect of *Herland* which I want to return to in closing, for it seems that in figuring Herland as an area which has (due to its natural boundaries) been able to resist invasion for two thousand years, having first overthrown patriarchy, Gilman may be establishing a lesbian pocket of woman-identified women who live and work together harmoniously.

At the 1995 conference on Gilman at Liverpool University at which this chapter was first presented as a paper, it seemed that there was considerable uneasiness about discussing Gilman's sexuality. Most particularly, difficulties arose around debates over Gilman's passionate friendship with Martha Luther. It seemed that to suggest that Gilman may have been lesbian or bisexual, or that she may have had relationships with women which might be read as lesbian, was sacrilege: even to include her as part of a lesbian continuum seemed to cause enormous anxieties. Yet reading through her diaries it is clear that she was devoted to Luther—the pair agreed to wear matching bracelets 'as a badge, ornament, bond of union, etc' on 14 May 1881, and on 13 December 1881 Gilman wrote (but never sent) a moving poem to Luther who had become engaged to Charles Lane.[24] Though my primary interest in this chapter is not to establish exactly what the nature of the friendship between the two women was, or to argue that Gilman saw herself as lesbian, I do think that it is crucial to allow for possibilities of interpretation, and at least not to stifle debate. By using the metaphor of the pocket in these short notes to suggest both something hidden and something on the boundaries, I hope to suggest that Gilman's writing allows for many possibilities for women, and that her insistence on the primacy of relationships between women (mothers and daughters, women of similar ages, mother-in-law and daughters-in-law) is an important pocket of resistance for women.

Notes

1 See indexed references in Charlotte Perkins Gilman, *The Diaries of Charlotte Perkins Gilman*, ed. Denise D. Knight, 2 vols (Charlottesville and London: University Press of Virginia, 1994).

2 Cited in Larry Ceplair, ed., *Charlotte Perkins Gilman: A Non-Fiction Reader* (New York and Oxford: Columbia University Press, 1991), p. 281.

3 Ann J. Lane has noted the optimism and didacticism which are characteristic of Gilman's writing. See 'The Fictional World of Gilman' in *The Charlotte Perkins Gilman Reader*, ed. Ann J. Lane (London: The Women's Press,

1987, first published 1981), pp. xviii-xix.

4 I have always found *Herland* very funny.

5 In 1923 Gilman's *His Religion and Hers: A Study of the Faith of Our Fathers and the Work of Our Mothers* appeared.

6 Susan Gubar has already described the relationship between Rider Haggard's *She* (1886) and *Herland*. See Susan Gubar, '*She* in *Herland*: Feminism as Fantasy' in *Charlotte Perkins Gilman: The Woman and her Work*, ed. Sheryl L. Meyering with a foreword by Cathy N. Davidson (Ann Arbor and London: UMI Research Press, 1989), pp. 191–202. Gilman subverts the conventions of the masculine adventure novel throughout the novel, but most explicitly in the escape sequence in which the three men run away from their place of hospitable captivity only to find that their plane had been neatly sewn up in a bag by the women of Herland. Immediately after this Terry attacks the literature of the country, only to be ironically rebuked by Van who says: '"Can't expect stirring romance and wild adventure without men, can you?"' (H p. 44) The difficulty of interpretation here centres on those two words 'without men'. Is this an allusion to male authorship or male agency? Elaine Showalter makes a similar point about Freud's encounter with Louise N., a patient of his who asked him to lend her something to read. 'Freud had recommended *She*: "a strange book... full of hidden meaning... the eternal feminine"', yet Louise N. replied, '"I know it already. Have you nothing of your own?"' Freud's reply suggests that he believes her to want something written by himself yet, as Showalter points out, her 'remark might also be taken to mean that she already knows about the eternal feminine and its hidden meanings better than he did; didn't he have anything to give her about the hidden meanings of the eternal masculine?' Elaine Showalter, *Sexual Anarchy: Gender and Culture at the Fin de Siècle* (London: Bloomsbury, [1990] 1991), pp. 137–38. See also Sandra Gilbert's discussion of Freud's subsequent dream cited on the same pages. Gilman seems to have loathed Freud, talking at one point of 'the solemn philosophical sex-mania of Sigmund Freud, now widely poisoning the world'. See Larry Ceplair, ed., *A Non-Fiction Reader*, p. 285.

7 Bill Brown, 'Science Fiction, the World's Fair, and the Prosthetics of Empire, 1900–1915' inAmy Kaplan and Donald Pease, eds, *Cultures of United States Imperialism* (Durham and London: Duke University Press, 1993), pp. 140–42.

8 Ibid., p. 141.

9 Ibid., p. 142.

10 Cited in Bill Brown, 'Science Fiction...', p. 145.

11 America itself might be figured as a gigantic woman as it is, for instance, in John Donne's 'Elegy on his Mistress Going to Bed' (1669).

12 'The poster produces an antithetical point of view from that produced by the model canal exhibition: a terrestrial (even subterrestrial) enlargement inverts the aerial miniaturization; the gigantic body becomes the visual alternative to the miniature machinery of the zone that operated "without" human bodies. This classical body subsumes the work of the 30–40,000 "white and negro workmen," primarily West Indians, employed to construct the canal'; Bill Brown, 'Science Fiction...', p. 146.

13 Mary Russo, *The Female Grotesque: Risk, Excess and Modernity* (New York and London: Routledge, 1994), pp. 24–25.

14 Susan Gubar, who also describes the land as a 'blank space', notes Freud's

association between the blank space and female genitalia. See Sheryl Meyering, ed., *Charlotte Perkins Gilman: The Woman and Her Work* (Ann Arbor: UMI Research Press, 1989), p. 192. In his analysis of Dora, Freud repeatedly notes Dora's fidgeting with the reticule (a small bag which serves as a pocket) which she wears. Later he associates it with her mother's jewellery case, and then links both to female genitalia: 'Perhaps you do not know that "jewel-case" ["*Schmuckkästchen*"] is a favourite expression for the same thing that you alluded to not long ago by means of the reticule you were wearing—for the female genitals, I mean.' Cited in *The Freud Reader*, ed. Peter Gay (London: Vintage, 1995), p. 74. I am grateful to Terry Lovell for suggesting this connection. As Showalter notes in *Sexual Anarchy* (1991), a common nineteenth-century metaphor for the medical investigation bodies was one couched in terms of exploration and colonization, 'While male novelists... describe their journeys into Kôr, Kafiristan, or the heart of darkness as sexual expeditions into a primordial female body, doctors describe their invasions of the female body as adventurous quests for treasure and power'; Elaine Showalter, *Sexual Anarchy*, pp. 129-30.

15 These sort of laboured verbal/visual puns take place throughout the novel. Terry, with somewhat forced humour, appropriates the name of one of his female teachers, Somel, and calls her '"Some 'ell"' (H p. 35).

16 Norris writes, 'It was the season after the harvest, and the great earth, the mother, after its period of reproduction, its pain of labour, delivered of the fruit of its loins, slept its sleep of exhaustion, the infinite repose of the colossus, benignant, eternal, strong, the nourisher of nations, the feeder of the entire world'; Frank Norris, *The Octopus: A Story of California* (New York: Doubleday, Page & Co., 1901), pp. 46–47.

17 In *The Woman's Bible* (1895) the etymology of woman is given as 'Womb-man', for woman 'was man and more than man because of her maternity'; Elizabeth Cady Stanton, *The Woman's Bible*, with an introduction by Dale Spender (Edinburgh: Polygon, 1985), p. 22.

18 See, for example, Christopher P. Wilson's comments: 'Perhaps this is why Gilman chose the possessive pronoun: ultimately, it is not "she-land", but Herland. And yet, even here, there is a sign of Gilman's enigmatic narration. We should remember that "Herland" is a name that *Terry* coins at the very start of the adventure. We never actually hear the country's real name'; Christopher P. Wilson, 'Steady Burghers: The Terrain of Herland' in Sheryl Meyering, ed., *Charlotte Perkins Gilman: The Woman and her Work*, p. 185.

19 Gilman uses the myths surrounding Herland to build up the men's expectations of what they are to see. This is not an uncommon fictional strategy and is one which was being used widely in the period to suggest the fantasies of migrants to the great American cities. In Harold Frederic's *The Damnation of Theron Ware* (1896), and Theodore Dreiser's *Sister Carrie* (1900), a key train journey to the city is accompanied by an anticipatory public invocation of that city's name by a passenger or a railway conductor who acts as an initiator. The approach to the city is both geographical and metaphorical, and is tied into a fantasy or mythology of the city. Gilman appropriates this in *Herland* and combines it with colonial fantasies of other lands and peoples.

20 He turns out to be a known criminal and is swiftly arrested: '"That's him, and he's wanted all right", said one of his captors, while the other, none too gently, removed his moustache' (R p. 46). In *Uncle Tom's Cabin* (1852) by

Gilman's 'Aunt Harriet', which she knew and loved, shaving and hair are discussed repeatedly, almost obsessively, for primarily they denote race. In the household of the Quakers, Simeon is engaged in 'the anti-patriarchal operation of shaving', and the contrasting descriptions of the wild and matted hair of Topsy (brutally cropped by Ophelia) and the soft blond ringlets of the angelic Little Eva (also cut to be given away as keepsakes to the slaves) take on a very particular significance. See Harriet Beecher Stowe, *Uncle Tom's Cabin: or, Life Among the Lowly,* ed. Elizabeth Ammons (A Norton Critical Edition—New York and London: W. W. Norton, 1994), pp. 122, 249-52, 206 and 209.

21 For a wonderful account of the significance of male wigs in the seventeenth and eighteenth centuries see Marcia Pointon, 'The Case of the Dirty Beau: Symmetry, Disorder and the Politics of Masculinity' in Kathleen Adler and Marcia Pointon: eds, *The Body Imaged: The Human Form and Visual Culture Since the Renaissance* (Cambridge: Cambridge University Press, 1993, rpt 1994), pp. 175–89. She notes that in 1677 a Northampton wigmaker called John Mulliner ceremoniously burned a wig on his conversion to Quakerism, (p. 175).

22 Shortly after this, Terry makes another sneering comparison between women, men, and facial hair: '"With so many old women you'd think there'd be some razors," sneered Terry. Whereat Jeff pointed out that he never before had seen such complete absence of facial hair on women' (H p. 73).

23 Van says of Ellador, 'The witch! If ever anybody worked to woo and win and hold a human soul, she did, great superwoman that she was' (H p. 130).

24 See indexed references to Luther in Gilman's diaries (Charlotte Perkins Gilman, *The Diaries of Charlotte Perkins Gilman*). The description of buying the bracelets is in Vol. I, p. 58. On looking at the language of her unsent poem it is easy to accuse Gilman of hyperbole, or even fantasy, yet to say that she fantasizes or exaggerates seems to suggest her attachment even more strongly than it might deny it. Among the expansive and impassioned lines are these:

> 'Sweetheart!' You were my sweetheart. I am none,
> To any man, and I had none to you...
> Think of the days when we could hardly dare
> Be seen abroad together lest our eyes
> Should speak too loud.

Charlotte Perkins Gilman and Women's Health: 'The Long Limitation'

JANET BEER

Marriage can make women sick. Married men live longer and are healthier than single men. We know these things now; they are statistically proven and have become acceptable truths and the basis for much of our theorizing as feminists.[1] More than a hundred years ago, Charlotte Perkins Gilman experienced in her own life and witnessed in the lives of others the dynamic association between gender relations and health and illness. The majority of her work is concerned with exegeticizing the body politic—that most ancient of metaphors—as a sick body, a body which will always be ailing in some or all of its parts while women are disabled and even diseased by their relegation to the living of partial lives, that is the lives of married women. Gilman's writing, both fiction and non-fiction, is permeated with metaphors of infection and sickness, with villains who have 'the Bad Disease' (R p. 62) and heroines who are disabled by their physical weakness, as well as by their ignorance and economic powerlessness. In this chapter I intend to examine the context of Gilman's depiction of disease and sickness in its intimate relationship with marriage through her use of a variety of different genres. I will begin with her autobiography, *The Living of Charlotte Perkins Gilman* (1935), mentioning only briefly the auto-biographically inflected story, *The Yellow Wallpaper* (1892), consider her unpublished detective novel, *Unpunished*[2] in some detail, look at a number of short stories and conclude with a short discussion of *Herland* (1915), the utopian story of a nation without illness or anger.

Gilman perceives a relationship of cause and effect between principles of social organization and individual health. In her fictions she plays with different forms and different genres in order to experiment, to create worlds where the organization sustains women in health rather than sickness. It is perhaps inevitable that the ideal body politic is the world arranged on the principles of the female body, constructed as science fiction or utopianism in *Herland*, although along the way Gilman's experimentations with quest, legend or fable, romance, gothic and the fantastic offer some alternative means of textual as well as cultural organization.

Gilman's autobiography resembles nothing more emphatically than Henry David Thoreau's *Walden* (1854) in its connections between the health of the nation and the health of the individual. 'Where I Lived, and What I Lived For'[3] could be the heading on any one of Gilman's pages, only where Thoreau is writing the self glorying in the expansion of soul, claiming the legacy of freedom which is his as a white, male New Englander, Gilman is scrambling to establish a personal position, both physically and intellectually. She is always coming from behind, even in terms of her genealogy, and in order to establish her credentials as a New Englander—abandoned as she has been by her father, the forebear with the most powerful connection to a Massachusetts intellectual élite—she lets us know at the outset what her antecedents are: 'The immediate line I am really proud of is the Beecher family' (L p. 3). Like Thoreau she is a thrifty manager of limited resources—'In one eleven months my total outlay was $5-11—including shoes!'—and, also like Thoreau, she is an over-reacher—'So far there was a good record of health, strength, cheerfulness and patience, and constant industry. Within, the splendid sense of power, the high though indefinite purpose, the absolute consecration to coming service' (L pp. 72–73). In the chapter 'Power and Glory', Gilman details her régime of exercise and her athletic abilities, even claiming: 'With right early training I could easily have been an acrobat, having good nervous coordination, strength, courage, and excellent balancing power' (L p. 64). In her youth there is no pyrotechnic—of mind or body—of which she is not capable; she is confident of her capacity to excel in all things: 'One of my Harvard boy friends told me no girl could read Clifford and understand him. Of course I got Clifford at once—and found him clear and easy enough' (L p. 99). The absolute difference between Thoreau's lists of equipment and costs, Thoreau's accounts of good husbandry and the nature of his relations with his fellow creatures in the woods, Thoreau's sensibility of the epic grandeur of the most mundane of his activities or observations and the life lived and aspired to by Gilman is, however, in the sense of an ending which haunts Gilman but is refuted by Thoreau. Despite its overt claims and ambitions, there is in the *Living* a subtext of closure, of confinement, of sickness, that curtails and reduces her every attempt to exercise the legacy of New England, of a fine, fit body and a brilliant intellect.

Thoreau walks at night, ignores or acknowledges his fellow fishermen on Walden pond if he so pleases; he lives alone and feels no need of protection. Gilman is warned not to go out at night: 'A stalwart man once sharply contested my claim to this freedom to go alone. "Any true man," he said with fervor, "is always ready to go with a woman at night. He is her natural protector." "Against what?" I enquired. As a matter of fact, the thing a woman is most afraid to meet on a dark street is her protector. Singular' (L p. 72). Thoreau fears only the incarceration of his soul; his mental and physical health are assured for as long as he can exercise the cosmic sweep of his imagination. His ending is thus: 'Only that day dawns to which we are awake. There is more day to dawn. The sun is but a morning star.'[4] Language which signals confinement of the body, the destruction of its health and the gathering darkness of the soul takes its place as a sometimes grim lexis; as she returns home to husband and baby from her restorative trip to California in 1885–86: 'Leaving California in the warm rush of its rich spring, I found snow in Denver, and from then on hardly saw the sun for a fortnight. I reached home with a heavy bronchial cold, which hung on long, the dark fog rose again in my mind, the miserable weakness—within a month I was as low as before leaving...' [Gilman's ellipses] (L pp. 94–95). *Walden* is one of the great philosophical tracts of American freedom of mind and body, *The Living of Charlotte Perkins Gilman* is its inverse sister text, a testament to the thwarting by marriage and motherhood of the potential of the woman who called herself at twenty one 'a philosophic steam-engine' (L p. 71).

The autobiography, substantially written in 1926 at the age of 66 (although not published until 1935, after her death) turns on the intimate association between marriage and debility. The chapter which deals with the great transforming illness of her early twenties is entitled 'The Breakdown'; her successful second marriage is barely mentioned in the chapter 'Three Flats and a House': 'I returned to Chicago June 8th, and on the eleventh went to Detroit, as usual to the house of a friend, where I was met by my cousin, G. H. Gilman of New York, and we were married—and lived happy ever after. If this were a novel, now, here's the happy ending' (L p. 281). The underlying dynamic of the autobiography is from health to sickness, not sickness to health or misery to happiness. She calls that illness 'the débâcle' (L p. 99)—and much of 'The Breakdown' is concerned with the emphatic assertion and reassertion of the transforming power which the post-partum collapse had upon her. Her words echo *The Yellow Wallpaper*: 'The mental agony grew so unbearable that I would sit blankly moving my head from side to side—to get out from under the pain' (L p.96) and she conjures the breakdown as damaging the ability to lead a properly productive life:

> That leaves out twenty-seven years, a little lifetime in itself, taken out, between twenty-four and sixty-six, which I have lost. Twenty-seven adult years, in which, with my original strength of mind, the

> output of work could have been almost trebled. Moreover, this life-time lost has not been spent in resting. It was always a time of extreme distress, shame, discouragement, misery. (L p. 103)

This then is one of the formative incidents in Gilman's life. Until the illness she has seen herself as a self-made woman: 'Worst of all was the rapid collapse of my so laboriously built-up hand-made character. Eight years of honest conscientious nobly-purposed effort lost, with the will-power that made it. The bitterness of that shame will not bear reviving even now' (L p. 101). The word that recurs here is 'shame'; Gilman had made herself something other than the shamefast woman who must apologise for her physical or intellectual weakness; she had literally trained herself out of dependence, out of weakness, and the collapse of this character then becomes one of the transforming incidents in her life. Autobiographers, and particularly women autobiographers, often pay tribute to a central, formative influence in their lives. In the process of self-mythologizing here, Gilman pays tribute to no single man or woman, rather it is the darkness of her illness, the power of mental and physical debilitation to which she attributes most influence. Its enduring legacy is not only in the recurrence of her ill-health but in the images and structures of disability and disease with which she subsequently spent her writing life, the most obvious example being in *The Yellow Wallpaper*.

In *Unpunished*, Gilman takes the genre of the crime novel and transmutes its plot and substance by means of a grand metaphor which speaks of the deformity and sickness which result from the tyranny of men over women. As Ann J. Lane says in her biography of Gilman: 'If she could not destroy patriarchy in reality, she could do it in literary fantasy'.[5] In *Unpunished* the female housekeeper is disabled and disfigured—her mobility and her beauty restored only at the end of the story—but she is kept in a state which keeps her imprisoned in the house, immobile and ashamed to be seen by others, both powerful metaphorical representations of the condition, as Gilman sees it, of housewife. Tyrannized over by father and then by husband/brother-in-law, the two Smith sisters dramatize between them the whole range of the possible injuries that patriarchy could deal them; in the words of the private investigator who is the first narrator of the story: 'Mrs. Booth shell-shocked so to speak, Mrs. Warner more or less crippled and disfigured. And while she was still unconscious—concussion of the brain and all that—Vaughn takes the whole lot to his house—father would not see 'em you know—and persuades the half-crazy Mrs. Booth to marry him, right off.'[6] Jacqueline Warner, the elder sister, spends eight years of her life subject to the tyranny of her father's favourite, Wade Vaughn; her sister only escapes the role of Vaughn's wife by hanging herself.

One of Gilman's most emphatic villains, Vaughn is portrayed as a man who enjoys power, whose pleasure is derived from his ability to make others afraid of him and to keep them suspended in misery for as long as possible. He is a torturer of anyone who has displayed a weakness at any point in their lives; a blackmailer, an extortionist, he is kept in health and happiness by the exercise of unrestrained and self-gratifying power for which he receives the praise and approbation of the community at large. Here in the context of his rushed marriage to Iris only two weeks after the death of her husband: 'He explained to people that he did it in order to take care of her, and got credit for devoted affection and benevolence.'[7] Gilman leaves us in little doubt that the crash itself, which kills both the chosen husbands of the sisters, cripples Jaqueline and deranges Iris, is the result of some plot of Wade Vaughn's. His sphere of influence is apparently limitless. However, Iris defies him by killing herself, Jacqueline ultimately defies him by a secret programme of physical improvement and strengthening exercises, reminiscent of those described by Gilman as forming a part of her youthful training, and finds sufficient strength in her twisted body to impersonate her dead sister and thereby frighten Vaughn to death. The murder of Vaughn is the incident with which the action begins, and although the narrative deals retrospectively with the events which lead up to his death, the multiple killing of Vaughn—poisoned, stabbed, shot, strangled and dealt a powerful blow to the head (and all these acts, in fact, carried out on a corpse)—is the symbolic overthrow of the oppressor by the oppressed. Unyielding patriarchy lies assaulted by all those denied a chance to develop their capacities as human beings or even to live their lives free of fear. As Jacqueline Warner says:

> And I could be cured, Dr Akers tells me, my feet and my face too—almost with this wonderful facial surgery they use now, but that would cost money, and Wade has it all. When I asked to have it done, humiliated myself and begged, urged that if I were straightened out I could earn enough to pay him back, he said I was sufficiently useful to him as I was, and more likely to stay! Like the Chinese women...[8]

Dr Akers is kept in thrall because Vaughn has knowledge of a euthanasia the doctor carried out on a patient dying in agony, and he therefore cannot marry and have a family of his own or develop and progress as a doctor, held, as he is, in suspension by blackmail. Dr Akers thus understands what it is to exist in a position of subservience, to have to have permission from another person as to whether he can marry, expand his practice, or otherwise conduct his life as an autonomous human being. The three servants are all talented individuals forced into lives of servitude by Vaughn's knowledge of their past weaknesses, and when Joe asks him to make a change in their arrangements the conversation progresses as would a dialogue between master and slave:

> 'If you will allow me to leave you and go to work for myself, I will undertake to pay you the hire of another servant, and an increasing amount over that as I get on. In the course of a few years I am sure I could make it well worth your while, sir'.
>
> 'Nothing doing, Joe. My income is good enough, and there are some things I like better than money, as you may have observed. It gives me more pleasure to see a ten thousand dollar man blacking my boots and putting in my studs, handing my soup and cleaning my silver, than I should get from that much more money'.[9]

Joe is perhaps Gilman's most emphatic demonstration of the waste of talent that results from the tyranny of one human being over another. He has had a man's opportunities: the education denied to the Smith girls by their old-fashioned father and the choice of a profession; he is an entrepreneurial spirit, made for better things than the domestic tasks which he performs, but the pleasure of the inappropriateness of such a man doing such work is the rationale given by Vaughn for Joe's being forced to continue. The case of Joe illustrates Gilman's point that the disposition of the individual household is typically organized to bring comfort and ease to one member of that household and in order to achieve that state for one person all others must be confined within too restricted a space for the exercise or development of their individual talents. Joe, like Dr Akers, becomes a subordinate; like the woman, he has no influence over the disposition of his talents and cannot exercise free will. Gilman says in *Our Androcentric Culture, or The Man-Made World*: 'What man has done to the family, speaking broadly, is to change it from an institution for the best service of the child to one modified to his own service, the vehicle of his comfort, power and pride',[10] and *Unpunished* is an extraordinarily powerful illustration of this belief, dramatizing a situation in which the family, its domestic employees and its physician are all in thrall to the gratification of one man's pleasure. In the working through of the action, Gilman shows the destructive effects on the whole of the social body when the educative, social and health needs of the child, the power and potential of the woman and those rendered helpless by the removal of their autonomy are subordinated entirely to the maintenance of the patriarch. Such an allegorical interpretation is consonant with the way in which we can read the majority of Gilman's fictions but here, in the detective story, she is able to yoke the features of the genre to a more emphatic moral than the eventual triumph of good over evil or the unravelling of a complicated crime by a superior investigative brain. The novel reaches what might be termed a female multiple climax, with six of the oppressed murdering Vaughn in one evening's work. Vaughn has made all those in thrall to him equal in terms of their confinement to the working out of his purpose; all have been made subordinate by their dependence, their helplessness, their lack of autonomy and their coercion into a single way of interpreting and even being in the world. Theorists like Luce Irigaray have, in recent years, associated subversive female desire with multiplicity, for example in 'Ce Sexe qui n'est pas un':[11] 'The geography of her pleasure is much more diversified, more multiple in its differences, more complex, more subtle, than is imagined—in an imaginary centered a bit too much on one and the same'.[12] In Gilman's work the same imperative is evident; all those oppressed within *Unpunished* are feminized, making explicit the necessity for a multiplicity in action which will destroy the power of the monolithic centre.

To introduce Irigaray on pleasure into a discussion of a brutal murder is not a means by which to glorify the act of homicide, but part of an attempt to wrench the significance of the event away from the taking of life to the recognition of the giving of life to all those subjugated by Vaughn's despotism; the movement is from gratification for the one to gratification for the many. In Irigaray's terms the experience of pleasure is removed from the single, the male, to the multiple, the female. We must read the detective story with an inverted eye; Vaughn is villain before he is victim and his single-minded villainy cancels out any claim he has upon compassion; the perpetrators of the crime were victims before they were murderers and the crime which Gilman is exposing is other than homicide. Gilman rewrites the terms of the genre of the detective story in order to reorientate our understanding of what forms a solution and what constitutes a crime; she subverts the narrative momentum of the tale so that it centres on the passage to freedom of those who have perpetrated the murder rather than on the solution of the murder, upon the multiple ending rather than the single. The murder is ultimately a collective act and the unravelling of the mystery is concerned not so much with the solution of the crime of murder but of the crime of patriarchy.

Marriage has been the instrument of the tyrant, and the organization of the nuclear family its accomplice, as is made explicit in this text. Iris refuses to marry Vaughn, the man of her father's choice, and so, along with her sister, is disinherited. After the accident Vaughn marries her anyway, because and in spite of her simple mind, and holds Jacqueline in thrall as his housekeeper because she has the children to consider. When little Iris is grown Vaughn seeks to force her to marry his henchman, Crasher, so that he can retain control of the fortune which will be hers when she marries the man of his choice. This final act of tyranny, however, leads to the peripeteia; the oppressor is killed and those who were in thrall are free to live their lives to the full, a freedom made literal by the operations which Jacqueline has to restore both her looks and her mobility. Gilman's detective story is concerned with examining the conditions of the home—a nightmarish place where Vaughn conducts his profession as lawyer, blackmailer, father, husband and employer all with equal ruthlessness and self-absorption; the young Iris is representative of all women here as she is forced into self-sacrifice because of feelings of responsibility for the lives of others. This is how he persuades her, while holding her on his lap:

> 'No, I can't make you, by force, but I will tell you what will happen if you disobey me. Listen carefully, for there is no avoiding these consequences. If you do not go to the city hall with Mr Crasher Wednesday morning, you not only lose your future share of your grandfather's estate, but I shall give Hal a command which he will refuse—something to hurt his mother perhaps, something he would not do, and being disobedient, he will lose his share too. Then I shall turn him and your Aunt Jack out of doors, at once, Hal will have to leave college and go to work at whatever he can do. He will find it hard to support his mother, to say nothing of you.
>
> 'Furthermore, as another painful consequence, I will foreclose the mortgage I hold on Dr Aker's house, and break up his business as well. I have criminal charges against him—I can put him in prison. I can do it...
>
> 'On the other hand, if you forget your likes and dislikes of Mr. Crasher like a good girl, you may be more or less unhappy at first, women often are. But I shall have to pay over quite a sizeable fortune, and if you are a satisfactory wife to him he may let you do a lot for your aunt and Hal with money. So you see it is merely a question between you doing something you don't want to and the misfortune of several people you are fond of.'[13]

Gilman makes explicit the blackmail which is exerted upon the young girl to perpetuate the system whereby she abdicates any chance of self-fulfilment in order to make life easier for others. Appealed to on grounds of duty, guilt and shame she would have accepted her lot quite meekly had Gilman's plot not allowed for the listening device with which Jacqueline has penetrated Vaughn's patriarchal sanctum and her subsequent intervention to save Iris from the fate of generations of women before her. The active woman is the agent of change here; monstrously handicapped as she is Jacqueline has made herself powerful by systematically gathering information and building up her own physical and moral strength as well as that of those around her. She makes herself anew—despite being apparently the most passive woman imaginable, hideous, wheelchair- and house-bound—she rebuilds her self in the face of monstrous male tyranny.

Gilman's women do not have to be oppressed by an outrageous tyrant like Vaughn in order to be ailing or under-developed. In 'The Vintage' (1916), Gilman again associates sickness and marriage. It is one of Gilman's most damning stories about the effects of sexually transmitted diseases and the society which allows such infections to remain a secret from young women and thus permit them to spread unchecked. 'The Vintage' is not the only story Gilman tells of the effects of sexually transmitted diseases upon women who are ignorant of their existence, never mind their effects. In her novel *The Crux*, serialized in *The Forerunner* (1910) and published separately by the Charlton Company (1911), she demonstrates the widespread devastation caused by syphilis. In the story 'Wild Oats and Tame Wheat' (1913)[14] she takes the genre of parable and uses it to demonstrate that where the sexually transmitted disease is concerned, there can be no simple or tidy meaning. In this parable she describes a 'Certain Man who followed the habits of his kind' (SS p. 218); he is a representative of his gender but not his species, and, instead of following to the usual ending of a parable about 'wild oats', that is to a reformation of character, Gilman demonstrates that there can be no forgetting and no real reform in cases such as these because, once acquired, the sexually transmitted disease does not disappear but endures and infects the unsuspecting 'damsel' who waits for 'her one hope—a husband' (SS p. 218).

In 'The Vintage' Gilman takes a girl at the height of physical health and shows her decline into sickness and misery, all the while remaining in ignorance of what afflicts her. She produces deformed children, dead children, 'blasted buds' (SS p. 107) as Gilman calls them, serially miscarrying and enduring the destruction of her future as well as her past glory. Gilman reveals the intimate relationship between the social and the individual health and the cultural malaise is perhaps nowhere more succinctly expressed than in this story. One of the most powerful of Gilman's images of the sick society is in the wedding scene in 'The Vintage' where the doctor, Howard Faulkner, the guardian of individual and community health, looks on at the wedding of Leslie Montroy and Rodger Moore: 'So he held his tongue, and saw the woman he had loved so long, all white and radiant in her bridal glory, marry the man with the worst of communicable diseases' (SS p. 106). The bride, here embodying all that is womanly in the culture, surrenders her physical health, her innocence, her love and devotion as well as her unborn children to the man who has the power to blight every single one of her hopes. The sick society is not only represented by the literal infection, however, but by a traditional system of male solidarity, or, as it is dignified here, 'professional honor' (SS p. 107); silent complicity in a culture which does not value the health of its women is as fatally infectious as sexually transmitted disease. In concentrating attention on the wedding ceremony Gilman dramatizes the fact that it is at this precise moment that the woman passes from a vigorous, healthy girlhood into a married state which will bring physical decline. Mirroring her own passage, detailed in the autobiography, from health to debility, Gilman here takes to the extreme her image of the married woman as an ailing woman. Awaiting her destiny, Leslie has been in perfect health; once married, her body is prey to whatever infection her husband chooses to deliver and, of course, it is the most terrible of infections, syphilis. Like other marriageable girls, Leslie has been kept in ignorance of such matters; her choice of a partner for life is based on notions of romantic love; the society which has inculcated her with the idea that emotional truth is transcendent has led her to make a choice which will blight not only her health but also the health of future generations.

At the beginning of 'The Vintage', Gilman deliberately problematizes generic boundaries: 'This is not a short story. It stretches out for generations. Its beginning was thousands of years ago, and its end is not yet in sight. Here we have only a glimpse, a cross section, touching sharply on a few lives' (SS p. 104). In telling the story of Leslie Montroy, Gilman is again adjusting the way in which we view the relationship between the generic and the specific; here is the tale of one set of blighted hopes, three or four ruined lives, but it is not enough for Gilman just to tell the tale; in the act of telling she seeks to break down the limits of the story and involve the whole of humanity in the search for an ending which will not take place at an altar.

When Gilman needs to demonstrate that a girl has been in receipt of an education and upbringing that distinguishes her from others of her sex; she usually has that girl raised by a father alone, given access to information and modes of behaviour not available to those who have been subject to conventional restraints. In her story, or legend, 'The Unnatural Mother' (1916) Gilman emphasizes that Esther Greenwood's knowledge about her own body allows her to understand the nature of womanhood in physical and spiritual terms and thus the implications of her commitment in marriage. Knowledge of these very matters, however, is what makes her both unwomanly and unnatural in the eyes of the village gossips and it is appropriate—if ironic—that the grounding in facts that Esther has received forms the substance of what is remembered about a woman whose actions in saving a whole community have become legendary. Esther's offence against the value system of the Toddsville dames is that the facts she has been educated in by her doctor father are most particularly about health and how to sustain it and as such they undermine the very principles of the social order:

> 'He taught that innocent girl about—the Bad Disease! Actually!'
>
> 'He did!' said the dressmaker. 'It got out, too, all over town. There wasn't a man here would have married her after that'.
>
> Miss Jacobs insisted on taking up the tale. 'I understand that he said it was "to protect her"! Protect her, indeed! Against matrimony! As if any man on earth would want to marry a young girl who knew all the evil of life! I was brought up differently, I assure you!' (R p. 62)

In 'The Unnatural Mother' Gilman enters into the genre of legend—from the very opening it is clear that the narrative is of note as one of the defining events in the life of the village of Toddsville—but the reason why the story of Esther is being retold is not to celebrate her life but to charge her with the neglect of her own child. That she saved the lives of fifteen hundred people is cast aside as the central expression of the local or national spirit that might usually be expected to emerge from such a story recounted as legend, in favour of the meaning of the event being manipulated by the local women to represent an individual case of bad mothering. That the story is clearly satirical, in dialogue throughout with the real humanitarian truth of Esther's heroic action, does not affect the point that Gilman can make in locating the story as legend. It is not myth—there are no dealings with the supernatural here—it is a story retold as a definitive expression of a local culture which refutes the heroic, based as it is on narrowness, bigotry, repression and ill-health.

Gilman often removes her heroines from their diurnal reality as women to achieve something different to the norm. Gilman manages these transformations through the use of a variety of genres: the fantastic, as in 'If I Were a Man' (1914) or 'When I Was a Witch' (1910), the fable or legend as has been seen in 'The Unnatural Mother', or romance, as in 'The Girl in the Pink Hat' (1916). In those of Gilman's stories which employ the supernatural, her heroines' fantasies illuminate conditions of oppression; the entry into the realm of the magical—the man's body for Mollie Mathewson and the power of wish fulfilment for the narrator of 'When I Was a Witch'—gives them access to the physical conditions of those who wield the power. In the body of Gerald in 'If I Were a Man', Mollie recognizes the handicaps she labours under in her attire and bearing as a woman: 'Everything fitted now. Her back snugly against the seat-back, her feet comfortably on the floor' (R p. 33). 'When I Was a Witch' demonstrates the pathology of city life, expressed through the torments of horses, cats and dogs, through the profiteers who control the food supply, through the mendacious newspapers and in the organization of trade and commerce in general. All these are the narrator's targets and the particular nature of her pact with the devil allows her to express her venom, declare the anger which is both disabling her and results from the disabilities of life as a woman, and to punish those who are running the country and ruining the future. It is only when she speaks aloud her vision of the lives of women—'the greatest power on earth, blind, chained, untaught, in a treadmill. I thought of what they might do, compared to what they did do, and my heart swelled with something that was far from anger' (R p. 31)—that the magic fails; the voice of compassion is insufficient, action is what is required. In his book *Genres in Discourse*, Tzvetan Todorov posits 'the "fantastic" speech act' as 'the speech act of a person reporting an event that falls outside the framework of natural explanations, when that person does not want to renounce the framework itself'.[15] In so far as autobiography is pragmatic and the detective story interrogative, they look for solutions—as Gilman's fictions most usually do—whereas the fantastic for Gilman expresses despair, the solution is beyond realism and she returns to the 'framework of natural explanations', as Todorov has it, in recognition of limitation. The fantastic here is the most powerful and apposite device Gilman can find to show that for the world to be re-arranged on decent, humanitarian principles the human imagination must break free of the constraints of experienced reality. The world where women are given 'full life and work and happiness!' (R p. 31) is, in these stories, even beyond that imagining, however. The workings of such magic would do more good than bad, would take power from the oppressors but would counterbalance this with the emancipation of the 'mothers of the world' (R p. 31) and thus the black magic fails.

In the story 'The Girl in the Pink Hat', read here as romance or quest narrative, the young girl who attracts the interest of the narrator is on the woman's quest for a conventional, respectable marriage. The story dramatizes her removal from familiar surroundings, the perils which beset her on the way, the influences which have deflected her from true understanding of her situation and the physical and spiritual danger into which her trusting nature and single-minded purpose have led her. Believing in the sincerity of her suitor, she has trusted herself to him in the light of very little real knowledge of his character or background. In this way Gilman illustrates the danger that exists for all women in the social organization whereby marriage itself and its accomplishment is more important than individual safety or security, never mind human development. Marsh is able to confuse Jess with his superior knowledge of the world, its administrative procedures—licences, business meetings, money, police-work—and it takes the unlikely combination of the two sisters as self-declared 'romantics' (R p. 39) to rescue her from her fate. Jess is described as 'girlish', 'trembling', 'pale' and 'ready to break down and cry' (R pp. 40–42) at any moment but her resolution in the face of his superior knowledge and excessive force is sufficient to enable her to open herself up to the taking of decisive action once the rescue plan is suggested to her. She is released from the ever-encircling arm of the man and restored to self-possession, freed from the physical threat of marriage. Instead it is Marsh who feels the encircling arm of the law in the shape of the handcuffs with which he is greeted at the station. Instead of marriage as grail, active womanhood is Jess's reward at the end of her journey; she loved and trusted Marsh sufficiently to marry him but, as in *Unpunished*, the multiple nature of both her disillusionment and his punishment opens up for her the complexities of the matter of female power and choice. Gilman does not even allow her to retain what she thought of as the physical certainties of her knowledge of him: '"There he is," she said. "He's just inside the gate. But how funny! He's got another hat—and another coat—how funny! But I'd know his moustache anywhere."' The policemen know a different man, however: '"That's him, and he's wanted all right," said one of his captors, while the other, none too gently, removed his moustache' (R p. 46).

Herland, Gilman's most successful utopian novel, offers—in terms of plot—another multiple solution, and one without ending as long as the action remains in Herland. The spectre of ill-health only threatens to close the story because the action removes to Ourland, such means of closure being non-existent in the women's land. Herlander society is based on equality and collectivity, and the narrative exposes nothing more starkly than the divisiveness and inequalities which reign in Ourland in terms of women's health. Gilman foregrounds the social causes of invalidism by highlighting the differences between leisured and working women; the simplest of questions asked by the male travellers reveal the inequalities not only in women's work and leisure but in their fitness, with those women who do not work, of course, being most subject to ill-health. Gilman experimented with utopian fictions throughout her long writing career, and as the genre is driven by the imperative to communicate the possibilities of universal well-being, Gilman is here able to identify the causes of illness in Ourland as isolation in the home, inadequate social and intellectual education, the denigration of motherhood and, most emphatically, marriage. The physical dangers that result from marriage yet are endorsed in Ourland are enacted in the attempted rape of Alima by Terry, and the solution, to expel him from Herland, maintains the body of the female state in a condition free from danger. This is articulated in the text as infection: 'I studied it awhile, thinking of the time they'd have if some of our contagions got loose there...' (H p. 146) and expelling the infection in the shape of Terry is the means by which they maintain the nation's health.

There is an ideal republic in Gilman's imagination and the health and fitness of its inhabitants haunts her fiction as she ranges between genres, practising the journey-work of writing, but repeating the same story. Her fictional utopia contrasts implicitly with her autobiography: 'I try to describe this long limitation, hoping that with such power as is now mine, and such use of language as is within that power, this will convince any one who cares about it that this "Living" of mine has been done under a heavy handicap...' (L p. 104).

Notes

1 M. Morgan, 'Marital Status, Health and Illness', *Social Science and Medicine*, 14A (1980), pp. 633–43.

2 Gilman completed *Unpunished* in 1929. It has been published by the Feminist Press, ed. D. Knight and C. Golden (New York, 1997). The manuscript is in the Gilman Papers in the Arthur and Elizabeth Schlesinger Library, Radcliffe College.

3 Henry David Thoreau, *Walden or Life in the Woods*, first published 1854 (New York: New American Library, 1960), p. 59.

4 Ibid., p. 221.

5 Ann J. Lane, *To Herland and Beyond: The Life and Works of Charlotte Perkins Gilman*, first published 1990 (New York: Meridian, 1991), p. 344.

6 Charlotte Perkins Gilman, *Unpunished*, Chapter 1, p. 8, ts., Gilman Papers, Arthur and Elizabeth Schlesinger Library, Radcliffe College.

7 Ibid., Chapter 7, p. 8, ts.

8 Ibid., Chapter 7, p. 1, ts.

9 Ibid., Chapter 10, p. 3, ts.

10 Charlotte Perkins Gilman, *The Man Made World; or, Our Androcentric Culture* (New York: Charlton, 1911), Chapter 1.

11 Elaine Marks and Isabelle de Courtivron, eds, *New French Feminisms: An Anthology* (Amherst: University of Massachussets, 1980).

12 Ibid., p. 103.

13 Charlotte Perkins Gilman, *Unpunished*, Chapter 10, pp. 8–9, ts.

14 In my book, *Kate Chopin, Charlotte Perkins Gilman and Edith Wharton: Studies in Short Fiction* (Basingstoke: Macmillan, 1997) I discuss the stories which deal with sexually transmitted diseases in considerable detail in comparison with Gilman's stories of female, communitarian health.

15 Tzvetan Todorov, *Genres in Discourse* (Cambridge: Cambridge University Press, 1990), p. 24.

The Sins of the Innocent: Breaking the Barriers of Role Conflict

ANNE E. TANSKI

The time during which Charlotte Perkins Gilman wrote was one in which English and United States societies struggled between a belief system deeply ingrained in their people and the Siren-like call of a new way of thinking and living. In *Love in the Machine Age* (1930), Floyd Dell explains, referring to women in particular, 'the fact... that we are in a transition period means that for multitudes of individuals there comes a change from the old order to the new at some time in their lives—that, having been trained to adjust to the old order, they are then called upon to live in the new'.[1] Although they felt the desire to live in the new, women blocked themselves with the restraints of patriarchal codes upheld by the older generations and many of their peers.

What came out of this transition was role-conflict which eventually resulted in an overwhelming sense of isolation. In the minds of the vast majority that still believed in upholding Victorian morals and ideals, to move away from 'women's appointed sphere' meant to commit a sin against the workings of tradition.

Role-conflict stemmed from changes in several areas including gender ideology, gender and social roles, as well as the institution of heterosexuality. In her work *Images of Women in Literature* (1974), Mary Anne Ferguson explains that 'role-conflict causes women great anguish; to be simultaneously wife, mother, and mistress to one's own husband causes stress for women that male role-conflict does not'.[2] Ferguson's evidence of this is that men did not see themselves (nor were they expected to) as spending most of their time in the roles of husband, father, and lover. Rather, emphasis was placed on the man's primary role as worker, relieving him of the stress and anguish of multiple roles.[3] As ideas about woman's multifaceted role began to change, their own anguish remained.

For women, the psychological and emotional turmoil associated with such changes in a society stubbornly bent on repression resulted in an overwhelming sense of isolation. Gilman, ahead of her time, realized this and sought to assuage women's feelings of social alienation and disconnectedness through her writings. As Mary A. Hill points out in her book *Charlotte Perkins Gilman: The Making of a Radical Feminist, 1860–1896* (1980), 'The emphasis in many of Charlotte's writings was becoming distinctly positive: there was less self-pity, more self-affirmation, less hostility directed against "enemies", more stress on cooperation with one's friends, less anti-male anger, more pro-female love.'[4] Hill quotes Gilman as declaring that it is time that women were '"united as a class—woman supporting woman... It is time we learned the one great secret of all human improvement—working together."'[5] Gilman's primary medium for this message was the short story, and to ensure that her stories would reach the reading public, she wrote and produced her own magazine, *The Forerunner*, from 1909 to 1916.

According to Mary Loeffelholz in *Experimental Lives: Women and Literature, 1900–1945* (1992), 'Gilman's reputation today rests less on her autobiography and nonfiction (although her 1898 *Women and Economics* is still read as a pioneering work of feminist theory) than on her short stories and utopian novels.'[6] *The Yellow Wallpaper* (1892) is the most well-known and widely read today, appearing in numerous literature anthologies, but each of her other stories presents a series of issues common to the inner turmoil, isolation, and anguish women of her time faced.

Two such fictions are 'Making a Change' (1911) and *The Crux* (1910). Gilman's style evolves over the nearly twenty years that span these narratives and *The Yellow Wallpaper*. As Loeffelholz points out, 'Gilman's later stories tend to wear their intentions on their sleeves, far more so than *The Yellow Wallpaper*.'[7]

'Making a Change' and *The Crux* are examples of Gilman's intention. The titles leave little chance of misinterpreting the themes of the stories, and the general message is highly optimistic in spite of the grim situations each one presents. 'The appeal of these stories lies precisely in their optimism; they attempt to persuade readers of Gilman's own belief that feminist reforms (like shared child rearing and a single sexual standard) were in reach because they were basically in everyone's interest.'[8] Loeffelholz is quick to point out, however, that such optimism limited Gilman's stories to problems that could be resolved by sheer will, energy, and imagination.[9]

Despite that limitation, Gilman's stories are no less valuable or influential. 'Making a Change' and *The Crux* address specific and distinct problems while simultaneously exhibiting common threads concerning role-conflict and isolation. The notion of biological sin also comes into question in both narratives.

In the short story 'Making a Change', Julia Gordins, a young wife, struggles with the change of new motherhood. Julia's beauty and musicianship initially attract her husband (and his mother). Yet, both qualities disappear with the arrival of the baby, Albert. The Victorians regarded this sacrifice as natural. Frank Gordins expects it, as does his mother, without a second thought. Julia, herself, expects it. However, Julia's biological sin lies in the idea that since woman's appointed sphere centres around motherhood, she should be a natural at the task when, in fact, she is not.

Gilman addresses this problem in her autobiography, *The Living* (1935). In the Foreword, written by Gilman's close friend, Zona Gale, she recalls Gilman saying, 'Women specialized to piano, specialized to voice, specialized to cooking—never to child-development. That "comes with the baby", forsooth!' (L p. xli). The music is a cultivated talent, and Julia 'had been an ardent musician before her marriage, and had taught quite successfully on both piano and violin' (R p. 67). Musicianship for single women was a social expectation, and an attractive quality, but nothing more was expected to come of it, especially after a baby.

Knowing that motherhood is her biological and social duty, Julia determines to fulfil it, and to do so she sacrifices her music:

> Here was a noble devotion on the part of the young wife, who so worshipped her husband that she used to wish that she had been the greatest musician on earth—that she might give it up for him! She had given up her music, perforce, for many months, and missed it more than she knew. (R p. 68)

Marriage and motherhood, a woman's true life work, replace musical talent. However, motherhood, or rather child-development as Gilman put it, is expected to come quite naturally. For both Gilman and her character Julia, the opposite is true. The ceaseless care of the baby takes its physical and emotional toll on Julia. She makes a solid effort, willing herself to the task of caring for a baby: 'The child was her child, it was her duty to take care of it, and take care of it she would. She spent her days in unremitting devotion to its needs' (R p. 67).

This stereotypical image fostered by patriarchy nearly kills Julia as she breaks under the pressure of repressing the artist in her while attempting to be wife, mother, and daughter-in-law: 'To any mother a child's cry is painful; to a musical mother it is a torment' (R p. 67). Psychologically and emotionally overcome, Julia inwardly seeks a release from the torment she feels: 'Julia was more near the verge of complete disaster than the family dreamed... [N]ow she looked at her husband, dumbly, while wild visions of separation, of secret flight—even of self-destruction—swung dizzily across her mental vision' (R p. 68). Julia's situation reflects in a subtle external way the inner turmoil she feels. She gives in to her husband's admonitions to let the elder Mrs Gordins take care of the baby. She does this out of her devotion to him as his wife and also out of complete weariness of mind and body.

In describing her own thoughts as weariness and depression overtook her, Gilman reveals:

> Prominent among the tumbling suggestions of a suffering brain was the thought, 'You did it yourself! You did it yourself! You had health and strength and hope and glorious work before you—and you threw it all away. You were called to serve humanity, and you cannot serve yourself. No good as a wife, no good as a mother, no good at anything'. (L p. 91)

This kind of thinking contributes to a growing sense of isolation. Gilman's thoughts here could easily become Julia's. She wants so much to be the perfect wife and mother, but her talents are artistically inclined, not domestically so. She isolates herself by giving the baby over to Mrs Gordins, then quietly locks herself in her room, and turns on the gas in a suicide attempt.

Two sins have now been committed: failing at her roles as a woman and attempting to take her own life. The one situation leading to the other, though horrifying to Victorian thinking, is, none the less, seen as a frequent tendency in women during that time. In his book on human secondary sexual characteristics of men and women called *Man and Woman* (1904), Havelock Ellis concluded that suicidal tendencies in women of that time were the result of either 'a sudden shock or... simply the last stage in a slow disintegration'.[10] For Julia, the latter is true. Ellis continues to explain that an often hidden contributing factor to 'the frequency of female suicides in early life generally is shame at the prospect of becoming a mother'.[11] Julia's shame is her belief that she is an inept mother, reinforced by her husband's nagging and her mother-in-law's insistence that she can do the job.

The prospect of motherhood is a connecting thread between 'Making a Change' and *The Crux*, but the concept of 'sin' is different. In *The Crux*, serialized in *The Forerunner* in 1910, Vivian Lane is a young woman who must struggle with a potentially life-threatening decision: whether or not to marry the syphilitic Morton Elder. The two choices she has force her to compromise both the possibility of marriage and of motherhood.

By choosing not to marry, Vivian risks committing the social sin of spinsterhood, shunning her biological duty to marry and produce children.

However, marriage to Morton commits the biological sin of the horrid and irreversible consequences motherhood would have for her as her friend, Dr Jane Bellair, points out:

> Another result... is to have children born blind. Their eyes may be saved, with care. But it is not a motherly gift for one's babies—blindness. You may have years and years of suffering yourself... You may have a number of still-born children, year after year. And every little marred dead face would remind you that you allowed it!... Dear girl, don't you see that's wicked?... Beware of a biological sin... for it there is no forgiveness. (R pp. 121–22)

At issue here, as well as in 'Making a Change', is the common practice in Victorian society of not acknowledging the existence of such things as depression, suicide, and sexually transmitted diseases.

Howard Mumford Jones, in his work 'The Comic Spirit and Victorian Sanity' (1962), states, 'Victorianism is the pretense that if you do not name a thing, it isn't there... The Victorians were so bent on being moral that they ignored the unpleasant aspects of life.'[12] Gilman breaks this Victorian sense of denial through the character of Dr Jane Bellair. Bellair forces Vivian to see the reality of the situation. She also derides her male colleague and Morton's physician, Dr Richard Hale, for his inaction, soundly blasting the male code of honour in the process.

When she asks Hale what he would do if it were his sister instead of Vivian, Hale tersely replies, 'I might kill my sister', to which Bellair responds coldly, 'A man's honor always seems to want to kill a woman to satisfy it... I won't leave you to the pangs of unavailing remorse... That young syphilitic is no patient of mine' (R pp. 118–19). Gilman's attitude toward male honour, couched in the terms of Victorian morals, is clear. Jones explains that 'to talk of duty, honour, the obligations of being a gentleman, the responsibilities of matrimony, or the sacredness of religious belief is to be Victorian'.[13] One would have thought that Dr Hale's position as a physician would override his staunch morality because he knows the consequences of syphilis.

Instead, he hides behind his oath to protect patient confidentiality in order to avoid the truth and keep his honour intact. Dr Bellair has no male moral obligation to put her in conflict. Further, she has the 'benefit' of first-hand experience to tell her that informing Vivian is the only honourable thing to do. Having herself fallen victim to the same kind of circumstance years before, Dr Bellair refuses to let the innocence of a young girl be the cause of years of misery and heartbreak when it could be avoided altogether. The key to releasing both Julia and Vivian from their 'sins' lies in breaking through their innocence.

Julia's innocence consists of inexperience reinforced by a husband and mother-in-law who exacerbate the situation rather than seeking to remedy it. Both Frank and Mrs Gordins rail about the older woman's experience in the realm of child-development. Instead of using this experience to help Julia learn, the knowledge becomes a weapon that creates Julia's isolation and leads to her near demise. Neither woman has a sense of the oppressive forces working against her. Mrs Gordins is just as much a victim of patriarchal thinking as Julia is because she does not have the means to support herself and must rely on her son.

Mrs Gordins experiences her own sense of role-conflict and isolation. Living under her son and daughter-in-law's roof, she is pulled in three directions. She struggles between her patriarchal role as mother to her son, which conflicts with Julia's role as wife; her own displacement as wife; and finally, the urge to be a mother/care-giver to the new baby. Because she is no longer grounded in the security of lady of the house, her attempts to help reveal themselves as bitter resentment.

The mutual resentment between Julia and Mrs Gordins estranges them at a time when each needs the other most. Mrs Gordins further isolates herself by retiring to her room to attempt to remind herself that she is *still* useful. When Julia leaves the baby with her, she becomes even more adamant in her self-approbation.

Ferguson addresses this problem of oppression upon Victorian women in general as created by role-conflict: 'Liberation for women begins with an understanding of the oppressiveness of role-playing based in stereotypes. Women must separate in their minds the stereotypical image a beloved person may have of them from the person himself.'[14] At first glance, Mrs Gordins reflects patriarchal society in so far as she fosters her son's notions of domestic propriety, which account for little.

Frank knows the baby cries all the time, so Julia must be doing something wrong. His solution: 'My mother knows more about taking care of a baby than you'll ever learn! She has the real love of it—and the practical experience. Why can't you *let* her take care of the kid—and we'll all have some peace!' (R p. 67). Misguided in his advice, Frank's words only succeed in driving a wedge between the two women and ultimately lead to Julia's attempt to take her own life.

As a result of Julia's drastic action, Mrs Gordins awakens to the fact that both she and Julia are victims. Ferguson explains: 'As they realize that they are not alone in finding old roles intolerable, women gain the strength to question not their own sanity but the validity of the stereotypes'.[15] The women in 'Making a Change' question the validity of woman's role, but they also take steps to redefine it. What is interesting about their process is that they keep the male head of the household in mind.

'Making a Change' does not exclude the presence of Frank in the new household plan. As a matter of fact, every change is made to provide for his comfort. Economic concerns (man's sphere) are carefully considered for the Gordins' household and for other families with the inception of the baby garden, for it saves women having to secure nannies at a higher cost. The welfare of the baby is top priority and extends again to the other babies under Julia's and Mrs Gordins' care.

Granted, the plan is effected without Frank's knowledge, and when he does find out by accident, his mother's logical, air-tight argument leaves him no choice but to approve. Julia's 'experience' in the music field is restored, and she adds her newly acquired knowledge of child-development through running the baby garden with Mrs Gordins. Thus, innocence transforms into experience.

In her introduction to *The Charlotte Perkins Gilman Reader* (1981), Ann J. Lane explains that innocence has no charm. This is especially true when innocence creates the insurmountable barrier of despair as it does for Gilman's Julia because she lacked the experience necessary to provide choices other than ending her own life. On the other hand, *The Crux*, according to Lane, 'Takes another look at innocence betrayed—or almost betrayed' (R p. xxiii). Lane adds, 'Innocent women are created in a male image to be fragile and vulnerable. What women need is education, sophistication, world experience, adventure—tools for their own protection' (R p. xxiii). Lane finds that Gilman refused to subscribe to the belief that women needed men to protect them. Gilman's contention was that women needed 'to be protected *from* men, and that protection comes from the self' (R p. xxiii). Innocence, defined here as ignorance, becomes a quality that invites dangers, as Gilman points out in many of her stories.

The Crux attacks innocence in terms of the institution of heterosexuality and relations prior to matrimony as viewed in Victorian society. Russell M. Goldfarb explores the Victorian notion of respectability concerning both public and private conduct. In his book *Sexual Repression in Victorian Literature* (1970), he states:

> From birth to death for the average Victorian the observance of respectability was not a way of life but *the* way of life. He was born into a prudish family that taught conformity, valued his chastity, and encouraged the homely virtues. He found these values rewarded in school, at work, and by the people with whom he associated. His church and his government, his laws and his betters made sure he would be a proper Victorian.[16]

Despite so many efforts from so many institutions, the question of morality among young people remained a problem. If anything, the pressures from so many sides upon the young people to be morally pure backfired, creating the very thing the movement sought to prevent.

Floyd Dell explains how the 'purity ideal' did not deter the problems of promiscuity, use of prostitutes, and even homosexuality. Rather, the whole idea of 'Victorian morality consisted largely in ignoring, forgetting or denying the homosexuality that existed in the sexually-segregated schools [and] the prostitution which still flourished as the solace of masculine youth'.[17] Stubbornly, the thinking persisted that by not naming a thing, it did not exist; meanwhile, it existed rampantly in many forms. Goldfarb admits that a minority of Victorian men and women 'compromised their standards and were occasionally promiscuous'.[18]

In speaking of the youth of the Victorian era, Dell takes the discussion of promiscuity further as he explains that a non-religious reason to avoid premarital sexual relations 'was venereal disease. This negative incentive... was not generally sufficient to produce results in actual conduct', meaning that the large majority of young people were unmoved by this fear.[19] Dell couples this with the 'purity ideal' which, in and of itself, posed a double standard that failed to prevent the spread of disease. He explains: 'Men were socially trained to require such "purity" of their womenfolk, but women were not trained to demand it of men. They did not ever in large numbers demand it as a pre-marital virtue in men; they were more inclined to laugh at it.'[20] This attitude is clearly reflected in *The Crux* through the character of Vivian.

The struggle between giving up a life she was socially trained to live and accepting a man such as Morton causes Vivian great conflict and distress. She admits to Dr Bellair that Morton had told her he had led a less than exemplary life. Unfortunately, Morton told only a half-truth. Vivian fails to grasp the gravity of his true condition, protesting to Dr Bellair, 'He *loves* me!... he says I am all that holds him up, that helps him make a newer, better life... He told me he had—done wrong. He was honest about it... I owe some duty to him. He depends on me' (R p. 121). In this passage, Vivian exhibits Victorian innocence and denial as she parrots the 'catechism' of beliefs held by a proper Victorian woman. Sacrifice and acceptance of that condition prevent Vivian from seeing the double standard.

Goldfarb provides an historical context which helps explain Vivian's denial and willingness to sacrifice herself. Goldfarb turns to the insights of Victorian physician, Dr William Acton, in reference to women of the time:

> The Victorian woman was dignified, and because she was rational, 'Love for her husband and a wish to gratify his passion, and in some women the knowledge that they would be deserted for courtesans

> if they did not waive their own inclinations, may induce the indifferent, the passionless to admit the embrace of their husbands'.[21]

In a premarital context, Vivian accepts Morton's wrongdoing. Complicating the matter further, she also accepts the role of moral agent. She will hold him up; it is her duty.

Goldfarb explains the nuances of this kind of thinking as he states that the Victorian woman 'became a living embodiment of sexual sanctions. She was perhaps more alienated from her own sexuality than any man because she had a constant role to play as moral guardian of her society, her relations, and her home.'[22] For Gilman, such thinking was completely unacceptable. She makes her feelings known clearly through Dr Bellair:

> This is no case for idealism and exalted emotion... You may have years and years of suffering yourself—any or all of those diseases 'peculiar to women' as we used to call them! And we pitied the men who 'were so good to their invalid wives'! (R pp. 121–22)

Bellair's comments reflect bitter feelings toward the simple fault of not knowing any better and reliance upon the notion that a woman's problems led to pity for the husband. With the weapon of hindsight, Bellair acts as Vivian's oracle.

Men should no longer be pitied for diseases they themselves bring upon their women. Women should no longer feel the need to play the role of man's moral agent with the almost certain promise of ending up sacrificial lambs to Victorian principles, simply because of their own ignorance. Such is Gilman's message. Vivian is one example of a woman who must do the honourable thing by taking responsibility where male morality falls short, but not in the way Victorian codes of conduct prescribe.

As Ann Lane has stated (see above, p. 74), protection must come from the self. Vivian must break the engagement herself, and she must take steps toward her own independence. In the larger work of *The Crux*, Vivian fulfils Lane's earlier statement about the tools women need for their own protection. She eventually gains world experience, adventure, and sophistication. Since sterility in women is a result of syphilis, it is interesting to note Gilman's choice in making Vivian at least symbolically sterile, for she bears no children of her own. Instead, she receives maternal fulfilment in running a kindergarten.

As characters, Vivian and Dr Bellair reinforce Gilman's message about breaking the bonds of restricted knowledge. This was no easy feat. Goldfarb puts it into perspective:

> Sex was a secret in Victorian households. Fathers did not tell their

> sons the facts of life, nor did mothers tell their daughters. The family physician would not broach the subject; husbands and wives would not be open with one another. Many adult Victorians were completely ignorant about whole areas of human sexual behavior.[23]

When reinforcement of restricted knowledge comes from so many sources as these that Goldfarb outlines, one can sympathize briefly with Vivian's anguish. But breaking Vivian of the compulsion to stand firmly by her syphilitic man is not an impossible task.

The way Gilman presents *The Crux* combines stern truth with optimism. The traditional choices of marriage and motherhood might not be open to Vivian, but this does not mean that she has failed as a woman. As with 'Making a Change', the solution for Vivian is one of adjustment and transition, surrounded by babies who may not be her own, but who still need her mothering care.

The trap of innocence as represented in 'Making a Change' and *The Crux* is the belief that when convention fails, there is nowhere left to turn. One woman is resigned to failure and seeks to end her life, and the other is ready to resign herself to a less than perfect, but wholly traditional marriage with the dark cloud of physical ruin looming in the distant future. Gilman wanted women to settle for neither.

Though the definition of innocence has changed over the years, its association with ignorance still exists today. In many ways, some of the same attitudes and denial that plagued nineteenth-century thinking plague twentieth-century thinking. The young people are full of hope for the future. Marriage and motherhood for women are still considered important roles. However, the disease is decidedly different. Syphilis still exists, but the new scourge is AIDS.

Sexual intercourse before marriage happens among the female population in a more readily accepted way; these young women are the new Vivians. Innocence for them and their male counterparts is more a sense of denial than a lack of knowledge. They know the facts about the disease but act under false impressions of whom the disease actually affects. AIDS is not strictly a homosexual disease as many have found out.

Two such cases appear in Barbara Kantrowitz's article 'Teenagers and AIDS' (1992). Krista Blake, age 18, was engaged to be married and about to start college. A doctor's physical examination revealed that she had been infected with HIV by a previous boyfriend. She says, 'He knew that he was infected, and he didn't tell me... And he didn't do anything to protect me from getting infected either.' Krista immediately broke off her engagement with her present fiancé explaining, 'I love him enough that I want him to have his options for life open'.[24]

In light of Vivian's love and sense of duty to Morton in *The Crux*, Krista's duty lies in protecting the man she loves from infection, something Morton should have done for Vivian had he truly loved her. In a sense, Krista is the Morton that Gilman's Dr Bellair was looking for. Krista took responsibility once she knew her circumstances. Moreover, like Dr Bellair, she is trying to educate others before it is too late.

A second modern-day example of Gilman's vision is teenager Bridget Pederson who had always made her boyfriends wear condoms, but whose older boyfriend Alberto Gonzalez refused. She gave in. After three years together, financial circumstances forced them to sell their blood at a plasma centre:

> The doctors there told Pederson and Gonzalez that they were both HIV-positive. There was worse news to come. Gonzalez's brother told Pederson that Alberto had known for years that he had the virus—and had already infected a previous girlfriend... Armed with that information, Pederson went to the authorities and [in October of 1991] Gonzalez became the first person in the [United States] to be convicted on assault charges for passing the virus.[25]

Pederson's message to teenagers is simple: 'Don't trust someone, even someone you love, to come clean. People aren't always honest about their past sex life or HIV status.'[26] Gilman's message is essentially the same, and not only does this attitude still prevail more than 80 years after Gilman's story, but the Victorian attitude of not naming a thing into non-existence prevails as well.

Kantrowitz points out that 'even in areas where AIDS is widely acknowledged as a serious problem, there is a powerful resistance to frank discussion of teenage sexuality—as if avoiding the issue will make it go away'.[27] In 'Making a Change' and *The Crux*, not discussing the problems does not make them go away. In fact, Gilman shows and history bears out that avoidance can be fatal, and the young female characters end up paying the price of patriarchal morality. For Julia Gordins, her husband's honour as sole provider for his family with a socially acceptable, conventional wife nearly kills Julia. For Vivian Lane, her future husband's condition poses the potential for destruction not only of Vivian, but also of their unborn progeny.

Gilman's words reach through the years, as relevant to today's social issues and ills as they were to those of her era. As a humanist, she sought to tell men and women alike that the 'sin' of the innocent is to remain ignorant. No longer can the attitude of avoiding or denying a problem out of existence be sufficient, nor can women continue to move in circles created by men for men.

In his essay, 'Charlotte Perkins Gilman on the Theory and Practice of Feminism' (1956), Carl N. Degler expresses Gilman's views about what is wrong with the sexual division of behaviour:

> Up until the nineteenth century rarely was woman allowed to break out of the restrictions imposed upon her by the economic dependence upon the male... For her there were only the ancient, simple duties of the home to be performed 'in private and alone'. Always 'the smothering "no"' of the male's world held her back from realizing her human characteristics as well as her female ones.[28]

Gilman's view was that men and women should work together collectively instead of against each other. She sought to give women the confidence and encouragement needed to effect positive change for themselves. Lane says: 'Men, who are redeemable, and Gilman does offer many such examples, are decent, sensitive, and well-meaning, though conventional; but they are capable, when pressed, of changing, a quality of conversion without which they are lost' (R p. xv).

Both sexes must take responsibility for actions and inactions alike, putting prejudices and blame aside. Both sexes must work together, collectively as Gilman saw it, to learn what each feels, what each needs—physical, emotional, and psychological survival depend on it. As both 'Making a Change' and *The Crux* show, it is never too late to change. The characters realize (even if it comes at a later stage in their lives) that they can achieve redemption from their own collective ignorance born of social habit, and in doing so give hope to future generations. Through stories such as these, Gilman showed that changes in attitudes and habits as strong as those of Victorian morality are, in fact, possible and worth attaining.

Notes

1 Floyd Dell, *Love in the Machine Age: A Psychological Study of the Transition from Patriarchal Society* (New York: Farrar & Rhinehart, 1930), p. 50.

2 Mary Anne Ferguson, *Images of Women in Literature* (Boston: Houghton Mifflin, 1973) p. 10.

3 Ibid., p. 10.

4 Mary A. Hill, *Charlotte Perkins Gilman: The Making of a Radical Feminist, 1860–1896* (Philadelphia: Temple University Press, 1980), p. 188.

5 Ibid., p. 188.

6 Mary Loeffelholz, *Experimental Lives: Women and Literature, 1900–1945* (New York: Twayne, 1992), p. 197.

7 Ibid., p. 197.

8 Ibid., p. 198.

9 Ibid.

10 Havelock Ellis, *Man and Woman: A Study of Human Secondary Sexual*

Characteristics (London: Walter Scott, 1904; New York: Arno, 1974), p. 328.

11 Ibid., p. 333.

12 Howard Mumford Jones, 'The Comic Spirit and Victorian Sanity', in Joseph E. Baker, ed., *The Reinterpretation of Victorian Literature* (New York: Russell & Russell, 1962), p. 20.

13 Ibid., p. 20.

14 Mary Anne Ferguson, *Images of Women*, p. 26.

15 Ibid., p. 26.

16 Russell M. Goldfarb, *Sexual Repression and Victorian Literature* (Lewisburg: Bucknell University Press, 1970), p. 45.

17 Floyd Dell, *Love in the Machine Age*, p. 57.

18 Russell M. Goldfarb, *Sexual Repression*, p. 46.

19 Floyd Dell, *Love in the Machine Age*, p. 58.

20 Ibid.

21 Russell M. Goldfarb, *Sexual Repression*, p. 39.

22 Ibid., p. 41.

23 Ibid., p. 35.

24 Barbara Kantrowitz, 'Teenagers and AIDS', *Newsweek*, 3 August 1992, p. 46.

25 Ibid.

26 Ibid.

27 Ibid.

28 Carl N. Degler, 'Charlotte Perkins Gilman on the Theory and Practice of Feminism', in Sheryl L. Meyering, ed., *Charlotte Perkins Gilman: The Woman and her Work* (Ann Arbor: UMI Research Press, 1989), p. 13.

Utopian Fictions and Political Theories: Domestic Labour in the Work of Edward Bellamy, Charlotte Perkins Gilman and William Morris

RUTH LEVITAS

In Gilman's utopia *Herland* (1915) there is very little discussion of domestic labour. It is peopled entirely by women, who live separately in two-roomed apartments without kitchens; food can be eaten at dining rooms or taken away as desired. Collectivized child care takes place in specially designed surroundings, supervised by professionally trained staff. But we are not told how catering, laundry and cleaning are organized—and of course the question of the sexual division of labour does not arise in an all-female society. Domestic labour is invisible in this text because it has been abolished. More detailed representation of the potential re-organization of society can be found in other fictional writings preceding *Herland*. Many of Gilman's stories recapitulate the theme of how women can be freed from the drudgery of domestic labour and enabled to find fulfilling work outside the home. Among them are 'Aunt Mary's Pie Plant' (1908), *What Diantha Did* (1909/10), 'The Cottagette' (1910), 'Making a Change' (1911) and *Moving the Mountain* (1911). The key elements in the stories are the removal of cooking from the home through the development of kitchenless houses and apartments, the professionalization of cleaning and laundry services as well as catering, and the creation of excellent day-care facilities for young children. Carol Farley Kessler observes that the stories which deal with domestic labour and child care are a working out in fiction of the theoretical arguments advanced by Gilman in *Women and Economics* (1898); and it was for her non-fiction work and her political lectures that Gilman was best-known in her lifetime.

This chapter examines the theoretical framework underpinning Gilman's utopian short stories. It locates these in the context of socialist arguments about labour and domestic labour at the turn of the century, comparing Gilman's position with those of Edward Bellamy and William Morris. Bellamy and Morris offered opposing images of socialist utopian futures, differing crucially in their representation of work. The three writers taken together raise questions of whether the problem of domestic labour is one of the intrinsic nature of the work or the social relations under which it is performed—and thus questions of equality, difference and the sexual division of labour. Morris provides a useful qualification to the positions adopted by Bellamy and Gilman by rejecting their productivist assumptions, and paradoxically permits a greater recognition of the skill and value of women's work than does Gilman's feminist but Fabian critique.

The dominant view of domestic labour taken by socialists throughout the nineteenth century was that it was petty, trivial, demeaning, unskilled drudgery, which should be abolished either through the use of technology, as argued by August Bebel and Bellamy, or through the socialization or commercialization of domestic labour, as argued by Gilman. Belief in the dignity of labour outside the home was not extended to domestic labour. The idea that domestic labour might be as satisfying or valuable as other work was—and is—substantially tied to anti-feminist, pro-family positions. In the case of the public sphere, the intrinsic nature of work was distinguished by socialists from the social relations of capitalism under which the work was performed; but the substance of domestic labour was not consistently separated from the conditions of patriarchy under which this was carried out.

Bellamy, Gilman and Morris all challenged these conditions by insisting on the fundamental importance of the economic independence of women, and in Bellamy and Morris's case, on their absolute economic equality. None of them challenges the sexual division of labour in relation to domestic work, although Bellamy and Gilman do so in relation to the public sphere. Morris makes no separation between public and private spheres. His treatment of domestic labour is more consistent with his treatment of other forms of work, implying that the removal of capitalist and patriarchal social relations will transform the nature of all work. Morris is less inclined to argue that domestic labour is intrinsically unskilled and demeaning, and less inclined to argue for its professionalization, since he is opposed to increased specialization and division of labour.

The impact of Bellamy's *Looking Backward* (1888), both in the United States and elsewhere, is well known. The sequel, *Equality* (1897), was less popular; it is longer, and more exclusively didactic. In both books, Bellamy presents a centralized, efficient, mechanized utopia in which domestic labour has been abolished, although the treatment of women and of domestic work differs. In *Looking Backward* the discussion of domestic labour is limited; its transference to the public sphere has however solved the servant problem afflicting middle-class America. In response to the question 'Who does your housework, then?', the reply is:

> There is none to do... Our washing is all done at public laundries at excessively cheap rates, and our cooking at public kitchens. The making and repairing of all we wear are done outside in public shops. Electricity, of course, takes the place of all fires and lighting. We choose houses no larger than we need, and furnish them so as to involve the minimum of trouble to keep them in order. We have no use for domestic servants.[1]

Meals are taken in the dining house (within which families have individual private dining rooms), and this is said to mean that 'everything is vastly cheaper as well as better than it would be if prepared at home'.[2] Nevertheless 'the two minor meals of the day are usually taken at home, as not worth the trouble of going out'.[3] We are not told who prepares these—or who is responsible for the 'residual' work of cleaning. The statement that married women have no housekeeping responsibilities is predicated on the assumption that there is nothing to do, not on the suggestion that men share these responsibilities.[4]

In the public sphere, work is conducted by an 'industrial army', highly organized for maximum efficiency. Everyone works. Women accepted relief from housework 'only that they might contribute in other and more effectual... ways to the common weal'.[5] However, they 'constitute rather an allied force than an integral part of the army of the men. They have a woman general-in-chief and are under an exclusively feminine regime.'[6] Moreover, they are confined to 'suitable' work.[7] What is not clear is whether this suitable work in fact entails those tasks previously carried out by women as domestic labour. The nature of the tasks reserved for women is not specified. Women leave the industrial army 'when maternal duties claim them'.[8]

In *Looking Backward*, then, Bellamy retains a marked sexual division of labour in both private and public spheres, but one which is obscured by his insistence on the abolition of domestic labour by its mechanization and socialization. His rationale for this treatment of domestic work is less a concern for the lives of women than a general insistence on productivity, efficiency, and the abolition of waste—the same grounds on which he objects to the capitalist system in general. Nevertheless, if he fails to challenge the sexual division of labour (and even reinforces it), he does significantly challenge the social relations under which all work is performed. For women are released from economic dependency on individual men; all citizens are guaranteed an equal allocation of economic credits by the State. This is not, as Bellamy claims, an abolition of money, or of buying and selling; but all transactions are between individuals and the State, and all citizens are equal in this respect. The insistence on sexual difference is accompanied by an insistence on economic equality.

Equality is an attempt both to elaborate some of the themes in *Looking Backward* and to answer some of its critics. Here, Bellamy abandons the sexual division of labour in the public sphere: women are no longer organized separately in the industrial army, and 'there is not a trade or occupation... in which women do not take part'.[9] The rationale of differential strength has been removed, both because women have become stronger (and there is considerable discussion of the cultivation of ideal physiques for men and women), and because work has grown lighter, through increased use of machines. This process is expected to continue: 'some day we may be able to work by sheer will-power and have no need of hands at all'.[10] This perhaps excessive confidence in the potential of technology is repeated in the extended discussion of the abolition of domestic labour. Now, rather than meals being taken in a local restaurant, cooked food is delivered to the home: 'delicious but mysterious articles of food... come by pneumatic carrier'.[11] There is no washing up to do, because the dishes in which the food is served are all made out of paper. This is also true of the dishes in which the food is cooked, since heating is 'no longer... from without but from within': Bellamy has anticipated the microwave and pizza delivery.[12] Recycling avoids waste of materials, as well as abolishing washing up; and clothes and soft furnishings are also discarded and recycled when dirty, thus abolishing washing and ironing. Cleaning is much simplified: 'when we clean out a room, we turn the hose on ceiling, walls and floor. There is nothing to harm—nothing but tiles and other hard-finished surfaces.'[13] It is not, however, clear who 'we' are, or who holds the hose. As in *Looking Backward*, women are expected to stop work to care for their children. The sexual division of labour thus remains.

The economic value of women's domestic work is not recognized. Bellamy's view of domestic labour attributes little value to it, and less skill. It is portrayed as unskilled, unpleasant drudgery. Even those aspects which he does not see as intrinsically unskilled—nutrition and cooking—are rendered so by being carried out by women in the domestic sphere.[14] In the early stages of the revolution, women were in some instances seen as sufficiently employed in housework for their own families and 'they were recognised as rendering public service until the new cooperative housekeeping was sufficiently systematised to do away with the necessity of separate kitchens and other elaborate domestic machinery for each family'; others were required to work in the industrial army.[15] The purpose of abolishing domestic labour is not to liberate women from a burden of unpaid work, but to release women's labour to be spent in more socially useful, less trivial forms of production. There is never a suggestion that domestic labour might itself be a form of production, nor any discussion of its relation to the care of children. Still less is there any suggestion that men might do domestic work. Bellamy echoes the arguments of August Bebel, whose work he has sometimes been accused of plagiarizing:[16]

> The question to be solved is how to attain the best results with the smallest expenditure of power, time and material... The small private kitchen in the individual household is therefore an obsolescent institution, in which time, power, and material are thoughtlessly and extravagantly wasted. The entire preparation of food will be undertaken by society in the future... The private kitchen will disappear... When, in addition to these central kitchens, we have central washing establishments, in which clothes are washed, dried, bleached and ironed by the help of machinery, and if we take into account that besides all this there will be central heating and lighting, a supply of cold and warm water laid on, a sufficient number of baths, and that all our clothing and underclothing will be manufactured in central factories, we find our whole household life radically changed and simplified.[17]

This depends on founding 'a society in which all the means of production are the property of the community, a society which recognizes full equality without distinction of sex'. And 'only thus can woman become as productively useful as man'.[18]

While *Looking Backward* became a socialist classic that has never been out of print in the United States, Charlotte Perkins Gilman's work is much less well known, although it underwent a partial rediscovery in the 1970s, and is currently undergoing a dramatic revival. The two non-fiction works primarily concerned with domestic labour, *Women and Economics* (1898) and *The Home: Its Work and Influence* (1903), were both republished in the late 1960s, and a long excerpt from *The Home* was reprinted in 1980 in Ellen Malos's *The Politics of Housework*.

There is a clear relationship between Gilman's work and Bellamy's. William O'Neill argues that she was converted to socialism (of a sort) 'by reading Edward Bellamy's great utopian novel *Looking Backward*';[19] and 'Aunt Mary's Pie Plant' was first published in *Woman's Home Companion* with an editorial note that the story 'will be found a realistic miniature *Looking Backward*'.[20] But Gilman also draws on another tradition, a continuing thread of materialist feminism in the United States throughout the second half of the nineteenth century.[21] The influence of Charles Fourier on this movement was very strong and there is a visible connection between Gilman's views and those of the utopian socialists, reflected in her awareness of the importance of architectural design to social processes.[22]

The question of domestic labour is central to Gilman's social critique. She shares the view that it is unskilled, isolating drudgery, which must be abolished, enabling at least some women to engage in 'real' work which is more productive, more socially useful and more fulfilling. Gilman partially challenges the sexual division of labour in the public sphere. She is adamantly opposed, however, to men doing household work; she too believes in a natural division of labour, in which women are equal but different, and retain responsibility for the home and the care of children. Her argument in *Women and Economics* is that this natural difference is socially exaggerated to the point of being dysfunctional. Women are confined to the domestic sphere; they are consequently prevented from using their abilities for the public good, and prevented from being fully human. This insistence on difference is reiterated in *The Home*. Gilman operates with a deficit model of women, repeatedly arguing that they need to be enabled to become more like men. Thus her otherwise incisive critique is undermined both by her essentialist model of gender difference and, equally importantly, by her productivist assumptions.

Like Bellamy and Bebel, Gilman seeks to abolish domestic labour. This is to be done in three ways. Firstly, there will be less cleaning to do in houses designed without kitchens: 'the cleaning required in each house would be much reduced by the removal of the two chief elements of household dirt,—grease and ashes'.[23] Secondly, it will be done more efficiently by specialists using appropriate technology: 'it would be a home where the cleaning was done by efficient workers, not hired separately by the families, but engaged by the manager of the establishment'.[24] This will liberate enormous productive potential:

> Where now twenty women in twenty homes work all the time, and insufficiently accomplish their various duties, the same work in the hands of specialists could be done in less time by fewer people; and the others would be left free to do other work for which they were better fitted, thus increasing the productive power of the world.[25]

Thus domestic labour is to be abolished primarily by its socialization, its removal from the private to the public sphere, and its efficient execution through increased specialization and division of labour. Thirdly, the relationship under which domestic labour is carried out by women will be abolished by the economic independence of women.

The kitchenless house is a central theme for Gilman, drawn from earlier materialist feminist writers:

> If there should be built and opened in any of our cities today a commodious and well-served apartment house for professional women with families, it would be filled at once. The apartments would be without kitchens; but there would be a kitchen belonging to the house from which meals could be served to the families in their rooms or in a common dining room, as preferred... In suburban homes this purpose could be accomplished much better by having a grouping of adjacent houses, each distinct and having its own yard, but all kitchenless, and connected by covered ways with the eating house.[26]

Gilman sees the preparation of food as one of the two chief elements of household work (the other being the care of children), to which she adds cleaning, washing and nursing. Her objections to individual kitchens are manifold. Central among these is waste—of labour, of the repetition of plant, of fuel, and of food.[27] Food preparation 'takes up half the working time of half the population of the world'.[28] The socialization of domestic labour will cut the cost of living by two-thirds and add to productive labour by a half.[29]

Yet the current wasteful organization does not result in the work being well done. Women are unable to carry it out in a skilled and efficient way for a variety of reasons: the average capacity of women limits the skill and knowledge available; women work only for their families, and thus have little stimulus to improve; they work in isolation; and they have constantly conflicting duties.[30] Gilman argues that home cooking is nutritionally unsound, frequently indigestible, and conducive to unhealthy self-indulgence.[31] How, she asks, 'can we reconcile ourselves to the continuance of a system not only so shamefully inadequate, but so ruinously expensive?'[32]

Gilman is a great advocate of specialization and the division of labour. Like Emile Durkheim, she sees the division of labour as the essential element in social progress:

> The savage works by himself, for himself; the civilised man works in elaborate independence with many for many. By the division of labour and its increasing specialisation we vastly multiply skill and power... The solitary savage knew neither specialisation nor organisation—he did his own work... Even in rich America, even in richest New York, in *nine-tenths* of families the housewife 'does her own work'.[33]

Lack of specialization and lack of skill go hand in hand. At present, domestic labour is 'a bunch of ill-assorted trades, wherein everything costs more than it ought to cost, and nothing is done as it should be done,—on a business basis'.[34] More vehemently, Gilman declares the home to be 'a swarming heap of rudimentary trades' and complains that 'our boasted industrial progress carries embedded in its very centre this stronghold of hoary antiquity, this knotted, stumpy bunch of amputated rudiments'.[35]

Gilman objects both to 'the maintenance of primitive industries in a modern industrial community', and to 'the confinement of women to those industries and their limited area of expression'.[36] Her starting point is that women must be involved in work outside the home: in an accurate criticism of the materialist feminist tradition she argues that 'attempts at cooperation so far have endeavoured to lessen the existing labours of women without recognizing their need for other occupation, and this is one reason for their repeated failure'.[37] Confined to the home 'the women of today... go mad by scores and hundreds'.[38] Even where they do not go mad, they are ignorant, weak, and narrow, and not suitable companions for men: 'the woman is narrowed by the home and the man is narrowed by the woman'; he is 'injured by constant contact with a smaller mind'.[39]

Yet Gilman's answer to this problem involves only a very limited challenge to the sexual division of labour, and a very ambivalent attitude to the skill and value even potentially involved in the tasks of domestic labour. It is quite clear that she sees these tasks, once socialized, as the province of women. There is one point in *Women and Economics* where, unusually, this is contradicted:

> as we socialize our functions, [cleaning] passes from her hands into those of man. The city's cleaning is his work. And even in our houses the professional cleaner is more and more frequently a man.[40]

This, however, is exceptional. Generally, the argument in *Women and Economics* assumes that commercialized or socialized domestic work is still to be carried out by women, although they will cease to be residential servants, paid or unpaid:

> Under the free development of these branches a woman could choose her position, train for it, and become a most valuable functionary in her special branch, all the while living in her own home: that is, she would live in it as a man lives in his home, spending certain hours of the day at work and others at home.[41]

Once the 'several professions involved in our clumsy method of housekeeping' are developed as independent specialisms, women would have a choice of occupation. They would of course choose professions compatible with their primary role as mothers (and be enabled to do so by the provision of excellent professional day care for their children).[42] Many women, indeed, 'would continue to prefer the very kinds of work which they are doing now, in the new and higher methods of execution'—although she also argues that many professions are more compatible with motherhood than is domestic work.[43] Although men and women should be equal, 'equal does not mean similar, remember'.[44]

Gilman is adamant that expecting men to share domestic labour is not a solution, that this is an unacceptable burden to lay upon men who are already overworked in earning the money to support the grossly inefficient system of private housekeeping, who 'do everything else that is done to maintain our civilisation':

> There will be some pathetic protest here that it is a man's duty to help women bear the troubles and difficulties of the home. The woman ardently believes this, and the man too, sometimes. Of all incredible impositions this is the most astounding... Granting that the care of body is women's especial work; the feeding, clothing and cleaning of the world; she should by this time have developed some system of doing it which would make it less of a burden to the man as well as the woman.[45]

It would be 'cruel as well as useless' to expect men to do more than they already do. Like Bellamy, Gilman sees women as economically dependent upon men, and does not see domestic labour as a form of production upon which men are dependent: 'The support of the family we have laid entirely upon the man, thus developing in the dependent woman a limitless capacity for receiving things, and denying her the power to produce them.'[46]

The enormous reduction of domestic work through its socialization would free a substantial proportion of women to share in the forms of work done by men. Gilman challenges the sexual division of labour only in terms of wanting to make women more like men. Her arguments about skill and value in relation to domestic labour bear the marks both of her assumption that what men do is superior to what women do, and her reluctance to concede that there is anything remotely dignified about women's present position. To concede that domestic labour is either skilled or valuable is to reinforce a myth which supports women's economic dependency:

> The economic dependency of women upon men, with all its deadly consequences, is defended because of our conviction that her labour in the home is as productive as his out of it... It is with a real sense of pain that one remorselessly punctures this beautiful bubble.[47]

Yet Gilman also insists on calculating the economic value of women's work in the wasteful single family household: in *What Diantha Did*, the eponymous heroine outrages her father by demonstrating that the value of her unpaid labour over many years, together with her direct financial contribution in the four years she has been teaching, outweighs his expenditure on her lifetime's upkeep.

Gilman is ultimately ambivalent about whether socialized domestic labour can be accorded the same skill and value as men's work—whether, in fact, the problem is the work itself or the social relations under which it is performed: 'Even cleaning rightly understood and practised, is a useful and honourable profession. It has been amusing heretofore to see how this least desirable of labours has been so innocently held to be women's natural duty.'[48] It is quite clear that she regards it as a necessary evil to be minimized in favour of other forms of work:

> Work the object of which is to serve one's self is the lowest. Work the object of which is merely to serve one's family is the next lowest. Work the object of which is to serve more and more people, in widening range, till it approximates the divine spirit that cares for all the world, is social service in the fullest sense, and the highest form of service that we can reach.[49]

Although Gilman's critique of the position of women sometimes appears very radical, the substance of it is not very different from Bellamy's arguments. What is different is the amount of attention she gives the issue. In addition, she writes at length about the care of children, which, like housework, she argues is done both badly and wastefully. All her arguments about women's work are predicated on the demand for properly equipped, properly staffed nurseries and schools for children. The kitchenless apartment block will have 'a roof-garden, day-nursery, and kindergarten, under well-trained professional nurses and teachers'.[50] Motherhood may be a natural role, but the care and teaching of children is properly a professional one. Gilman has little confidence in maternal instinct—for even if mothers naturally love their children, they are not necessarily very good at bringing them up. Mothers, after all, raise the 'growing crop of idiots, imbeciles, cripples, defectives, and degenerates, the vicious and the criminal; as well as all the vast mass of slow-minded, prejudiced, ordinary people who clog the wheels of progress'.[51] Her recognition of the extent of the problem of women's work and women's lives is infinitely greater than Bellamy's, but in the end, apart from the crucial recognition of the question of child care, her analysis is little different, and she too assumes that the residual work to be done in the home will be negligible once domestic labour is socialized.

While Gilman claims to address the question of women and economics, the economic basis of her solution is undermined by her attitude to the value of domestic labour. Whereas Bellamy solves the problem of women's economic independence through distributive equality, Gilman consistently writes of the need for socialized services to be provided on a commercial or business basis. This will ensure the economic independence of those women providing the services, as in *What Diantha Did*, as well of as those released into higher forms of work. Yet she does not (at least in the two books where one might expect it to be central) address the question of class division, of differential wages, of the sexual division of labour in the public sphere, in terms of the implications of these for women's ability to be genuinely financially independent. Although, like Bellamy, she insists that the economic basis of women's 'dependence' must be abolished, she does not attribute value to women's work in a way which makes this possible.

Both Bellamy and Gilman try to solve the problem of domestic labour by its abolition, through a mixture of technology and socialization. In so far as they challenge the sexual division of labour, it is to allow women to participate in work hitherto reserved for men. Both are committed to a version of social progress based on maximizing productivity and efficiency. Both, especially Gilman, express views about the organization of domestic work and its effect on women which were (and to an extent still are) radical and contentious. Gilman clearly felt it necessary to defend herself repeatedly against the potential criticisms of wishing to destroy the home and family privacy. Countering the suggestion that the loss of family mealtimes would undermine family life, she remarks that 'a family unity which is only bound together by a table cloth is of questionable value'.[52]

By comparison, William Morris's treatment of the position of women appears unenlightened, especially for a political writer of such acuteness. Morris is, with reason, usually seen as the most reactionary of the three on the subject of women, although he is otherwise the most radical. He was a revolutionary and Marxist socialist, whereas Bellamy called himself a nationalist rather than a socialist, and Gilman aligned herself with Fabianism and was antipathetic to Marxism. Morris's general analysis of work under capitalism and its potential transformation under socialism is far more penetrating than that of either Bellamy or Gilman: he argues against the division of labour, against the distinction between mental and manual labour, against untrammelled mechanization, and for the valorization of craft skills. Despite his endorsement of the sexual division of labour, the context in which this occurs means his overall arguments can fruitfully be extended to domestic work. With Morris, we have to add a rejection of the sexual division of labour; with Bellamy and Gilman, we have to add both this and a revision of the value placed on women's work.

Morris (1832–96) wrote *News from Nowhere* (1890) in direct reply to *Looking Backward*, which he reviewed in *Commonweal* on its first publication. Morris opposes the dominance of technology, as well as the attitude to work, demonstrated in *Looking Backward*. He is deeply suspicious of the idea that machinery is labour-saving, and will lead to a reduction in the hours of work (a suspicion borne out by the fact that the time spent by women on domestic labour has not been significantly reduced by the prevalence of domestic technology). Morris wrote in his review:

> Now surely this ideal of the great reduction in the hours of labour by the mere means of machinery is a futility. The human race has always put forth about as much energy as it could in given conditions of climate and the like... I believe that this will always be so, and that the multiplication of machinery will just—multiply machinery; I believe that the ideal of the future does not point to the lessening of men's energy by the reduction of labour to a minimum, but rather to the reduction of *pain in labour* to a minimum, so small that it will cease to be a pain... the true incentive to useful and happy labour is and must be pleasure in the work itself.[53]

News from Nowhere is constructed around this ideal, and thus is properly read as a critique of alienated labour. There are machines in Nowhere, and Morris's political lectures repeatedly argue that machines are a good thing as long as they are our servants and not our masters. Their purpose, however, is not to eliminate work, for work, including necessary work, is to become a pleasure, the expression of human creativity. Morris is also adamant that everyone must take responsibility for both the practical and political details of life. The former cannot be shuffled off onto others, any more than the latter can be shuffled off onto 'an abstraction called the State'.[54] Taking responsibility for the practical details of life—which contemporary feminists argue many men are unable or unwilling to do—necessitates reducing rather than increasing the division of labour. In 'The Society of the Future', Morris argues for 'a non-ascetic simplicity of life', and one in which the role of technology is greatly reduced. This will necessitate everyone possessing a wide range of skills: everyone should be able to swim, ride, sail a boat; have carpentry and smithying skills, and a range of agricultural competences. They should also learn 'cooking and baking, sewing, and the like, which can be taught to every sensible person in a few hours, and which everyone ought to have at their fingers' ends'.[55] In this society, the 'division of labour would be habitually limited: men (and women too, of course) would do their work and take their pleasure in their own persons'.[56]

If the social division of labour is to be reduced, what of the sexual division of labour? In *News from Nowhere*, Morris describes woman in the new society as 'respected as a child-bearer and rearer of children, desired as a woman, loved as a companion, unanxious for the future of her children' and hence possessed of an enhanced 'instinct for maternity'.[57] Women are not exclusively confined to domestic labour, although the range of work they undertake is narrower than that of men; but domestic labour is seen as something for which women are particularly fitted, and something which is highly valued. The sexual division of labour is intact. On the basis of *News from Nowhere*, feminist critics commonly dismiss Morris's attitude to women as unacceptable.[58] In a more considered analysis, Jan Marsh concedes that 'it could be argued that... Morris is at least taking housework seriously', but goes on to observe that 'this gendered division of tasks is not what socialist feminists would regard as utopian'.[59]

Morris's insistence on the sexual division of labour is repeated elsewhere; in 1886, he insisted that while 'we must claim absolute equality of condition between women and men... it would be poor economy setting women to do men's work (as unluckily they often do now) or vice versa'.[60] To another correspondent he wrote that 'women as a rule are very feeble on the artistic side; their line is business and mathematics'.[61] But an interview in 1894 showed Morris's position to be more complex. He argued that women's talents varied, like those of men, and that people should do what they are suited to. His objection was to women competing with men in manual work 'for which they are manifestly not suited', and thus being underpaid and driving down the general level of wages.[62] Although Morris was agnostic about 'what strength of muscle and strength of limb women might acquire by training' in a differently ordered society, he continued to argue that women were in fact weaker. But 'when married women are also industrial workers, they... have the double burden upon their shoulders of tending the home and helping to earn a living too... Women suffer terribly under the present system.'[63] Morris and Gilman were both opposed to the 'double shift': Morris's solution was to exempt working-class wives from work in the public sphere, Gilman's to exempt men from domestic labour.

Morris's comments in 'The Society of the Future' that the skills of domestic labour can be taught in a few hours might be seen as dismissive and trivializing. However, he takes a similar attitude to many of the other activities listed as essential for all. It is rather a reflection of his belief that people when not under duress have a capacity to enjoy acquiring and using practical skills. He can therefore be read as insisting on the importance of all those activities which contribute directly to the maintenance of daily life, particularly when they are direct and unmediated. This is consistent with Morris's general emphasis on the importance of practical, craft skills, and thus his refusal to valorize mental above manual labour, or to endorse their separation.

A key element in Morris's argument is the transformation of the conditions under which domestic labour in performed. Like Bellamy, he insists on absolute material equality between men and women. Unlike Bellamy—and unlike Gilman—he does not suppose that the nuclear family will necessarily remain intact. Whereas the Leete family in *Looking Backward* is a conventional bourgeois family despite the supposedly transformed economic relationships, and whereas Gilman says in *The Home* that 'the place of the one initial and undying group of father, mother, and child will remain to us',[64] in *Nowhere* people live in groups of various sizes, as they please, and the nuclear family is not necessary: 'the social bond would be habitually and instinctively felt, so that there would be no need to be always asserting it by set forms: the family of blood-relationship would melt into that of the community and of humanity'.[65] In consequence, domestic work is not performed in isolation, but neither are people regimented into large communal organizations.

The implication of Morris's position is that the negative aspects of domestic labour—like those of other work—derive from the social relations under which it is carried out; and that it is skilled, valuable, important work, rather than something nasty and demeaning which should be abolished. Combined with his acceptance of the sexual division of labour, it is easy to see why this appears reactionary, since, as Gilman was only too well aware, the dignity of domestic labour is routinely mobilized as part of an anti-feminist position. Taken in the context of his general critique of labour under capitalism, it is clear that Morris's argument cannot be assimilated to such an anti-feminist stance. His analysis is clearly inadequate in so far as he assumes a natural sexual division of labour, but it is no more inadequate in this respect than that of Gilman or Bellamy. In terms of according worth to the processes of support for material life, Morris is considerably better.

The questions raised by Gilman, Bellamy and Morris remain important for contemporary feminism. In the 1970s, feminists sought to establish that domestic labour is economically productive, and that women engaged in unpaid housework and child care are exploited by private and/or public patriarchy. In the 1980s and 1990s, they continued to argue that men, both individually and as a class, appropriate the unpaid labour of women.[66] There is a cluster of related issues, which can only be touched on here: the intractability of the sexual division of labour; the value of domestic labour, the skills involved, and the relationship between these; whether those tasks are performed on a paid or an unpaid basis; and the relationship between housework and child care. But domestic labour is still almost all performed by women. As Marilyn Waring has shown, the economic value of work performed in the private sphere goes unrecognized in the very specific sense that it does not count as work for the purposes of calculating Gross Domestic Product.[67] This is true whether it be child care and housework, tasks concerned with the reproduction of labour power, or (as is typically the case in many developing countries) subsistence agriculture and the carrying of water. The same tasks conducted in the public sphere would be counted as productive, since they would be incorporated into the market system. In the public sphere, segregated labour markets mean that women are confined to areas which are low paid and defined as low in skill—often precisely those areas of work closely related to domestic labour. What constitutes 'skill' is socially constructed and negotiated, and women's skills are consistently underrated; women collude in this process when they accept or reproduce arguments that domestic work is unskilled.

Gilman's vision of the kitchenless house has not become a reality. Indeed, George Ritzer, discussing fast food as an example of Weberian rationalization in *The McDonaldization of Society*, is like most people unaware that early technocratic socialists aspired to this:

> Given the efficiency of the fast-food restaurant, the home kitchen has had to grow more efficient or it might have faced total extinction. Had the kitchen not grown more efficient, a comedian could have envisioned a time when the kitchen would have been replaced by a large, comfortable telephone lounge used for calling Domino's for pizza delivery.[68]

But such changes as have taken place since Gilman and Bellamy were writing have been largely upon the lines they envisaged, in the sense that some tasks have moved from the private, unpaid sphere to the public, paid one. We do not have the excellent, professionally-staffed day-care centres designed as appropriate environments for young children, and the inadequacy of public day-care (especially in Britain, where it is less available than almost anywhere in Europe) places a severe limitation on women's participation in paid labour, and consequently on their economic independence. Nor do we have Bellamy's distributive equality. For that part of the population who have homes and decent incomes, parts of domestic labour have moved outside the home in various ways. The kitchens of the affluent are equipped with dishwashers, washing machines, freezers, and microwave ovens. Supermarkets provide prepared and processed foods. Cooked food for consumption at home is readily available (at least in cities). This food may be nutritionally undesirable and often horrible, but it is certainly available. Drawing this work (including the manufacture of kitchens appliances) into the public sphere does indeed mean an increase in the division of labour, an increase in specialization.

The changes are ambiguous. As domestic washing machines replaced the launderettes which replaced public laundries (where everything was washed, ironed and folded), work was brought back into the home in a different form. Moreover, the expectation that domestic labour would diminish to a rump, the execution of which (and the sexual division of which) was unimportant, has shown no signs of being fulfilled. Rather, Morris was right. Women spend as much time on domestic labour as they always did, but they spend it differently. This is not a matter of choice (except in a marginal sense), since standards and expectations are socially set. The way in which the reproduction of labour power takes place is not a private matter. There are informal sanctions against those who do not keep themselves, their families and their homes in a 'proper' state—and, especially where children are concerned, sometimes formal sanctions as well.

Increased specialization and division of labour may increase productivity as measured by the highly questionable economic indicators available, such as Gross Domestic Product. What is less clear is that this increase represents an overall improvement in the quality of life, or that it is ecologically sustainable. The benefits of technology at the point of use (in this case in the kitchen) have to be offset against the consequences of their production, in terms of materials and the human effects of the labour processes involved in their manufacture. This does not mean we should dispense with machines altogether, but if there were more time, perhaps fewer would do.

The claim by Gilman and Bellamy that things can only be done well on the basis of a high degree of specialization should also be treated with some scepticism. Sometimes Morris's notion of 'doing your own work' may seem to carry opposition to specialization too far, although as Paul Thompson insists, he was advocating the reduction rather than the abolition of the social division of labour.[69] It is clear that Morris shared Gilman's recognition that human labour is necessarily and properly social, and embedded in specific structures of social relations. Nevertheless, people are indeed capable of acquiring a range of skills, and most of us do, although they may not be the ones Morris listed. And domestic work is indeed skilled (although like any work, it can be done well or badly); these skills have to be learned; and they are essential to human survival and comfort. The degree of skill which can be applied (again, as in all work) depends on the material and cultural resources available.

The political problem is that insisting on the skill and value of domestic labour may be used to justify or deny the subordinate position of women within patriarchy, and to legitimate the sexual division of labour. The two separate themes of the sexual division of labour and the contested skill and value of domestic labour are conflated in the view that domestic labour is a burden unfairly borne by women, which men should share. Women who can afford to do so have increasingly given up the struggle to make men do their share, and bought more technology and hired help from cleaners (and nannies). This, together with the unfashionableness of any concern with material production, may be one reason why domestic labour has lapsed from its central importance in feminist theory. It also encourages the definition of domestic labour as unskilled, as this justifies the low wages it commands.

It is not true that domestic work is unskilled. Moreover, it is politically futile to tie demands for men to do more of the tasks of domestic labour to an assertion that the tasks (rather than the relations under which they are currently executed) are intrinsically oppressive and unskilled. These two assertions work politically in opposite directions. For domestic work *not* to involve the exploitation and oppression of women, it is necessary simultaneously to challenge the sexual division of labour, and insist on the skill and value of domestic work in both private and public spheres. What is important is to insist on a proper recognition of the economic and human value of the processes of life support which constitute much of women's work—and to continue to insist that men do their share.[70]

Notes

1 Edward Bellamy, *Looking Backward,* first published 1888 (Harmondsworth: Penguin, 1986), p. 102.

2 Ibid., p. 123.

3 Ibid., p. 118.

4 Ibid., p. 184.

5 Ibid.

6 Ibid., pp. 184–85.

7 Ibid., p. 185.

8 Ibid., p. 184.

9 Edward Bellamy, *Equality* (London: Heinemann, 1897), p. 39.

10 Ibid., pp. 39-40.

11 Ibid., p. 46.

12 Ibid., p. 46.

13 Ibid., p. 46.

14 Edward Bellamy, *Looking Backward,* p. 257.

15 Ibid., p. 327.

16 See Nancy Snell Griffith, *Edward Bellamy: A Bibliography* (Metchuen, NJ: Scarecrow, 1986), pp. 69-70 and Arthur Ernest Morgan, *Edward Bellamy* (New York: Columbia University Press, 1944).

17 August Bebel, *Woman in the Past, Present and Future,* first published 1883 (London: Zwan, 1988), p. 227.

18 Ibid., p. 111.

19 William O'Neill, Introduction to Charlotte Perkins Gilman, *The Home: Its Work and Influence*, first published 1903 (Urbana: University of Illinois Press, 1972), p. ix.

20 Carol Farley Kessler, *Charlotte Perkins Gilman: Her Progress Towards Utopia* (Liverpool: Liverpool University Press, 1995), p. 118.

21 See Dolores Hayden, *The Grand Domestic Revolution* (Cambridge: MIT Press, 1981).

22 See Polly Wynn Allen, *Building Domestic Liberty* (Amherst: University of Massachusetts Press, 1988)

23 Charlotte Perkins Gilman, *Women and Economics*, first published 1898 (New York: Harper and Row, 1966), p. 244.

24 Ibid., p. 242.

25 Ibid., p. 245.

26 Ibid., pp. 242–43.

27 Charlotte Perkins Gilman, *The Home*, p. 117.

28 Ibid., p. 95.

29 Ibid., p. 289.

30 Ibid., p. 90.

31 Ibid., p. 137; 181.

32 Ibid., p. 117.

33 Ibid., pp. 84–85.

34 Ibid., p. 70.

35 Ibid., p. 97; 117.

36 Ibid., p. 10.

37 Charlotte Perkins Gilman, *Women and Economics*, p. 247.

38 Ibid., p. 267.

39 Charlotte Perkins Gilman, *The Home*, p. 277.

40 Charlotte Perkins Gilman, *Women and Economics*, p. 247.

41 Ibid., p. 245.

42 Ibid., pp. 245–46.

43 Ibid., p. 246.

44 Charlotte Perkins Gilman, *The Home*, pp. 286–87.

45 Ibid., pp. 286–88.

46 Ibid., p. 289.

47 Ibid., p. 52.

48 Charlotte Perkins Gilman, *Women and Economics*, p. 246.

49 Ibid., p. 279.

50 Ibid., p. 243.

51 Charlotte Perkins Gilman, *The Home*, p. 59.

52 Charlotte Perkins Gilman, *Women and Economics*, p. 244.

53 William Morris, 'Looking Backward', in A. L. Morton, ed., *Political Writings of William Morris* (London: Lawrence and Wishart, 1984), p. 252.

54 Ibid., p. 253.

55 William Morris, 'The Society of the Future', *Political Writings of William Morris*, p. 197.

56 Ibid., p. 201.

57 William Morris, *News from Nowhere*, first published 1890 (London: Longmans, Green, 1902).

58 See Angelika Bammer, *Partial Visions: Feminism and Utopianism in the 1970s*

(London: Routledge, 1991), p. 29; Christine Delphy and Diana Leonard, *Familiar Exploitation* (Cambridge: Polity, 1992), p. 7 and Nicholas Salmon, Introduction to *William Morris, Political Writings: Contributions to Justice and Commonweal 1883–1890* (Bristol: Thoemmes, 1994), pp. xviii-xix.

59 Jan Marsh, 'Concerning Love: *News from Nowhere* and Gender', in Stephen Coleman and Paddy O'Sullivan, eds, *William Morris and News from Nowhere: A Vision for Our Time* (Bideford: Green Books, 1990), pp. 114–15.

60 Norman Kelvin, *The Collected Letters of William Morris: Volume 2* (Princeton: Princeton University Press, 1987), p. 545.

61 Ibid., p. 824.

62 Sarah Tooley, 'A Living Wage for Women', *The Women's Signal*, 19 April, 1894, *The Journal of the William Morris Society* 10 (4) Spring 1994, pp. 5–9.

63 Ibid., pp. 6–7.

64 Charlotte Perkins Gilman, *The Home*, p. 64.

65 William Morris, 'The Society of the Future', p. 203.

66 See Ellen Malos, *The Politics of Housework* (London: Allison and Busby, 1980), Deborah Tong, *Feminist Thought* (London: Routledge, 1992), Christine Delphy and Diana Leonard, *Familiar Exploitation* (Cambridge: Polity, 1992), and Sylvia Walby, *Theorizing Patriarchy* (Oxford: Blackwell, 1990).

67. Marilyn Waring, *If Women Counted* (London: Macmillan, 1988).

68 George Ritzer, *The McDonaldization of Society* (Thousand Oaks, CA: Pine Forge Press, 1993), p. 45.

69 Paul Thompson, *The Work of William Morris* (Oxford: Oxford University Press, 1991), p. 269.

70 A version of this chapter first appeared as an article in *Utopian Studies*, 6 (1) 1995. I am grateful to the editor for permission to republish it here in a shortened and slightly altered form. I am also grateful to Caroline New, Ellen Malos, and the members of the Women's Research Group at the University of Bristol, and the *Utopian Studies* reviewers and editor for their comments on earlier versions of the article; and to participants in the 1995 conference on Gilman, and the editors of this volume, for their responses.

Gender and Industry in *Herland*: Trees as a Means of Production and Metaphor

ALEX SHISHIN

Three-quarters of the way through Charlotte Perkins Gilman's *Herland* (1915), the narrator, Vandyck (Van) Jennings, confesses, 'I see I have said little about the economics of the place [Herland]; it should have come before' (H p. 99). The intimation is that he will presently have a great deal to say about this subject. This, however, is not to be. While the author of *Women and Economics* (1898) devotes an entire chapter to the religion of her all-woman utopia, we are left to deduce what Herland's industry and political economy are like by piecing together clues scattered throughout the novel. This creates contradictions and ambiguities. The biggest ambiguity concerns the actual level of industrial development in Herland. There are indications that the means of production are as sophisticated as those in the modern capitalist world, if not more so. Yet, at the same time, strong implications suggest that Herland's society had reached a plateau and its technological sophistication is essentially that of a flowering but fundamentally unchanging traditional culture. There are also questions of the nature of governance. In many ways Herland, particularly in the operation of its work groups, seems to be a pure democracy close to anarchism. Yet it has authoritarian elements, most noticeable in relation to the breeding of children. Coupled with this is the question of how much these ambiguities and contradictions owe to accident and/or intent. Do they exist simply because serial publication of *Herland* in Gilman's monthly magazine, *The Forerunner*, prevented her from revising the novel as a single piece? (*Herland* only appeared in book form in 1978.) Or could it be that at least part of the confusion exists deliberately, because Gilman was frightened by the subversive implications of some of her ideas—particularly those pertaining to private property and the centralized State—and wanted to obscure them? Was the reformer Gilman, in other words, a closet revolutionary? This chapter cannot answer that question. Neither will it attempt to reconcile *Herland's* contradictions nor unravel its ambiguities. It will only explore the overall effect that Gilman's political and economic clues produce and leave the reader to pass judgement.

Our initial clue to the state of the industrial art in Herland comes in the first chapter. Travelling in a remote part of the world, Terry, Jeff and Van find a mountain pool with evidence of dyes and fragments of 'a well-woven fabric, with a pattern, and of a clear scarlet that the water had not faded'; the narrator concludes they could not have been produced by any local 'savage tribe' (H p. 4). Van tells the others, 'Somewhere up yonder they spin and weave and dye—as well as we do' (H p. 7). Later, when the three adventurous men have penetrated Herland by airplane (a new and daring invention) and have been gently but decisively made prisoners by the Herlanders, they learn that the country is centred around the production and caring of children. But how exactly is that 'well-woven fabric' made? This we never find out.

At one point Van assures us that the Herlanders had a 'daring social inventiveness far beyond our own, and a mechanical and scientific development fully equal to ours' (H p. 81). And indeed when the three men try to escape to their airplane and are recaptured, the women return them to their place of confinement in automobiles: 'Back we went... skimming along in electric motors enough like ours to be quite recognizable...' (H p. 42) (Electric autos were popular as the proper ladies' cars at the time of *Herland's* writing.[1]) But how do the Herlanders build those briefly-mentioned electric cars? To produce them Herland would need an industrial base like the one that existed in the advanced capitalist world of 1915. If such an industrial base exists in Herland, we do not see it, nor hear or smell it. The same pleasant condition—a pronounced lack of industrial pollution and ugliness—is present in the two seminal utopian novels which preceded *Herland*: Edward Bellamy's *Looking Backward* (1888) and William Morris's *News from Nowhere* (1890). But while Bellamy and Morris offer explanations for this, Gilman does not.

When Julian West awakes from over a century-long hypnotic sleep in *Looking Backward* and first looks at twentieth-century Boston, he remarks on the lack of smoking chimneys. His host and future father-in-law, Dr Leete, tells him they have been out of use for nearly a century because 'the crude method of combustion on which you depended for heat became obsolete'.[2] If Herland has passed through a similar industrial development, we are not informed. The bucolic, ignored except in passing by Bellamy, is decidedly emphasized in *Herland*, even more than in Morris's *News from Nowhere*.

Morris's hatred of industrialism is more vehement than Bellamy's. The narrator, William, upon waking up in twenty-second century Hammersmith, marvels with delight, like Julian West, at the lack of industrial mess: 'The soap works with their smoke-vomiting chimneys were gone; the engineer's work gone; and no sound of riveting and hammering came down the west wind from Thorneycroft's.'[3] But what he sees in their place are not the vestments of a high-tech centralized state socialism, as anticipated by Bellamy, but a society whose aesthetics have gone back to those of the fourteenth century. He first notices a stone bridge which he thinks more beautiful than Florence's Ponte Vecchio and remarks: 'I had perhaps dreamed of such a bridge but never seen such a one out of an illuminated manuscript.'[4] Morris's Communists ('Socialism' and 'Communism' were used interchangeably in the nineteenth century) have consciously destroyed virtually every last vestige of industrialism; there is not even the hum of an electric motor to be heard. Gilman does not exhibit Morris's love for the archaic, nor outwardly share his revulsion with heavy industry. Yet while she accepts technological innovation as something that raises civilization above the society of 'savages', she seems to have but passing interest in how things are produced. *News from Nowhere* is devoted to an alternative handicraft technology. This is not the case with *Herland*, although like Morris, Gilman does not clutter her utopia with factories.

Although Van says that the Herlanders' scientific and technological sophistication equals that of patriarchal capitalism, he also says that they 'were ignorant as Plato and Aristotle were, but with a highly developed mentality quite comparable to that of Ancient Greece' (H p. 85), indicating that the Herlanders have reached the pinnacle allowed by the limits of their isolation from the evolutionary processes of the outside world (it would make Herland somewhat similar to the highly developed but isolated cultures like Jomon Japan and pre-Columbian Aztec, Mayan and Inca societies). This exposes a major contradiction. If the Herlanders are as 'ignorant' as Plato and Aristotle, then no matter how sophisticated their culture might be, the manufacture of electric cars and even 'well-woven fabric' like those of the twentieth century would be beyond them.

Gilman's writings display a naive faith in the moral as well as material benefits of scientific progress.[5] She tries hard to convince us that progress is paramount in Herland. She even rolls out the racial argument, saying that the women of Herland are of superior 'Aryan' stock, of far better blood than the 'savages' who live in the surrounding country and fear them. This has led one critic, Lois Rudnick, to in effect accuse Gilman of anticipating Hitlerian racism: 'The novel is marred by the implicit fascism of an imagined world in which Aryan women, living in a Latin American country [*sic*], are attempting to create the "perfect race".'[6] (Gilman was racist, ethnocentric and anti-Semitic, but, as Lane points out, she was neither rabid nor consistently bigoted.[7])

How aware was Gilman of the contradictions she created in the political economy of Herland? We can only guess. Fortunately, her better instincts as a novelist, if nothing else, prevented incongruities from destroying either the dramatic or thematic credibility of her novel. And, as we shall see presently, Gilman chose finally to emphasize one productive art which a sophisticated but isolated culture could develop better than a technologically advanced one: forestry. It is this industry (in the broad meaning of the word) that Gilman most extensively elaborates on, and the one which most acts as a catalyst for the creative expression of the ideas that had been gestating in her previous work.

Virtually all the themes we encounter in *Herland* can be found in *Women and Economics* (1898), Gilman's first major and best selling non-fictional work. In this book, Gilman argues that for thousands of years men have treated women like expensive ornaments and second-rate nursemaids and housekeepers. This has retarded women's mental development. She writes:

> Men can cook, clean, and sew as well as women; but the making and managing of the great engines of modern industry, the threading of earth and sea in our vast systems of transportation, the handling of our elaborate machinery of trade, commerce, government,—these things could not be done so well by women in their present degree of economic development. This is not owing to lack of the essential human faculties necessary to such achievements, nor to any inherent disability of sex, but to the present condition of woman, forbidding the development of this degree of economic ability. The male human is thousands of years in advance of the female in economic status.[8]

This argument is based on the false premise that women have been inexperienced in working outside the home. Ruling-class wives and daughters fit the Gilman model, but not peasant and working-class women. 'Most women, in the nineteenth century, as well as throughout history, were not removed from the process of production', writes Lane. 'They continued to produce, while at the same time they were subordinated, sexually and economically, to men.'[9] However insightful Gilman's analysis of the conditions of privileged women under the industrial capitalism of her day, Lane adds, Gilman is guilty of oversimplifying history and anthropology.[10] The class struggle and the oppression of working people by capitalists is not a major issue in *Herland*, just as it is not in *Women and Economics*.

Embedded in the passage quoted above is Gilman's belief that acquired traits are passed on by parents to their children through heredity. Gilman took this point of view from the pre-Darwinian naturalist Jean-Baptiste Lamarck and clung to it though it had been decisively refuted by August Weismann. In challenging Weismann's argument 'that however many generations of pigs have their legs amputated, each new generation has the same original number', notes Lane, Gilman insisted on differentiating between mutation and acquired traits, writing that, 'An acquired trait is something that one uses and develops, not something that one has lost.'[11] In *Herland*, Gilman uses an indirect *ad hominem* to attack Weismann by having her least likeable character, Terry, pompously declare that Weismann proved 'acquired traits are not transmissible' (H p. 78). A Herlander's response, 'If that is so, then our improvements must be due to mutation or solely to education', reflects what Lane calls Gilman's own 'relaxed' attitude toward Lamarkianism.[12]

In any event, Gilman sets up a situation in *Herland* where women are not only separated from men for centuries but also do not need men for the perpetuation of the race. Miraculously—or perhaps because of latent acquired traits—they are able to give birth through parthenogenesis. In so doing, she has created a society in which women are not limited in acquisition of positive acquired characteristics by patriarchal oppression and are, therefore, able to pass down to their children traits which are superior to those passed down to children in patriarchal societies.

Given this premise, one can imagine the temptation a female utopian writer might have felt to create a male-baiting anything-you-can-do-we-can-do-better novel in terms of mechanized industrial development. While in a few instances Gilman skirts this—creating inconsistencies—she does not succumb to the temptation. For one thing, Gilman's anthropological sense probably told her that a community living in isolation was in no position to develop a high-tech society similar to that of industrial capitalism. For another, she probably realized that if she were to create a high-tech paradise, imitating Jules Verne and H. G. Wells, *Herland* would lose a major moral point, that peace, freedom and intelligence prevail when one gender does not oppress another. Herland's women do not need a better mechanized capitalistic industrial model. They already have an ecologically-friendly industry and a restful, caring and, seemingly, an unauthoritarian—near anarchist—kind of socialism.

Though *Herland* is about women independent of men, Gilman takes pains not to be anti-male. After their violent liberation from captivity, the women of Herland are isolated from the rest of the world by a natural catastrophe, an earthquake. They do not reject the world of men outright as do, for example, the women in Sarah Robinson Scott's novel *Millennium Hall* (1754) or as did in real life the American Sanctified Sisters, later the

Woman's Commonwealth (1867–1983).[13] After the three men are captured, ever so gently like runaway children, the Herlanders see their presence among them as an opportunity to re-establish the 'bisexual state of our people' (H p. 88). (That the women, who have not married for some two millennia, did not actively seek out the 'savage' non-Aryan men in the vicinity of Herland is another indication of Gilman's racism.) Gilman even leaves the sexually predatory and woman-hating Terry with a few positive qualities. He is at least forthright and a man of his word. He promises in the end not to betray the location of Herland and presumably does not. Given the pervasive gentleness of *Herland,* Gilman's choice to give significant emphasis to forestry is not coincidental.

Herlanders are virtually pure pacifists. They do not make wars of conquest to get more living space (H p. 68); they are horrified at the idea of killing the unborn (H pp. 69-70) and they become nauseated by the men's descriptions of animal slaughter (H p. 48). The women do not eat meat. That their primary nutrition come from fruits and nuts, which fall naturally from trees, shows to what extent they try not to destroy life to sustain themselves. Looking further, one finds that forestry is a metaphor not only for the gentle and well-planned world of Herland but of the mental universe of Charlotte Perkins Gilman. Above all, Gilman presents Herlander forestry as an ecologically necessary solution for the space- and resource-limited mountain nation.

Because Herland is small, its people have eliminated grazing cattle, Van says, and 'worked out a system of intensive agriculture surpassing anything I ever heard of, with the very forests all reset with fruit- or nut-bearing trees' (H p. 68). Herlanders 'had early on decided that trees were the best food plant, requiring far less labour in tilling the soil, and bearing a larger amount of food for the same ground space; also doing much to preserve and enrich the soil' (H p. 80).

The Herland forest constitutes the three male intruders' first encounter with that country. They also meet the three young women, presently to be their significant others, climbing trees. This causes Van to remark: 'Civilized and still arboreal—peculiar people' (H p. 19). Just prior to that, Terry has said enthusiastically, 'Talk of civilization... I never saw a forest so petted, even in Germany. Look, there's not a dead bough—the vines are trained actually!' (H p. 15). Jeff and Terry, after some exploration, announce that nearly all the trees bear food, and: "The rest, splendid hardwood. Call this a forest? It's a truck farm' (H p. 14). Van concludes: 'These towering trees were under as careful cultivation as so many cabbages' (H p. 14). Suggestively, *Herland's* trees are also rich with metaphors.

Trees are exemplary socialists in certain ways. They are autonomous, yet communal. Also a rough classless equality exists in forests. While socialist Gilman does not directly call Herland a socialist society, a socialist atmosphere pervades it. The life of the country is grounded in what Peter Kropotkin called 'mutual aid'.[14] Herland is a classless society, and peaceful for that reason: 'You see, they had no wars', Van narrates. 'They had no kings, and no priests, and no aristocrats. They were sisters, and as they grew, they grew together—not by competition, but by united action' (H p. 60).

Trees require cross-fertilization to procreate. But their procreative process is purely utilitarian; it is carried out without elaborate courtship, fickle passions, or gender dominance. Herlanders procreate like trees in that sense, except that they have taken biological utility one step further by having virgin births. Furthermore, trees are without families and homes. They grow where they are planted. In terms of political symbolism this is important because by eliminating the irrational and oppressive male factor from the procreative process, Gilman gets rid of the family and the home (both of which she criticized in previous writings as retarding of personal growth and responsibility to the whole of society). 'They had no exact analogue for the word *home*, any more than they had for our Roman-based *family*', Van relates (H p. 95). The women have no surnames because they belong to one 'family', the community. Children are communally nurtured (like saplings) with no particular mother claiming a particular child. And thanks to their educational system, 'their children grow up as naturally as young trees' (H p. 96). In this way, Gilman aligns herself with the pre-revolutionary secular and religious socialists, communists, associationists and other communalists—Robert Owen's New Harmony in Harmony (Indiana), the Perfectionists, and various celibate Christian communities, for example, who believed social progress demanded the destruction of the nuclear family.[15] But she goes beyond them in making Herlanders without personal homes: 'Our work takes us around the country', says Celis, the beloved of Jeff. 'We cannot live in one place all the time' (H p. 96).

Furthermore, none of the women appear to own personal property. The concept of possession does not even seem to occur to the Herlanders, who give up their babies to communal nurturing as easily as trees surrendering their seeds to the earth. Whenever Terry flashes jewellery in front of them, they are mildly interested but not seduced.

In abolishing family, home and all private property, Gilman also seems to have abolished the centralized State. *Seems to* because it is never fully discussed. Gilman does not vehemently underscore the abolition of central government as does Morris in *News from Nowhere*, who has the British Parliament building turned into a 'dung-market' and declares that 'the whole people is our parliament'.[16] On the other hand, she does not declare that Herlanders belong to an Industrial Army in the service of the national state as does Edward Bellamy in *Looking Backward.* We hear references to 'Overmothers', Herland's 'nearest approach to an aristocracy' (H p. 69)—perhaps an indirect influence from fellow Lamarkian, Friedrich Nietzsche. But we do not meet them nor learn what powers, if any, they have. Elsewhere Modine says Herland has a 'Landmother' who is 'what you call president or king, I believe' (H p. 76). As with the 'Overmothers', the Landmother remains backstage, her duties a mystery. One must wonder whether the Landmother's position is like the low profile office of the Swiss president or a ceremonial job like that of a European 'bicycle monarch'. The Landmother is, in fact, mentioned only once. We are constantly shown, however, Herlanders working together in informal and specialized groups in an atmosphere of equality and without any apparent leaders or hierarchies. Herlanders, explains Modine, 'have no law over a hundred years old, and most of them are under twenty' (H p. 64), implying a near-anarchist society (why they need any laws at all at this late date isn't explained). Thus, while Gilman avoids the inflammatory language of William Morris, the text strongly suggests that in her own quiet way Gilman is as radical as Morris and that she abolishes centralized authority in *Herland* by making it conspicuously absent.

There is another link between the Gilman of *Herland* and the Morris of *News from Nowhere*: the acceptance of violence as a procreative force in social change. In *News from Nowhere,* Hammond tells William: 'It was war from beginning to end: bitter war, till hope and pleasure put an end to it'.[17] And when William inquires whether this means 'actual fighting with weapons' or with 'strikes and lock outs', Hammond answers and then proceeds an attack on 'men who called themselves Socialists' who vainly sought to bring about the change through reform 'by hook or crook'.[18] This is a reference not only to the British Fabians, but also to Bellamy's *Looking Backward.* When Julian West says that the great change to socialism 'did not, of course, take place without great bloodshed and terrible convulsions', Doctor Leete replies that, to the contrary, 'there was absolutely no violence. The change had been foreseen. Public opinion had become full ripe for it, and the whole mass of the people was behind it.'[19] But more than that, Bellamy has Doctor Leete tell Julian that the 'followers of the red flag', meaning anarchists, not only hindered the change but were in the pay of the capitalists to cause trouble so that the great reform would not come about (Julian says in a footnote on the same page that 'this theory is whole [*sic*] erroneous' but he cannot account for the role of the anarchists except as capitalist henchmen).[20] Gilman, like Bellamy, eschews violence in her first utopian novel, *Moving the Mountain* (1911). She has the people voting in a socialist government in 1920 and then moving beyond socialism to establish a religion of 'Living and Life'.[21] Not so in *Herland*. The liberation of Herland's ancestors from their polygamous and slave-owning masters comes at the end of 'a succession of historic misfortunes', beginning with debilitating wars and ending with a devastating earthquake (H p. 54). With the power of the men weakened, the women revolt: 'There were many of them, and but a few of those would-be masters, so the young women, instead of submitting, rose in sheer desperation and slew their brutal conquerors' (H p. 55).

Gilman begins and ends her revolution in one sentence. She does not describe the violence as in any way glorious. Van is quick to say, 'This sounds like Titus Andronicus, I know, but that is their account. I suppose they were about crazy—can you blame them?' (H p.55). Importantly Gilman does not blame them—though she does not advocate killing oppressive men or ruling classes of men. Again quietly—and cautiously—she is hinting at something. The hint is that it is all right to slay tyrants, albeit in extreme circumstances.

At the time of the writing of *Herland*, American socialism's mainstream —that is the Socialist Party—was solidly behind reform. There were individuals and organizations, notably the anarcho-syndicalist International Workers of the World (IWW), which did advocate direct action, that is violent protest and revolution. At least one organization, the Socialist Labor Party, advocated a peaceful revolution through the ballot box and the organization of industrial unions to back the socialist vote. Gilman, from all the evidence I have seen, was never anything but a reform socialist. In Chapter XIV (pp. 198–214) of her autobiography (1935) in which she recounts her experiences as the California delegate to the International and Socialist and Labor Congress of 1896, Gilman does mention that she went to hear Peter Kropotkin, Elisee and Louise Michel the evening of the day that they and other anarchists were refused admission to the Congress and that she found them 'desperately earnest souls' (L p.202). But, in the same breath she says she found the anarchist literature the 'funniest' she had received at the Congress and that the way in which anarchist groups squabbled their way out of existence the best 'exposition of the essential weakness of that philosophy' (L p. 202). The Fabian Society, who 'honored me with a membership', she found to be a 'group of intelligent, scientific, practical and efficient English Socialists' (L p. 203). Yet the fact remains that Herland's peaceful world is not achieved through Fabian or Bellamy-like reforms but through the shedding of blood, as in *News from Nowhere*. And that Gilman chooses not to dramatize a dominant centralized state in *Herland* and that she does choose to emphasize essentially decentralized and unhierarchical work groups might mean that Kropotkin and the other anarchists had some kind of influence on her. We don't know as she does not record what they talked about that evening. Gilman also mentions meeting William Morris (L p. 209) and mourning his sudden death (L p. 112). But though she praises Morris, she says nothing about *News from Nowhere* and how it might have influenced her.

There is one thing Gilman is unambiguous about: her rejection of sex for pleasure. As Lane points out in her biography, Gilman stated explicitly in her 1904 book *Human Work* that nature intended sex to be for reproduction only, and that once we understood it we would be a lot happier; she also said humanity progressed despite male sexual excesses.[22] In *Herland* Gilman not only presses this point by making motherhood self-generating, she also makes a radical contrast between the destructive sexuality of Terry (who in the end attempts to rape his beloved, Alima) and Van whose love for Ellador is based primarily on friendship, not sexual attraction. Significantly, he says, 'That friendship grew like a tree' (H p. 90).[23]

Gilman wrote in *Women and Economics* that the inequalities between the genders had made people 'over-sexed', that is, made them exaggerate their sexual differences. It was Gilman's belief that this hindered both sexes from embracing those traits which would be of benefit to the human race as a whole. In *Herland* this is echoed by Sommel speaking to Van: 'Of course in a bi-sexual race the distinctive features of each sex must be intensified. But surely there are characteristics enough which belong to People, aren't there?' (H p. 90). One way sex differences are exaggerated is through dress and ornamentation. Herland's women, frequently called 'sexless' by Terry, dress simply for comfort in outfits that seem like a combination of togas and bloomers. Again, they are like trees whose foliage is purely utilitarian. This fosters a lack of vanity in the Herlanders and thus accounts for their lack of possessiveness.

Besides being eminently practical in procreation, trees are also highly mutable. They can be pruned, twisted or made to grow straight. Branches from different trees can be grafted on to others and they can be hybridized. The Herlanders replant forest areas 'with different kinds of trees', which to Van seems 'the simplest common sense, like a man's ploughing up an inferior lawn and reseeding it' (H p. 80). The Herlanders' creation of people follows a similar route. Gilman makes a pointed Lamarkian connection between human bio-social engineering and agriculture. When the men ask the Herlanders 'how they accounted for so much divergence [in their population] without cross-fertilization, they attributed it partly to the careful education, which allowed each slight tendency to differ, and partly to the law of mutation. This they had found in their work with plants, and proven in their own case' (H p. 77).

By manipulating acquired traits through bio-social engineering, the

Herlanders have bred cats that neither 'sing' nor catch birds (H p.69) and babies that do not cry (says Van: 'I never heard a child cry in Herland, save once or twice after a bad fall' [H p. 103]). Potential bad seeds have been bred out through appeals to bad women not to have babies (H p. 82). It is here that Gilman's totalitarian tendencies come out—in contradiction to the general libertarian atmosphere of her novel. While indeed, as Rudnick says, there is something fascistic in *Herland*, it is important to underscore that she was influenced by prevailing Social Darwinistic ideas of her day—though Gilman explicitly rejects the 'survival of the fittest' philosophy in *Herland* (H p.68). Importantly, there are strong correlatives between the bio-social engineering in *Herland* and Bellamy's *Looking Backward*.

Bellamy's bio-engineering is poignantly class-conscious—a satiric reversal of class prejudices that judge a male's marital eligibility by how wealthy he is. Dr Leete tells Julian West that 'Each generation is sifted through a little finer mesh than the last' because '[w]ealth and rank no longer divert attention from personal qualities'; thus 'race purification' has been enabled by 'untrampled sexual selection'.[24] Dr Leete also tells Julian that 'our women sit aloft as judges of the race and reserve themselves to reward the winners'; therefore, 'Celibates nowadays are almost invariably men who have failed to acquit themselves creditably in the work of life'.[25] This barb against present ruling-class manhood is successful as far as it goes. But it shows that his utopia is still male-dominated. Also by including 'beauty', 'wit', and 'eloquence', along with (and ahead of) 'kindness', 'generosity' and 'courage' as qualities that women seek in men, Bellamy proves that he is still very much under the influence of bourgeois attitudes of marriage eligibility.[26] Beauty, wit and eloquence are all public-relations ploys in a world where one must merchandise one's self to be mated and to reproduce. At least Gilman has pared down the requirements for reproduction to those surrounding basic decency. But that Bellamy and Gilman can talk in terms of race purification with such seeming carelessness is as much an indication of the Western world's intellectual naivety before Hitler as it is of any authoritarian tendencies in these writers and others like them.

Gilman anticipates rational family planning by making Herlanders 'Conscious Makers of People'. They have the power of will over their biological functions to have or not have babies. 'When a woman chose to be a mother, she allowed the child-longing to grow within her till it worked its natural miracle. When she did not choose she put the whole thing out of her mind, and fed her heart with others' babies' (H p. 71). Population control is a conscious act of social will over biology. Van tells us that the Herlanders 'sat down in council together' and thought out just how many people their country could support 'with the standard of peace, comfort, health, beauty, and progress we demand'. Then they made a conscious and essentially industrial decision regarding how many virgin births they would have (H p. 68).

Herland's ability to have and manipulate virgin births is an acquired trait. Its entry into the early Herland community is first called a 'direct gift from the gods', but Van adds that the early Herlanders developed 'unknown powers in the stress of new necessity' (H p. 56). Could this be a recessive acquired trait come to the fore? Gilman's intellectual mentor was Lester Ward whose gynaecentric theory of evolution declared that humankind descended from an original mother. Being the first human, this ur-mother would by necessity (without an ur-father) have given birth through parthenogenesis (according to Ward, the human male followed the female in the evolutionary process, but became the master gender after first achieving sexual parity). Gilman, who was religiously loyal to Ward, despite his disrepute in mainstream scientific circles, has all of the women of Herland 'all descended from a single mother' (H p. 57).[27]

There are many ironies attendant to *Herland*. One is that Gilman was inspired as an artist by dogmatically clinging to Lamarkianism and Ward's evolutionary theories, which at the same time hampered her intellectual development. Another irony is that though in certain respects Gilman was a scientific reactionary, she was at the same time ahead of her era in making *Herland* a 'green' utopian novel, embracing what would subsequently be called the Conservation Ethic and which evolved into the current ecological consciousness. *Herland* (like Morris's *News from Nowhere*) anticipates contemporary ecological utopias, notably Callenbach's *Ecotopia* (1975), which also tries to incorporate a feminist perspective (albeit from a male point of view).[28] Marvelling at the environmental wisdom of the Herlanders, Van tells us: 'These careful culturists had worked out a perfect scheme of refeeding the soil with all that came out of it. All the scraps and leavings of their food, plant waste from lumber work or textile industry, all the solid matter from the sewage, properly treated and combined—everything which came from the earth went back to it.' The result was 'like that in any healthy forest; an increasingly valuable soil was being built, instead of the progressive impoverishment so often seen in the rest of the world' (H pp. 80–81). Thus do the women of Herland create an industry superior to the capitalist product of patriarchy.

Utopian literature does not only propose ideal answers to the world's problems but also asks ideal questions. The question *Herland* asks is about what society would be like if women were allowed to develop unhindered by patriarchy. Gilman's utopia is a self-contained and isolated world. In this way, *Herland* is typical of most utopian novels. Yet unlike the novels of many (perhaps most) utopian thinkers, *Herland* is not a blueprint for the future. Rather it is like a Swiftian exaggeration which is extreme in its improbability but proves a point about real life. Gilman's point is that the oppression of women by men is the source of all oppression. Take away this source, she argues, and you will build a reasonable society.

Gilman removes men from her utopia by having the women kill them off—after the men have greatly weakened themselves by slaughtering each other in successive wars. Left alone, the women are able to mature as they have not been able to in patriarchal society. Yet when men—white men, anyway—appear in Herland, their presence is welcomed as a way of establishing again what Gilman naively calls a 'bi-sexual' society. In *Herland* there is a reconciliation between separatism and integration. Women need to be alone, away from the primary source of their oppression, to find out who they are, so that they can not only become whole human beings but also contribute through a fully developed intelligence to creating a better world, *Herland* says in effect. But the separation from men need not be a divorce. Gilman's message is that when women have developed themselves—when they can demonstrate they are as clear thinking and industrious as the best of men—they can re-integrate with them. They can do so bearing gifts whose greatness the world has never known. But the men must become like Van—mature enough to receive them.

Notes

1 Floyd Clymer writes: 'Electrics were favored by the weaker sex [sic] because they required no cranking and there were no obnoxious exhaust fumes to be counted with. Their top speed was fifteen to twenty miles per hour, and most electrics would travel twenty to twenty-five miles on one charging of batteries' (Floyd Clymer, *Those Wonderful Old Automobiles* [New York: McGraw-Hill, 1953], p. 24).

2 Edward Bellamy, *Looking Backward*, first published 1888 (New York and Toronto: The New American Library, 1960), p. 45.

3 William Morris, *News from Nowhere: An Epoch of Rest*, first published 1891 (London and Boston: Routledge & Kegan Paul, 1970), pp. 5–6.

4 Ibid., p. 6 .

5 Ann J. Lane, *To Herland and Beyond: The Life and Work of Charlotte Perkins Gilman*, first published 1990 (New York: Meridian, 1991), p. 295.

6 Lois Rudnick, 'The New Woman', in Adelle Heller and Lois Rudnick, eds, *Nineteen Fifteen: The Cultural Moment* (New Brunswick: Rutgers University Press, 1991), p. 74.

7 This 'implicit fascism' was in fact mainstream American racism which prevailed in Gilman's time and was only decisively challenged after the Second World War. The worst of Gilman's racism, anti-Semitism and ethnocentrism was confined to her personal writings but, as Ann J. Lane writes, they 'inevitably limit and scar her theoretical work as well'. But, continues Lane, Gilman's racism 'while always limiting and always inexcusable, has a quality

of ambivalence and uncertainty about it. She did, for example, vigorously dissent from the newly revived eugenics movement, which was rooted in the belief that most human traits were irrevocably genetic in origin and therefore unchangeable' (Ann J. Lane, *To Herland and Beyond*, p. 255). Lane also points out that 'despite her racist ideas, Charlotte's was the only voice raised at the 1903 convention of the National American Woman's Suffrage Association against a literacy requirement for the vote, the device commonly used to disenfranchise black citizens'. Ten years later, in the April 1913 issue of her magazine *The Forerunner*, she wrote 'That we have cheated the Indian, oppressed the African, robbed the Mexican... is ground for shame' (Ann J. Lane, *To Herland and Beyond*, p. 256).

8 Charlotte Perkins Gilman, *Women and Economics: A Study of the Economic Relation Between Women and Men*, first published 1898 (Amherst, NY: Prometheus, 1994), pp. 8–9.

9 Ann J. Lane, *To Herland and Beyond*, p. 296.

10 Ibid., p. 296.

11 Ibid., p. 256.

12 Ibid. Lane writes: 'Common sense tells us, [Gilman] says, and parents and teachers know that "as the twig is bent, the tree's inclined".' She is fairly relaxed about the explanation: 'Inherit we must to some degree; and whatever comes to us by that method must belong to the parent before he is a parent'' (ibid., p. 256).

13 For the former, see Linda Dunne, 'Mothers and Monsters in Sarah Robinson Scott's *Millenium Hall*', in Jane L Donawerth and Carol A. Kolmerton, eds, *Utopian and Science Fiction by Women*, (Syracuse: Syracuse University Press, 1994), pp. 54–72, and for the latter see Wendy Chimielewski, 'Heaven on Earth: The Woman's Commonwealth, 1867–1983' in Wendy E. Chimielewski, Louis J. Kern and Marlyn Klee-Martzell, eds, *Women in Spiritual and Communitarian Societies in the United States* (Syracuse: Syracuse University Press, 1993), pp. 52–67.

14 Peter Kropotkin, *Mutual Aid: A Factor of Evolution*, first published 1902 (London: Freedom Press, 1987).

15 See Raymond Lee Muncy, *Sex and Marriage in Utopian Communities in Nineteenth Century America* (Bloomington: Indiana University Press, 1973).

16 William Morris, *News from Nowhere*, p. 63.

17 Ibid., p. 88.

18 Ibid., p. 89.

19 Edward Bellamy, *Looking Backward*, p. 54.

20 Ibid., p. 170.

21 Ann J. Lane, *To Herland and Beyond*, p. 292.

22 Ibid., p. 283.

23 Gilman's extreme romanticism, exemplified by the rational love between Van and Ellador and her literal and metaphorical use of trees, can be psychologically appreciated when we look at her early juvenile notebook story 'A Dream'. In this story she imagines herself an adventurer come to a mysterious forest in which elves watch her from trees - much as the three male intruders are watched by the three young Herland women at the beginning of the novel. See Carol Farley Kessler, *Charlotte Perkins Gilman: Her Progress Toward Utopia and Selected Writings* (Liverpool: Liverpool University Press, 1995), p. 85.

24 Edward Bellamy, *Looking Backward*, p. 179.

25 Ibid., p. 180.

26 Ibid., p. 179.

27 In most of her books, writes Lane, 'Gilman expressed her indebtedness to the work of Lester Ward', mentioning that in her 1911 book, *The Man Made World; or Our Androcentric Culture*, she went so far as to declare that 'nothing so important to humanity [as Ward's Gynaecentric Theory] has been advanced since the Theory of Evolution, and nothing so important to women has ever been given to the world'. She does, however, concede that Ward's conclusions are 'disputed by the majority of present-day biologists' (Ann J. Lane, *To Herland and Beyond*, pp. 278–79).

28 Ernest Callenbach, *Ecotopia: The Notebooks and Reports of Edward Weston* (Berkeley: Banyan Tree Books, 1975). Bellamy sprinkles *Looking Backward* with ecological metaphors, most notably when Julian West returns to the nineteenth century in a dream and tells his beloved's shocked family and friends about socialism: 'Let but the famine-stricken nation assume the function it had neglected, and regulate for the common good the course of the life-giving stream, and the earth would blood like one garden, and none of its children lack any good thing' (Edward Bellamy, *Looking Backward*, p. 217). Yet, unlike Gilman and Morris, Bellamy's ecological consciousness, such as it is, remains primarily metaphorical. Bellamy's overwhelming concern is urban life and the production and distribution of machine-made goods and related services.

Herland: Definitive Ecofeminist Fiction?

AMANDA GRAHAM

'Ecofeminism' has been defined by Christine Cuomo as 'a radical environmentalism which incorporates both ecological and feminist concerns', and which 'emerged from the global feminist movement of the 1970s'.[1] Although the initial connotations of the term were political (it was formulated in 1974 by Françoise d'Eaubonne, who was writing about the role of women in a proposed ecological revolution[2]), it has since incorporated a wide range of contexts, listed by Karen Warren as 'historical, empirical, conceptual, religious, literary, political, ethical, epistemological, methodological, and theoretical', the common factor being that of connection between women and nature.[3]

Examining the question of 'what makes ecofeminism feminist', Warren argues that the crucial element is 'its twofold commitment to the recognition and elimination of male-gender bias wherever and whenever it occurs, and to the development of practices, policies and theories which are not male-gender biased'. This differentiates ecofeminism from other environmental theories such as deep ecology, which not only 'does not explicitly take the perspectives of women as integral to its analysis', but which takes a completely non-anthropocentric approach to environmental issues.[4] Placing ecofeminism within the broader context of feminist theory, Val Plumwood points out that 'since the theory of ecofeminism results from the application of feminist perspectives to problems of ecology, it is as complex and diverse as feminism itself'.[5] Plumwood pinpoints two major versions of ecofeminism—cultural ecofeminism and social ecofeminism. Cultural ecofeminism is seen as 'stress[ing] the links, historical, biological and experiential, between women and nature, and see[ing] their joint oppression as the consequence of male domination', whilst 'social ecofeminists tend to emphasize the social and political aspect of ecofeminism rather than the spiritual aspects', 'not see[ing] women's difference as either biologically determined in their relationship to nature or to one another'.[6] Whilst cultural ecofeminists see the solution to ecological and feminist problems as being 'the creation of an alternative women's culture' 'based on revaluing, celebrating and defending what patriarchy has devalued, including the feminine, non-human nature, the body and the emotions', the social ecofeminist perspective is one of 'nature as a political rather than a natural category', the proposed solution being 'the construction of a less oppositional culture'.[7]

This is a neat, and perhaps somewhat simplistic, division; Warren maintains that 'ecofeminism refers to a plurality of positions', explaining that this 'is because there is not one ecofeminism, any more than there is one feminism', and suggesting that 'ecofeminist positions are as diverse as the feminist ones from which they gain their strength and meaning'.[8] For the purposes of this chapter I shall, however, be referring to Plumwood's identification of social and cultural ecofeminism which, though crude, is most readily applicable to Gilman's work. The main justification for the retrospective application of ecofeminist theory to works of literature is that ecofeminism has been (and is) a theory in the making since long before d'Eaubonne formulated the term. The idea of a connection between women and nature is clearly not new, and its expression in literature has not been limited to a romantic point of view. As early as 1837, Lady Stuart-Wortley was suggesting, in verse, that the principle of freedom for all men might well be extended to women and animals.[9] Val Plumwood highlights the relevance to ecofeminism of utopian works such as *Herland*, pointing out that 'the story of a land where women live at peace with themselves and with the natural world is a recurrent theme of feminist utopias'[10] (admittedly, the 'natural world' of *Herland* is not only controlled, but exploited in ways which this chapter will examine). Sarah Lefanu, stressing the importance of what she terms 'the dream of elsewhere', cites Joanna Russ's identification of 'concern for ecology and the natural world' as a motivating factor in the writing of feminist utopias.[11] Plumwood, using the metaphor of the enchanted forest for life (as opposed to the 'technological desert' which she aligns with maleness: this is admittedly a simplistic division), examines some of the problems inherent in ecofeminism, asking the following questions:

> Is ecofeminism giving us a version of the story that the goodness of women will save us? Is it only women who can know the mysterious forest, or is that knowledge, and that love, in principle accessible to us all? Do we have to renounce the achievements of culture and technology to come to inhabit the enchanted forest? Can we affirm women's special qualities without endorsing their traditional role and confinement to 'women's sphere'? Can a reign of women

> possibly be the answer to the earth's destruction and to all the other related problems?[12]

Elusive though some of these questions are, Plumwood is recognizably addressing the very issues with which Gilman was concerned in 1915; Lefanu points out that *Herland* 'anticipates a central theme of the feminist utopias of the 1970s', particularly in its presentation of 'a vision of a community of women and children'.[13] The significance, from an ecofeminist perspective, of Gilman's choice of the utopian fantasy as a medium through which to express her concerns has already been pointed out. Gilman's use of a male narrative voice serves to highlight her arguments, effecting a constant juxtaposition of ideal (Herland) and reality (contemporary America), and facilitating the ironic contrasts exposed by the women's interpretations of the men's heavily-edited account of their society. The men's resistance to any exposé of their dominant ideology is outlined in Van's account of the women's interrogative processes:

> I wish I could represent the kind, quiet, steady, ingenious way they questioned us. It was not just curiosity—they weren't a bit more curious about us than we were about them, if as much. But they were bent on understanding our kind of civilization, and their lines of interrogation would gradually surround us and drive us in till we found ourselves up against some admission we did not want to make. (H p. 50)

From the very first page of *Herland*, men are aligned with science and theory of the most inflexible and destructive type (suggested by the narrator's comment that 'Terry had come armed with a theory'). This is contrasted with the women's more judicious employment of technology. Confident in their identity as male middle-class Americans (H p. 7) and sure of their self-worth, their expectations of the women of Herland are coloured solely by their personal fantasies (Terry claims his version by naming his fantasy land 'Feminisia', an appellation which manages to imply coy femininity without denoting the firm sense of ownership conveyed by 'Herland'). Observing (whilst taking in few of the finer details) that Herland is 'a *civilized* country', the narrator assumes that 'there must be men' (H p. 11). This assumption is reinforced by Terry when the men later come to a road 'as perfect as if it were Europe's best' (H p. 18) (the link between sexism and nationalism established by this observation will be discussed later). Although the narrator does admit that he has 'often groaned at home to see the offensive mess man [has] made in the face of nature' (H p. 18), only Jeff is prepared to concede implicitly that the women may have attained the status of civilization in their own right. Again, however, he defines 'civilization' in Western technological terms: 'If they've got motors, they *are* civilized' (H p. 29). Concepts of 'woman', 'nature' and 'civilization' remain, to the men, almost irreconcilable. 'Civilized and still arboreal—peculiar people', muses the narrator (H p. 17).

Going back to Plumwood's questions about women, culture and technology, Gilman is adopting, in ecofeminist terms, what is identifiable as a social ecofeminist position, suggesting that (in her utopia, at least) women are as capable as men of scientific and technological achievement. Advancements in these areas are seen, furthermore, as being viable without having to entail social or environmental damage. It is in her treatment of the issues of maternity and child care that Gilman's perspective inclines more towards cultural ecofeminism, which Plumwood sees as advancing 'the creation of an alternative women's culture' as the solution to feminist and ecological problems.

Victoria Davion, in her essay 'Is Ecofeminism Feminist?', argues that because the domination of women and that of the environment are 'conceptually linked', 'those fighting to save the environment should, as a matter of consistency, be working to overthrow patriarchy' and vice-versa.[14] In Herland, patriarchy has not been overthrown; a combination of tribal war and natural causes has simply wiped out the male population, conveniently (this is, after all, utopia!) enabling the establishment of a matriarchal society. Lefanu argues that in utopias 'such as *Herland*, separatism is of prime importance, indeed it is a prerequisite for any other form of social change'.[15] Although *Herland* is fantasy rather than hypothesis (Margaret Whitford, writing on the works of Luce Irigaray, who has in turn been linked with ecofeminism, argues that most feminist utopias 'do not seek to offer blueprints of the ideal future' but 'are intended more to bring about shifts in consciousness'[16]), Gilman's perspectives on maternity and the environment are concurrent with ecofeminist ethics (these issues are, as we shall see, explored more 'realistically' in the short stories). Christine Cuomo, writing on ecofeminism and population, dismisses the deep ecological argument that personal attachments are egoistic and need to be overcome, concluding that 'Women must be empowered with regard to their own bodies, their role as creators of culture'.[17] In *Herland*, this position is arrived at collectively, rather than autonomously. Despite Terry's assertion that it is 'against nature' for women to cooperate (H p. 67), the women of Herland have overcome their initial fear that 'the loss of everything masculine' would be synonymous with the loss of 'all human power and safety' to develop, not only their capacity for virgin birth, but a religion described by the narrator as 'a sort of Maternal Pantheism' (H p. 59).

This label encapsulates the dual importance, to Herland culture, of maternity and the environment. Although the narrator is initially dismissive of the concept of an exclusively female society, remarking that 'you'll find it's built on a sort of matriarchal principle, that's all', and concluding that 'the men [must] have a separate cult of their own' (H p. 7), he is later forced to acknowledge the power of 'Maternal Pantheism', seeing in his relationship with Ellador a return to the primal mother (H pp. 41–42). (Interestingly, Lefanu cites Carol Pearson's use, in writing on *Herland* among other feminist utopias, of the term 'coming home' to signify 'both coming home to the self and coming home to mother').[18] Maternal Pantheism is seen to have evolved through the gradual eradication of polytheism ('deities of war and plunder' having proved to be especially antipathetic to the Herland ethos of non-violence) and eventual centring 'on their Mother Goddess' (H p. 59). Gilman is anticipating, in *Herland*, the revival in goddess culture which Plumwood identifies as an integral part of cultural ecofeminism. Plumwood explains that:

> Women are seen [by cultural ecofeminists] as having a superior relation to nature which is sometimes taken to be biologically determined, so that only a society in which women can limit or control the number and influence of men will be free of aggressiveness and destruction of nature. For many, the new approach to nature also turns out to be an old one, that of celebrating fertility and creativity through feminist paganism, a religion celebrating community with the Earth as maternal and alive or as a powerful Goddess immanent in the world.[19]

Goddess worship in Herland is seen to have evolved, 'as [the women] grew more intelligent', into the 'sort of Maternal Pantheism' which the narrator describes (it is interesting to note that Gilman sees monotheism, in this instance, as a developmental stage surpassable by 'intelligence'). This is analogous with Plumwood's identification of 'a religion celebrating community with the Earth as maternal and alive'. The contrast, in *Herland*, between this state and the aggressive stance of the interlopers is highlighted in the account of their attempted escape. Having gathered, from a 'friendly nut-tree', plenty of 'large, satisfying, soft-shelled nuts' for nourishment on their journey, they fill up all the pockets of their serviceable Herland garments until, in the words which Gilman attributes to her male narrator, '[they] bulged like Prussian privates in marching order' (H p. 12). The combined products of women and nature are translated by the men into martial imagery. Women, by contrast, are specifically linked with nature and its products, the 'fair foresters and fruit-gatherers' being described by Terry as 'peacherinos—apricot-nectarines!' (H pp. 14–15). Later, woman and nature are less facetiously linked as the narrator analogizes his relationship with Ellador with the discovery and exploration of 'a strange [and fertile] land' (H p. 89). Although such perceptions are presented to us as masculine constructs, Gilman does alert us to her own awareness of such constructs, making her narrator conclude that those 'feminine charms' we are so fond of are not feminine at all, but mere 'reflected masculinity' (H p. 59). There is, perhaps, a hidden caveat in some of the narrator's observations on the women's cultivation of their environment: what, for example, are we to make of the suggestion that they '[care] for their country as a florist cares for his costliest orchids'(H p. 18)? Does the suggestion of artifice qualify or question the apparent affinity between women and nature, or does the narrator's automatic assumption of masculine involvement negate his whole analogy? The subsequent account of the 'parklike beauty' of the 'first-seen city' (H p. 43) is similarly problematic.

None the less, Herland culture as constructed by its women does seem equally to revere fertility of women and of earth. Organic farming methods are outlined in some detail:

> These careful culturists had worked out a perfect scheme of refeeding the soil with all that came from it. All the scraps and leavings of their food, plant waste from lumber work or textile industry, all the solid matter from the sewage, properly treated and combined—everything which came from the earth went back to it. (H p. 80)

The notion of continuity and regeneration is fundamental also to the Herland ethos of maternity, which encompasses not only 'a deep, tender reverence for one's own mother', but 'the whole, free, wide range of sisterhood' (H p. 96). We are told that 'life to them was growth; their pleasure was in growing, and their duty also' (H p. 102). Respect for growth is seen to have informed the Herland philosophy of child-rearing, an issue central to the novel, as well as to several of Gilman's short stories. The women of Herland regard child-rearing as a communal responsibility, with 'each hav[ing] a million children to love and serve' (H p. 71). Leaving aside for the moment the problematic stage of socially engineered evolution from which this situation has evolved (the fine dividing line between the 'splendid service of the country' engendered by 'reverence for one's own mother' and outright nationalism will be discussed later), the extension of individual maternity to a sense of communal responsibility and to concern for the environment is clearly concurrent with ecofeminist thought. Plumwood, writing on 'Ethics and the instrumentalizing self', draws the following analogy between personal and social concern:

> When the mother wishes for the child's recovery, the child's

> flourishing is internal to her desires, not merely an external, interchangeable means to some other end, such as her own happiness. She wants health and happiness *for* the child for its sake, as well as for her own. Such intrinsic or essential relationships are not confined to the private sphere, and the sense of loss and despair brought about in most of us by the future prospect of a devastated natural and social environment cannot be explained in terms of isolable individual interests.[20]

In her short story 'The Unnatural Mother' (1916), Gilman portrays a woman who has progressed well beyond 'isolable individual interests'. As in *Herland*, she uses the narrative voice (in this case wholly unsympathetic) to highlight the contrast between radical and received ideas. Having always shown an instinctive empathy with children in general, Esther, the 'unnatural mother' of the title, does not discriminate, in the face of disaster, between her own child and those whom she sees as communal children. Patriarchy in its highest form is cited in condemnation of Esther's actions, with a neighbour asserting that 'the Lord never gave her them other children to care for' (R p. 65). Interestingly, Esther has herself been raised, in the absence of a mother, by a father representative in his common-sense approach to child care of Gilman's faith in men's capacity for change.

Gilman's extension of relationships beyond 'the private sphere' is also evident in her concern with the issue of animal rights. Plumwood, discussing the relevance of animals to what she terms 'human/nature continuity', points out the ways in which animals are subject, in common with women and the environment, to 'dualistic assumptions':

> Under the sign of the Same or Self, animals are assimilated to the human or seen as reduced or impoverished versions of humans; under the sign of the Different or Other, animals are treated after the fashion of Descartes, in ways involving radical exclusion, and constructed as alien. In both treatments they emerge as inferiorized, because dualism cannot allow a non-hierarchical or unassimilated concept of otherness.[21]

Gilman can be seen to deal with each of these positions. We see the treatment of animals as 'self or same' in the short story 'When I Was a Witch' (1910), in the description of the 'poor, wretched, artificial little dog' (R p. 25) seen by the narrator in the car, wearing clothes (down to a pocket-handkerchief) and jewellery in imitation of his 'gaudily dressed' owner (R p. 25). (It is interesting to note that the narrator of 'When I Was a Witch' is able to improve the lot of animals, if only by killing the most miserable among them, but not of women.) In *Herland*, inferiorization of animals as 'different or other' is implicit in the narrator's account of the dairy and meat industries. The reaction of the women to this account is to turn white and leave the room. Somel, identifying with the lactating animal, asks 'Has the cow no child?' and, even when answered in the affirmative, assumes that there must be sufficient milk both for calf and human. She is initially quite unable to comprehend 'the process which robs the cow of her calf', which seems a terrible transgression of the maternal ethic, human or otherwise (H p. 48). No such awareness of animal rights is expressed in *Women and Economics* (1898), in which Gilman, questioning the adequacy of 'unaided maternal love and instinct in the simple act of feeding the child', asks whether 'maternal instinct' alone can 'discriminate between Marrow's Food and Bridge's Food, Hayrick's Food and Pestle's Food, Pennywhistle's Sterilized Milk, and all the other infants' foods which are prepared and put on the market by—men!'[22] Here, Gilman is arguing that, though 'maternal love is an enormous force', 'force needs direction'; the perceived necessity for 'intelligent effort' does not take into account those aspects of milk production which elicit revulsion from the Herlanders. However, husbandry in Herland has been phased out, not as a result of awareness of animal rights, but in the interests of preserving land for the growth of crops, and the Herland outlook remains largely anthropocentric, evincing few scruples as to the modification of animal nature to human requirements. The cats of Herland, for example, whilst being loved and respected (in contrast to the 'thousands of hungry, hunted cats who slink and suffer' in 'When I Was a Witch'), have none the less been bred 'by the most prolonged and careful selection and exclusion '(H p. 49) to human advantage. The result is a 'race of cats' which is quiet, selective towards its prey, and 'devotedly attached to their special owners'. Such modification is not far from the dog-breeding condemned as 'man's insolence' in 'When I Was a Witch'.

The issues of selective breeding and inferiorization of the Other bring us to an aspect of Gilman's work which is problematic not only from an ecofeminist point of view. Ann J. Lane, discussing 'With Her in Ourland', points out that Gilman 'shares many odious attitudes upheld by the intellectual community of a hundred years ago... express[ing] beliefs that are anti-Semitic, chauvinist, and racist' (R p. 200). Gilman's attitude towards race is crucial to an ecofeminist critique of her work, especially of *Herland*. Racism and colonization are among the principal concerns of ecofeminist theory, which sees them as being inextricably linked to other forms of inferiorization and oppression. Plumwood terms 'the oppressions of gender, race, class and nature' the 'four tectonic plates of liberation theory', and points out that ecofeminism has at various stages 'engaged with all four forms of exploitation encompassed in race, class, gender and nature'.[23] This stance has arisen largely from critiques of mainstream environmentalism, which is seen by ecofeminists as having 'failed to examine issues of race', let alone 'the way these structures [of class, gender and race] relate to environmental issues'.[24] Ecofeminist positions on issues of race have evolved also from critiques of feminist theory in general. Jim Cheney points out that 'taking up residence in the arms of theory provides safety and wholeness—of a sort. It provides a well-rounded world in which certainty prevails. The cost, however, is a continuation of alienation, the (however inadvertent) colonization of others, the maintenance of class privilege, and blindness to difference.'[25] Cheney goes on to argue that there is a danger of 'white, feminist theorists tend[ing] not to hear criticism from women of color as an attack on white *racism*, but as an attack on the activity of *theorizing*'. Whilst Cheney sets the attacking of racism apart from the attacking of theorizing, it is possible to identify links between the motives for racism and theorizing. Ecofeminism has been seen as being by definition anti-theory, or at the very least untheorized. However, this seeming deficiency can be read rather as openness, flexibility, and willingness to acknowledge and accommodate difference. Plumwood argues that 'reason in the western tradition has been constructed as the privileged domain of the master, who has conceived nature as a wife or subordinate other encompassing and representing the sphere of materiality, subsistence and the feminine which the master has split off and constructed as beneath him'. This has meant that 'the concept of reason provides the unifying and defining contrast for the concept of nature, much as the concept of husband does for that of wife, as master for slave'.[26] The reason/nature dualism has been extended so that 'racism, colonialism and sexism have drawn their conceptual strength from casting sexual, racial and ethnic difference as closer to the animal' (similarly, Whitford argues that 'modern forms of racism and political sectarianism are as much products of the Enlightenment as feminism', concluding that 'reason has not lived up to its emancipatory promises'[27]). Plumwood goes on to identify the ways in which colonies have been treated as being 'outside' civilized or Western society, with indigenous peoples being dismissed as 'savages', citing Kantian theory as representing 'the anthropocentrism of the western tradition'.[28] According to Plumwood, 'Kant's racist account of African people and people of colour' denied them even the 'measure of reason' attributed to women, seeing mental capacity as being directly proportionate to colour. Examining the origins of human/nature dualism, Plumwood argues that 'it is not only a masculine identity as such which underlies the Platonic conception of reason and of the life of reason, but a master identity defined in terms of multiple exclusions, and in terms of domination not only of the feminine but also of the slave (which usually combines race, class and gender oppression), of the animal, and of the natural'.[29]

Going back to the relevance to *Herland* of ecofeminist theory, it is not difficult to see that, whilst Gilman has successfully challenged the exclusion and domination of women and, to some extent, nature, her attitudes to race remain problematic. Sarah Lefanu suggests that there is a rejection in *Herland*, among other feminist utopias, of a dualistic pattern of ownership, denial and repression.[30] This is debatable, since those aspects of Gilman's work identified by Lane as 'anti-Semitic, chauvinist, and racist' (see above) cannot all be justified by their attribution to a male narrative voice. It is admittedly possible to read Terry's several references to 'savages' as being intentionally consistent with his overall chauvinism. This, in an ecofeminist reading, is tempting; the links between misogyny and racism as forms of oppression add significance to the narrator's parodic rendering of native speech—'Big Country, Big Houses, Plenty People—All Women' (H p. 3)—and to Jeff's humorously expressed regret of the dearth of 'husky black slaves' (H p. 9), not to mention Terry's deliberate singing of 'The things that I learned from the yellow and black' during the run-up to his attempted rape of Alima (H p. 131). It must, however, be acknowledged that the insistence on the Aryan origins of the Herlanders is Gilman's (Lefanu cites Ann J. Lane as pointing out that Mary Bradley Lane's *Mizora*, published in 1890, similarly features 'well-bred beautiful blonde women'[31]). 'There is no doubt in my mind', affirms the narrator, 'that these people were of Aryan stock, and were once in contact with the best civilization of the old [male?] world' (H p. 54). This point is reinforced by the further statement that 'they were "white", but somewhat darker than our northern races because of their constant exposure to sun and air '(H p. 54). Perhaps Gilman is anticipating the fashionable sun-tan. The women's ethnic origin is certainly linked, implicitly if not explicitly, to their capacity for development. Although the initial assumption of the male interlopers is that the women's achievements are 'on the plane of children, or of savages', they are eventually 'forced to admit... that they were as ignorant as Plato and Aristotle were, but with a highly developed mentality quite comparable to that of Ancient Greece (H p. 85). In the light of Plumwood's identification of the Platonic concept of reason as being instrumental in racial domination, it is significant that Herland culture has its roots in a patriarchal civilization. Plumwood argues that nature/culture and other dualisms have their origins in Ancient Greece, pointing out that whilst 'the society of classical Greece is so often viewed benignly, by both liberal and environmental writers, as the cradle of western civilization', 'the denial, exclusion and devaluation of nature can be traced far back into the intellectual traditions of the west, at least into the beginnings of rationalism in Greek culture'.[32] Gilman, in documenting the cultural and technological achievements of the Herlanders, is admittedly suggesting that some gender differences are socially constructed, and, from an environmentalist point of view, mechanization has been realized in Herland without necessitating what Plumwood describes as 'a flight from the female cosmos'.[33] Although the men see scientific achievement and femininity as being incompatible, the older (and therefore not truly 'feminine'?) women who first greet the intruders are described as resembling 'a vigilance committee of women doctors', suggesting that, to the masculine eye at least, scientifically accomplished women are by definition cold and sterile (H p. 20). However, Gilman's deliberate connection of her alternative women's culture with a philosophy which can be seen to class non-elite women with 'slaves, children and "other animals"' remains disturbing.[34]

Concurrent with these suggestions of élitism is the Herland practice of selecting only 'suitable' women for the bearing and rearing of children. The 'really high degree of social development' demonstrated by Herland culture (H p. 67) has been facilitated by the willingness of the women to cooperate in 'mak[ing] the best kind of people' (H p. 59). (Disconcerting links between maternity, nationalism and racism are uncovered in Chapter 9, 'Our Relations and Theirs'.) The feeling of sisterhood which promotes the 'appalling sacrifice' of 'negative eugenics' is significantly described as 'National' and 'Racial', as well as 'Human' (H p. 59). The system of 'negative eugenics' provides, from an ecofeminist point of view, an interesting parallel with the Herland programme of selective cat breeding, a connection which is reinforced by the narrator's likening of the Herlanders to lynxes (H p. 143), and subsequent speculation as to whether 'lynxes watch any better than (genetically inferior?) mousing cats'. Jeff, speaking of Western society, says that it is 'a law of nature' that what Moadine terms the 'inferior one-third' of society should produce the most children (H p. 63). Plumwood specifically links the concept of sacrifice with that of dualism, stating that 'just as a slave requires a master, just as instrumental value requires a non-instrumental goal, an end in itself, so self-sacrifice requires a set of primary, non-altruistic interests to sacrifice itself for. The concepts of egoism and altruism therefore build in inequality and asymmetry.'[35] Even when cloaked in sisterly and environmental concern, the Herland ethos remains, in ecofeminist and, indeed, feminist terms, rooted in dualism.

Why is this so? Does Gilman's use of the male narrative voice confer upon *Herland* a maleness which goes beyond intentional irony? Gilman *is* capable of transcending dualism: Georgia Johnston points out that the female narrator of *The Yellow Wallpaper* (1892) 'imagin[es] that part that is not visible to her within a patriarchal system of language'.[36] In *Herland*, the 'patriarchal system of language' remains largely unchallenged; despite the absence of men, the women are operating in a male world. Gilman implicitly adopts the socialist feminist position that gender differences are socially and historically constructed; in her eagerness to prove this point, she inevitably compromises her creation (admittedly unusual: Lefanu points out that 'the latter half of the nineteenth century saw a large amount of utopian writing, but even women writers tended not to address the specific problems of women'[37]) of an alternative women's culture and society, the solution to societal ills advanced by cultural ecofeminists. *Herland* ends on several ambiguous notes which are not altogether attributable to the uncertainties invoked by its plot. The women are attracted to Western scientific and technological achievement, and to the idea of rejoining 'the family of nations' (H p. 144). The means of achieving this objective is seen necessarily to entail 'civilizing—or exterminating—the dangerous savages' who inhabit the forest hinterlands of Herland. Although a distinction is drawn here—it is the men, and not the women, who suggest the killing—'civilizing' still smacks dangerously of colonialism, especially when approved by 'Aryan' women who have been 'well posted [by the men] as to the different races'. Perversely, however, the inability of Gilman's 'enchanted forest' to resist the encroachment of 'technological desert' may be read as one of *Herland's* most coherent strengths. Margaret Whitford identifies 'two views of utopia, either a kind of political romanticism (harmony with nature, Elysian future) or else a view of the future "in process", the struggles taking different forms, but never finally eliminated'. Whitford then cites Nora Rathzel as criticizing 'the first kind... from within feminism'. Rathzel argues that both 'romanticized versions of the past' and 'rosy visions of the future... take the contradiction out of life'; 'a Utopia in which there are no struggles' is analogous with an individual life in which no mistakes are made; this, according to Rathzel, is 'to opt out of living'.[38] In these terms, *Herland* is a resounding success, accounting not only for past struggles (the establishment of a workable ethos and culture), but for those of the present (coping with the intruders), whilst also anticipating the potential difficulties of a return, partial or entire, to a bisexuate society. Finally, Whitford cites Kristeva's argument that if utopia hinges on 'the omnipotence of an archaic, full, total, englobing mother with no frustration, no separation, with no break-producing symbolism', it is impossible 'to defuse the violences mobilized through the counter-investment necessary to carrying out this phantasm, unless one challenges precisely this myth of the archaic mother'.[39] Perhaps Gilman, in shifting her focus from the separatist 'Maternal Pantheism' of Herland, is simply anticipating Kristeva; not so much pandering to dualism, as debunking the myth.

Notes

1 Christine Cuomo, 'Ecofeminism, Deep Ecology, and Human Population', in Karen Warren, ed.,. *Ecological Feminism* (London: Routledge, 1994), p. 88.

2 Françoise d'Eaubonne, 'Feminism or Death', in Elaine Marks and Isabelle de Courtivron, eds, *New French Feminisms: An Anthology* (Amherst: University of Massachussets Press, 1980).

3 Karen Warren, ed., *Ecological Feminism* (London: Routledge, 1994), p. 1.

4 Ibid., p.1

5 Val Plumwood, 'Feminism and Ecofeminism: Beyond the Dualistic Assumptions of Women, Men and Nature', *The Ecologist* 22 (1) 1992, p. 10.

6 Ibid., p. 10.

7 Ibid., p. 10.

8 Karen Warren, *Ecological Feminism*, p. 2.

9 Lady Emmeline Charlotte Elizabeth Stuart-Wortley, 'REFORM—LIBERTY—MARCH OF INTELLECT—EQUALITY', Impressions of Italy and Other Poems (London: Saunders and Otley, 1837), *English Poetry Full-Text Database*, rel. 5, CD-ROM (Cambridge: Chadwyck, 1993).

10 Val Plumwood, *Feminism and the Mastery of Nature* (London: Routledge, 1993), pp. 8–9.

11 Sarah Lefanu, *In the Chinks of the World Machine: Feminism and Science Fiction* (London: The Women's Press, 1988), pp. 53–54.

12 Val Plumwood, *Feminism and the Mastery of Nature*, pp. 8–9.

13 Sarah Lefanu, *In the Chinks*, p. 57.

14 Victoria Davion, 'Is Ecofeminism Feminist?', in Karen Warren, ed., *Ecological Feminism* p. 11.

15 Sarah Lefanu, *In the Chinks*, p. 55.

16 Margaret Whitford, *Luce Irigaray: Philosophy in the Feminine* (London: Routledge, 1991), p. 20.

17 Christine Cuomo, 'Ecofeminism, Deep Ecology, and Human Population', p. 102.

18 Sarah Lefanu, *In the Chinks*, p. 54.

19 Val Plumwood, 'Feminism and Ecofeminism', p. 10.

20 Val Plumwood, *Feminism and the Mastery of Nature*, p. 1.

21 Ibid., p. 123.

22 Charlotte Perkins Gilman, *Women and Economics*, ed. Carl N. Degler (New York: Harper and Row, 1966), p. 196.

23 Val Plumwood, *Feminism and the Mastery of Nature*, p. 1.

24 Douglas J. Buege, 'Rethinking Again', in Karen Warren, ed., *Ecological Feminism* pp. 42–63.

25 Jim Cheney, 'Nature/Theory/Difference', in Karen Warren, ed., *Ecological Feminism*, p. 162.

26 Val Plumwood, *Feminism and the Mastery of Nature*, p. 3.

27 Margaret Whitford, *Luce Irigaray*, p. 17.

28 Val Plumwood, *Feminism and the Mastery of Nature*, p. 169.

29 Ibid., p. 72.

30 Sarah Lefanu, *In the Chinks*, p. 54.

31 Ibid., p. 56.

32 Val Plumwood, *Feminism and the Mastery of Nature*, p. 72.

33 Ibid., p. 74.

34 Ibid., p. 78.

35 Ibid., p. 143.

36 Georgia Johnston, 'Exploring Lack and Absence in the Body/Text: Charlotte Perkins Gilman Prewriting Irigaray', *Women's Studies*, 21, 1992, p. 77.

37 Sarah Lefanu, *In the Chinks*, p. 56.

38 Margaret Whitford, *Luce Irigaray*, p. 18.

39 Ibid., p. 19.

'In the Twinkling of an Eye': Gilman's Utopian Imagination

VAL GOUGH

Many recent theorists of utopian thinking have pointed out that the strength of a literary utopia lies not so much in the particular social structure it portrays, but rather in *how* the utopian vision is portrayed. Since narrative strategies and formal devices encode ideological messages, the form of the literary utopia is at least as significant as its content. As Tom Moylan says:

> ... the utopian process must be held open as a symbolic resolution of historical contradictions that finds its importance not in the particulars of those resolutions but in the very act of imagining them, in the form of utopia itself.[1]

Not surprisingly, then, analyses of Gilman's most well-known literary utopia, *Herland* (1915), have shown how the novel's formal and structural properties contribute decisively to its subversive utopian message.[2] The fundamental premise of such approaches is that imagined utopias are most effective and most subversive when they function less as blueprints than as thought experiments which throw critical light upon the status quo, and open up space for imagining new possibilities. Hence recent critics have tended to privilege and even prescribe a form of 'critical' utopian thinking which eschews narrative closure, authority and monologism in favour of emphasizing process, relativity and dialogism. Moylan, for example, argues that:

> The task of an oppositional utopian text is not to foreclose the agenda for the future in terms of a homogenous revolutionary plan but rather to hold open the act of negating the present and to imagine any of several possible modes of adaption to society and to nature based generally upon principles of autonomy, mutual aid, and equality.[3]

Valuable as such theories are, they undoubtedly reflect the current postmodern distrust of master narratives, and have led to the privileging of some utopian texts over others. In Gilman studies, the current appeal of *Herland*'s self-reflexive narrative strategies has led to a critical neglect of her other utopian novels, *Moving the Mountain* (1911) and *With Her in Ourland* (1916). These two novels are less easy for critics to embrace because of their range of politically incorrect messages (especially about race and class), and their programmatic mode of utopian thought. Most recently, Carol Farley Kessler has described *Herland* as a 'full-blown utopia for women' which, she says, was prepared for by Gilman's previous utopian works, including *Moving the Mountain*.[4] Thus Kessler says: 'In *Moving the Mountain* Gilman sketches social changes that she would present more fully in *Herland*.'[5] But if Gilman called *Moving the Mountain* a 'baby Utopia',[6] it was not because she saw its vision as incomplete, but rather because she wished it to 'grow' in the minds of its readers. In fact, Gilman presents the utopia of the novel (America in the 1940s) precisely as a blueprint for the reader, an outline of a whole, workable society, or what Riane Eisler has called a 'pragmatopia'.[7] *Moving the Mountain*—much more than *Herland*—aims to provide a whole picture and a broad scope. Whereas the fictional utopia in *Herland* functions not primarily as blueprint but as a narrative strategy to facilitate social critique, the utopia portrayed in *Moving the Mountain* functions above all as an authorized and naturalized 'realizable utopia'.[8]

According to Moylan, such fictional utopias, designed to function as blueprints, fail to operate oppositionally but rather remain complicit within hegemonic power structures. He says: 'a specific, homogenous utopian vision would be a betrayal of radical utopian discourse and would only end up serving the instrumentalization of desire carried on by the present structures of power'.[9] But by looking closely at Gilman's conception of the nature of utopian thought, we can begin to see why she chose this particular narrative form for her novel. It enables us to see this choice not so much as a failure to appreciate the relationship between narrative form and content, but rather precisely as the desire to marry the two together as intimately as possible.

Moving the Mountain—this neglected novel—written only four years before the critically acclaimed *Herland*, surely raises the question of how utopias which are presented as blueprints are to be viewed critically today. Are such utopias to be written off as failures and written out of theories of utopian thinking? One way of avoiding this is to re-emphasize the importance of content (as opposed to—or as well as—form) in utopian texts. Whilst theories of utopian thought which centralize the importance of form are without doubt necessary and valuable, the tendency of many readers is nevertheless to focus primarily on content (*even when* the text demands attention to form). This means, I believe, that utopian texts whose purpose is to function as a blueprint can still have subversive effect, an effect that arises less from their form than from their thematic content.

My purpose, then, is not to write *Moving the Mountain* off as a failure because of its non-conformity to the currently privileged paradigm of critical utopia, but rather to examine the novel to see *why* Gilman chose to make her utopia function as a blueprint, and to examine the ideological implications of such a strategy. As I shall show, Gilman's narrative strategies were deliberately chosen because of her theories about religion, social evolution, the utopian potentials of America and the nature of utopian change.

In 1898, Gilman had written to her future husband, Houghton: 'I am immensely interested in finding sound sociology as I see it in the teachings of Christ; because I have long felt that our next advance must come through development of existing religious feeling and not in contradiction to it.'[10] Her last published book was *His Religion and Hers* (1923) in which she argued that religion, as presently practised, did not direct people towards their real divine purpose as she saw it: that of 'race improvement'. Consequently, she said, they would have to be taught to replace 'the remote, uncertain, contradictory view concerning a book-derived God' with a 'sense of social responsibility, a social conscience, hope and purpose for society, knowledge of the laws of social evolution, lives governed and guided in accordance with those laws'.[11] It is undoubtedly indicative of Gilman's central concern with religion that *Moving the Mountain's* protagonist, John Robertson, returns to America from exile in Tibet, a place always associated in popular consciousness with esoteric religion and other-worldly spirituality. *Moving the Mountain* explicitly fuses the concept of utopian change with that of religion and spiritual revelation, by depicting utopianism as a 'New Religion' which makes real in the here-and-now the hitherto distant, always deferred, possibility of heavenly bliss. The 'Preface' to the novel makes explicit Gilman's conception of utopian thinking as a counter-discourse to the Judeo-Christian religious tradition:

> One of the most distinctive features of the human mind is to forecast better things... This natural tendency to hope, desire, foresee and then, if possible, obtain, has been largely diverted from human usefulness since our goal was placed after death, in heaven. With all our hope in 'Another World', we have largely lost hope of this one.[12]

The novel's portrayal of utopianism as a form of non-theistic 'Religion', as the 'right expression' of the primordial life-force', or 'Social Energy',[13] places Gilman within a tradition of feminist utopian writers for whom envisioning alternatives is a political and spiritual imperative and for whom, as Adelaide Proctor says, 'Dreams grow holy when put into action'.[14] She can be seen as a precursor of late twentieth-century feminist writers like Ursula Le Guin, Penny Casdagli and Sally Miller Gearhart, for whom utopianism is intrinsically spiritual and theologically revisionary. Gilman's belief in the ability of the 'change of mind' effected by utopian thinking to change 'real people, now living'[15] corresponds to Gearhart's belief, as a spiritual feminist, that utopian envisioning can be visionary in a way which directly effects change. Gearhart's depiction of a lesbian-separatist utopian community in her 1979 novel, *The Wanderground*, is premised upon the assumption that utopian ideas become real, and that utopian envisioning is itself a political act. In Gearhart's utopia, to dream, to imagine, and to 'envision' are all to create reality: one of the utopian Hill-women's dream-vision of snakes takes place in the narrative as a 'real' experience; another 'envisions' a plant which physically and actually exchanges her fatigue for energy.[16] These episodes function as meta-commentary upon the process of utopian envisioning itself, asserting that envisioning can create reality, can make 'what is not yet' into 'what is'.

Similarly, the crux of Gilman's utopian philosophy in *Moving the Mountain* is the reality of ideas. One of the utopians insists:

> Ideas are the real things, Sir! Brick and mortar? Bah! We can put bricks and mortar in any shape we choose—but we have to choose first! What held the old world back was not facts—not conditions—not any material limitations, or psychic limitations either. We had every constituent of human happiness, Sir—except the sense to use them. The channel of progress was obstructed with a deposit of prehistoric ideas. We choked up our children's minds with this mental refuse as we choked our rivers and harbors with material refuse, Sir.[17]

The precise change which has enabled the utopia to come about is nothing more, and nothing less, than a change in ideas: 'It involves no other change than a change of mind, the mere awakening of people, especially the women, to existing possibilities'.[18] Gilman's narrative purpose is, of course, to change the ideas of her readers, and she aims to do this by providing them with the information, the conceptual 'bricks and mortar' with which to build a concrete utopian reality. Thus Gilman's textual decision to depict a blueprint in *Moving the Mountain* is illumined by her conception of utopian thought as a counter-religion based not on mystery and unknowing, but on total knowledge and full, unimpeded vision:

> 'In place of Revelation and Belief,' she said slowly, 'we now have

> Facts and Knowledge. We used to believe in God—variously, and teach the belief as a matter of duty. Now we know God, as much as we know anything else—more than we know anything else—it is The Fact of Life.'[19]

Hence the novel's narrative is conceived as a broad overview, a 'species of digest' written by John Robertson (as he returns to America from an amnesiac sojourn in Tibet lasting thirty years) in order to 'establish... a coherent view of what had happened'.[20] After reading Edward Bellamy's *Looking Backward* (whose utopian figure also to a large extent functions as a blueprint), Gilman commented, 'I like a few salient and relevant facts—and then far seeing generalisation', and as Carol Farley Kessler points out, *Moving the Mountain* provides a 'panoramic view' of a utopian society.[21] John travels widely, experiencing the delights of the utopian world. But these experiences are largely reported to us, in the guise of his totalizing digest, rather than 'experienced' by the readers themselves. The status of John's narrative as a generalizing and totalizing one parallels the nature of the novel's utopian state, which is a totalitarian régime, albeit enforced not by violence or tyranny but by consensus and 'common sense'.

To be 'far seeing' functions throughout the novel as both metaphor for and literal enactment of utopian thought. 'Those far-seeing women were pioneers', says Hallie, John's niece; and his friend, Frank, asserts, 'ideas can be changed *in the twinkling of an eye!*' (emphasis mine).[22] The utopians are described as 'able to see' and benefiting from 'the outlook broader'.[23] Visual scrutiny is the primary means by which John first encounters the utopian world, which is itself organized to enable maximum surveillance:

> It was a big, handsome place. The front windows faced the great river, the rear ones opened on a most unexpected scene of loveliness... They gave me a room with a river window, and I looked out at the broad current, changed only in its lovely clearness, and at the changeless Palisades.
>
> Changeless? I stared, and seized the traveling glass still on the strap.
>
> ... The water front was green-parked, white-piered, rimmed with palaces, and the broken slopes terraced and garlanded in rich foliage. White cottaged and larger buildings climbed and nestled along the sunny slopes as on the cliffs at Capri. It was a place one would go far to see.
>
> I dropped my eyes to the nearer shore.[24]

Because Gilman views travel as both a means of and a metaphor for acquiring the 'far-seeing' utopian vision, she makes use of some of the conventions of travel writing in her narrative. Like the European male subjects of previous centuries' landscape discourse, whose imperial eyes scanned the lands they visited, John's primary encounter with the utopia is via visual scrutiny of the landscape. Yet Gilman reverses the power dynamic of much travel writing, whose specular subjects installed their own imperial discursive order and projected their own fantasy of dominance and appropriation in the act of seeing. Instead, Gilman portrays the visitor/observer as one who is *to be* assimilated.

Moreover, Gilman's narrative seeks to rehabilitate America as the fabled utopia, as a 'new world' of imaginary alternatives and utopian possibilities. This fable had been somewhat tarnished by late eighteenth- and nineteenth-century travel writers, who had found the reality of America less impressive than the myth. François-René de Chateaubriand's *Travels in America,* for instance, found the reality of American cities a disappointment: 'The aspect of Philadelphia is cold and monotonous. In general the cities in the United States are lacking in monuments, especially old monuments'.[25] The narrative continues: 'A man landing as I did in the United States, full of enthusiasm for the ancients, a Cato seeking everywhere for the rigidity of early Roman manners, is necessarily shocked to find everywhere the elegance of dress, the luxury of carriages, the frivolity of conversations, the disproportion of fortunes, the immorality of banks and gaming houses, the noise of dancehalls and theatres.'[26] Most particularly, English travellers who visited America in the 1830s and 1840s had constructed America as anti-utopia. Books such as Frances Trollope's *Domestic Manners of the Americans* (1832), Harriet Martineau's *Society in America* (1837), Captain Marryat's *A Diary in America* (1837) and Charles Dickens' *American Notes* (1842) all portrayed America as an uncouth and vulgar nation. Gilman's fictional 'foreign' traveller observes an America which is designed to reverse such dystopian images. That she located her fictional utopia not 'elsewhere' but in an American 'here and now' only thirty years distant, testifies to her optimism and faith in the utopian potentialities which she believed to be latent within American social reality.

If Gilman's fictional visitor to America-as-utopia encounters it primarily through visual scrutiny, the utopians themselves are portrayed as uniquely observant—'Nellie, [was] always unobtrusively watching me'—and the utopian society reproduces itself via mechanisms of surveillance.[27] The children, for example, are 'observed intelligently' by the baby culturists in order to fit their environment to their needs.[28] Myopia is symbolic of dystopian lack of vision: '"I see no child in glasses!" I suddenly remarked one day... I recalled the Boston school children and the myopic victims of Germany's archaic letter-press; and freely admitted that this was advance.'[29] Education ensures that, we are told, 'In the mind of every child is a clear view.'[30] When John encounters his cousin Drusilla, her 'reactionary' lifestyle is reflected in her inability to see clearly and look closely—'she dropped her eyes and flushed faintly'—whilst her potential for utopian thought is hinted at by her ability to 'flash... a grateful look' when John criticizes her family.[31]

Such an emphasis on seeing reflects Gilman's belief in the possibility of a perspective of rational objectivity, one which she portrays as essential for the achievement of a utopian vision. Early on in the novel, Nellie asserts the difference between 'subjective' bias ('the objection and distaste you feel is only in your personal consciousness'), and supposedly 'objective' fact ('Everything *is* better').[32] Throughout the novel, Gilman portrays travel, particularly travel within utopia, as a supremely valuable mechanism for achieving this supposedly broad and objective point of view. All the technological innovations described in the novel (noiseless airships, electric trains and boats, well-organized roads) are ones which facilitate efficient travel. Whilst goods are no longer needlessly transported over long distances, nevertheless people are encouraged to travel, and all the utopian children spend a year travelling as they approach maturity. In this, Gilman again hints that the fictional utopia has its potential in the actuality of early twentieth-century America, which afforded unique opportunities for country-wide travel.[33]

Most particularly for Gilman, the broad, objective view is both literally and metaphorically a 'flight of the mind'. As John Robertson explores his home afresh, he notices particularly the impact of the noiseless airships that have been developed, which, he says, 'opened up a new world of delight to me'.[34] Time and time again, there is in the novel (often gratuitous) mention of these airships, whose ubiquitousness has turned the utopians, so we are told, into 'a race of flying men [*sic*]'.[35] From these airships, John develops a theory that links the achievement of utopia with the assumption of a supposedly objective, all-encompassing point of view. He says to his companion:

> Look here, Owen, I think I have the glimmer of an idea. Didn't the common use of airships help to develop this social consciousness you're always talking about—this general view of things?

Owen replies in the affirmative, saying:

> You see few people are able to visualize what they have not seen. Most of us had no more idea of the surface of the earth than an ant has of a meadow. In each mind was only a thready fragment of an idea of the world—no real geographic view. And when we got flying over it commonly, it became real and familiar to us—like a big garden.[36]

Roberta F. Weldon has pointed out that much of the American literature of the nineteenth century is a 'literature of movement', most particularly a literature fascinated by speed:

> The characteristic American journey tends to be imagined in at least two common ways. The first of course, is that the American journey moves westward, and the second, that the mode of conveyance which the traveler chooses probably depends upon how quickly it can bring him [sic] to the destination.[37]

Yet she also draws attention to a flourishing tradition, the 'Literature of Walking' represented by authors like Thoreau and Hawthorne, who portrayed walking as an imaginative and redemptive process set against the detachment from nature produced by the railroad. Gilman too treats travel as a metaphoric inner journey, but is fascinated by the difference of view enabled specifically by air travel. Bridget Bennett points out (in her chapter in this volume) that the advent of the aeroplane profoundly affected concepts of ways of seeing, providing a model for a universal view. As Paul Virilo says: 'By 1914 aviation was ceasing to be strictly a means of flying and breaking records... [I]t was becoming one way, or perhaps even the ultimate way of *seeing*.'[38] In the novel, John flies over the land and this provides him with an overview of the utopians' social structure. Constantly we see him scrutinizing the utopian landscape from above: 'looking down at the lovely green fields and forests beneath'; 'that quiet river garden which was so attractive from above'; 'all the beauty spread below me'; 'We kept our vehicle gliding slowly above it while Nellie pointed things out.'[39] Such a view functions as a metaphorical model for the transcendence of ideological boundaries Gilman portrays in *Moving the Mountain* as necessary to the achievement of utopian change. Later in the novel the message is made even more explicit. John says: 'The airships did make a difference. To look down on the flowing, outspread miles beneath gave a sense of the unity and continuous beauty of our country, quite different from the streak views we used to get. An airship is a moving mountain-top.'[40] Thus to 'see over' the land is a literal enactment of, and metaphor for, the transcendence of dystopian ideology. Nellie says to John: 'If you can... see over your own personal attitudes it will not be long before a real convincing *sense* of joy, of life, will follow the intellectual perception that things are better.'[41] Thus Gilman legitimizes her utopian vision by constructing it as objective, as a transcendence of personal bias. Again we see the religious component of her thinking in the linking of utopianism and transcendence.

Yet of course, to 'see over' is also in some senses to oversee, to supervise and control, and also to overlook, to obscure. Gilman reveals the ideological basis of the dystopian present, with its 'false theories of industry',[42] but she deliberately overlooks and obscures the ideological nature of her own utopian theories. *Moving the Mountain* engages resolutely in a 'hermeneutics of supervision' as William V. Spanos defines it:

> By the hermeneutics of supervision, I mean the imposition of meaning from the normative/panoptic perspective on the subversive aporetic elements—the differential force—to make them conform to the larger (imperial) design.[43]

Thus Gilman is happy to include in her utopia the kind of social policing and coercion that Michel Foucault has shown is achieved precisely through surveillance. In *Discipline and Punish,* Foucault examines how power is shown to take the forms of surveillance and assessment of individuals, realized in the practice of state institutions such as prisons, schools, the army and the workplace. These institutions discipline the body, mind and emotions, constituting them according to the needs of hierarchical forms of power such as gender and class. The utopia Gilman envisages in *Moving the Mountain* relies upon the very same panoptic mechanisms of social coercion and surveillance which constitute the gender identities she seeks to deconstruct. Individuals who do not socially conform are stigmatized, even pathologized. Owen describes the way that women who do not conform to current norms of sexual behaviour are seen as 'cases for medical treatment, or perhaps surgical'.[44] Thus Gilman is not averse to legitimizing through naturalization the very same operations of power which reinforce the gender structures she seeks to dismantle. Owen says: 'In visible material progress we have only followed simple lines, quite natural and obvious, and accomplished what was perfectly possible at any time.'[45] In this way, the naturalized absolutes of the present world are merely replaced by different naturalized absolutes; indeed, normativity is portrayed as the mechanism by which utopian change is achieved: 'We have a standard of citizenship now—an idea of what people ought to be and how to make them so.'[46]

By privileging the objective, transcendent eye, *Moving the Mountain* remains complicit with the monologic nature of much utopian thinking (i.e. *not* critical utopias), and shares with it the symptom of narrative stasis.[47] Mary Ann Caws argues that 'the aim of free seeing would be a flexibility of function able to accommodate images both ordinary and askew, straight or with perceptual shifts, and to translate them liberally into nourishment for new ways of seeing'.[48] But Gilman's concept of utopian thinking as the collective 'twinkling of an eye' involves the suppression of errancy and the foreclosure of true dialogue. John functions as the errant exile finally brought 'home', through the gradual loss of his dystopian ideological baggage. His assimilation into the utopian consensus is achieved via a series of 'dialogues' which actually function as monologic statements of utopian 'truth'. Thus Gilman's concept of utopian vision as unanimity has much in common with Richard Rorty's delineation of the repressive nature of visual metaphors. For Rorty, visual idioms are associated with a desire to indicate 'accurate representation' and 'objective truth', elements that foreclose rather than sustain genuine conversation, and function as obstacles rather than catalysts to creativity and freedom.[49]

The narrative strategies of *Moving the Mountain* reproduce the concept of the utopian vision as an objective, universal one. Although we are frequently reminded that John Robertson is not a detached, objective observer, but comes with all his dystopian biases, ultimately his narrative is legitimized and authorized, particularly by the plot device which makes the novel into his written digest of all that he sees and is told. Thus he is an authoritative male voice speaking largely to other male voices, despite the novel's *thematic* insistence on the centrality of women. The utopians insist that literature must change in order to function efficiently as 'nourishment' for growing utopian subjects, yet John's method of narration remains static and unchanged even as his own attitudes are seen to gradually change. While thematically, the novel asserts the necessity to reconceptualize identity and reconfigure the subject ('It dawned on us that life was not an individual affair'[50]), formally the novel produces a conventional, monologic, individualistic reader whose function is to be assimilated into the utopian consensus. The blueprint-like quality of the fictional utopia comes partly from the utopian's insistence upon the *reality* of their world, its factual basis as opposed to the illusory quality of dystopian beliefs. Again the notion of objective perspective is called up to reinforce the factuality of the utopian world: 'Don't you remember what Lester Ward calls "the illusion of the near"—how the most familiar facts were precisely those we often failed to understand?'[51] In creating a fictional 'realizable utopia' which functions on a 'literal' basis, as a literalization of all Gilman's utopian ideas, Gilman must leave the tensions and contradictions of such a project unacknowledged. The 'hermeneutic of supervision' whose logic organizes the narrative of *Moving the Mountain* works instead to assimilate all aporetic elements into the overall design.

Gilman's next novel, *Herland*, develops similar ideas but employs a different textual practice. The fictional utopia functions not as a blueprint, but as a strategy for provoking questions in the reader. And the way metaphors of vision are employed in the novel implies that Gilman's concept of the utopian imagination had changed too. No longer is the view from the mountain the metaphor for the utopian perspective. Instead, the all-women utopia dubbed 'Herland' by one of its male visitors is enclosed by mountain ranges and has survived precisely because it has been shielded from the surveillance of the outside world. In its geography, Herland recalls Tibet, that land enclosed by mountain ranges which in the previous novel functioned to symbolize dystopian isolation. But now, the utopian space is conceived of not as a place of panoptic surveillance, but as a separated—and separatist—haven. Flight no longer symbolizes the transcendence of dystopian ideologies, but rather symbolizes precisely the colonialist and masculinist nature of pretensions to objectivity which Gilman had concealed in *Moving the Mountain*. The three male would-be explorers get into their biplane equipped with instruments designed to aid their desire to specularly penetrate the female space of Herland: 'So we got the big biplane and loaded it with our scientifically compressed baggage: the camera, of course; the glasses' (H p. 10). Their plan is to 'spy out the land' (H p. 10) and map its borders, but Gilman reveals that the supposed objectivity of their airborne surveillance is coloured by male fantasies and projections, by gradually revealing the disparity between the conclusions they derive from their fly-over and the true nature of Herland. Far from being an objective perspective, to 'see over' is now overtly to overlook and to project subjective, patriarchal assumptions.

The specularity of male surveillance is contrasted with the methods of surveillance employed by the Herlanders, who merely observe the men as they try to escape, and sew up their biplane in a bag. Van explains:

> ...all they did was to call the inhabitants to keep an eye on our movements all along the edge of the forest between two points. It appeared that many of those nights we had been seen, by careful ladies sitting snugly in big trees by the riverbed. (H p. 44)

Rather than naturalize the utopian vision, Gilman reveals that 'seeing' always has an agenda, be it a utopian or dystopian one. Later in the novel Van comes to realize the effectiveness of the Herlanders' methods of observation, which 'see through' male specularity:

> Little had we thought that our careful efforts at concealment had been so easily seen through, with never a word to show us that they saw. They had followed up words of ours on the science of optics, asked innocent questions about glasses and the like, and were aware of the defective eyesight so common amongst us. (H p. 144)

Gilman still uses the metaphor of the view from the mountain top, but crucially, she relativizes it by making visible the positionality of its originator. Van uses the image to describe Ellador's reaction to his love-making:

> She trembled in my arms, as I held her close, kissing her hungrily. But there rose in her eyes that look I knew so well, that remote clear

> look as if she had gone far away even though I held her beautiful body so close, and was now on some snowy mountain regarding me from a distance. (H p. 138)

Thus whereas in *Moving the Mountain* the metaphor functions as a sign of absolute value, utopian envisioning, and is legitimized as such by the narrative, in *Herland* its value is shown to be a relative and subjective one: it tells us about Van's attitude toward's Ellador reaction. And like Van, the reader views Ellador's perspective ambivalently, despite the fact that she is a utopian: is she admirably detached and objective, or is she cold and unemotional? Utopian thinking is presented not as a blueprint for our own, but as a goad to questioning and critique. And the novel constructs a reader aware of the narrator's positionality, and therefore aware of the provisionality of his discourse.

In *Herland*, then, Gilman relativizes the process of utopian envisioning which she had conceived as an objective perspective in the previous novel. The reading position produced by the novel is one which necessarily involves awareness of the relativity of reading positions. And utopian change is depicted as taking place, not in 'the twinkling of an eye' but over many years of patient effort. If *Moving the Mountain* functions paternalistically as a kind of Father-Text which secretly coerces its readers into a utopian consensus, *Herland* functions as the kind of Over-mother it fictionally depicts, by gently and wittily encouraging its readers to grow through questioning and thought-experiment.

Does this then mean that *Moving the Mountain* is a failure, particularly in comparison with the critical utopia which is *Herland*? Such a conclusion would certainly, as we have seen, reproduce current thinking about utopian writing. Yet to stop there would be to ignore the importance of utopian content and Gilman's own aim to produce a 'realizable' utopia. *Herland* works less well if read on these terms, for its quasi-lesbian separatist community, kept safe by an impossible geographical isolation, does not represent any kind of realistic proposition for utopian living: but of course it does not aim to. Because of the element of fantasy, Gilman can portray a society which reproduces parthenogenetically and with the aid of a kind of natural eugenics (Herlanders can 'will' themselves not to fall pregnant). But Gilman's aim in writing *Moving the Mountain* was very different: to portray a pragmatopia, one which she saw as a realistic proposition or blueprint for future social change. On this level, the novel functions exceedingly well, portraying a society which, whilst not perfect, is certainly plausible and pleasant. Because Gilman presents the utopia as a blueprint, she is committed to a literary technique based on verisimilitude and realism, which creates the illusion of familiarity necessary to engender belief in the alternative, utopian world. As J. R. R. Tolkien said, 'the moment disbelief arises, the spell is broken; the magic, or rather art, has failed'.[52] Thus the inevitable contradictions (inevitable in any utopian vision) could not be resolved or concealed using fantasy elements, but rather had to be concealed by narrative form. Gilman always wrote for a purpose, and because her purposes were different when she wrote *Moving the Mountain* and *Herland*, she produced two very different kinds of novels. Our current critical privileging of *Herland* reflects current critical trends, and there is no doubt that it is a very good novel. But *Moving the Mountain*, with its convincing and inspirational portrayal of an America which—if not perfect—is certainly more pleasant for the majority than it was then or is now, reminds us of the power of ideas, however they are mediated, to take root and perhaps 'grow'—if not as speedily as Gilman would have wished—in the human mind.

Notes

1 Tom Moylan, *Demand the Impossible: Science Fiction and the Utopian Imagination* (New York: Methuen, 1986), p. 39.

2 See Anne Cranny-Francis, *Feminist Fiction: Feminist Uses of Generic Fiction* (Cambridge: Polity Press, 1990); Laura E. Donaldson, 'The Eve of De-struction: Charlotte Perkins Gilman and the Feminist Re-creation of Paradise', *Women's Studies*, 16, 1989; Val Gough, 'Lesbians and Virgins: The New Motherhood in *Herland*', in David Seed, ed., *Anticipations: Essays on Early Science Fiction and its Precursors* (Liverpool: Liverpool University Press, 1995), pp. 195–215.

3 Tom Moylan, *Demand the Impossible*, pp. 26–7.

4 Carol Farley Kessler, *Charlotte Perkins Gilman: Her Progress Toward Utopia with Selected Writings* (Liverpool: Liverpool University Press, 1995), p. 9.

5 Ibid., p. 63.

6 Charlotte Perkins Gilman, *Moving the Mountain* (New York: Charlton, 1911), p. 6.

7 See Carol Farley Kessler, *Her Progress*, p. 7.

8 This term is taken from Kessler, *Her Progress*, p. 8, but I use it to support a very different argument from hers.

9 Tom Moylan, *Demand the Impossible*, p. 28.

10 Quoted in Larry Ceplair, ed., *Charlotte Perkins Gilman: A Non-Fiction Reader* (New York: Columbia University Press, 1991), p. 273.

11 Ibid., pp. 273–4.

12 Charlotte Perkins Gilman, *Moving the Mountain*, p. 5.

13 Ibid., p. 243.

14 Quoted in Carol Farley Kessler, ed., *Daring to Dream: Utopian Stories by United States Women: 1836–1919* (Boston, MA.: Pandora-Routledge & Kegan Paul, 1984), p. 19 (2nd edition, subtitled *Utopian Fiction by United States Women before 1950* [New York: Syracuse University Press, 1995]). Several analyses of utopias by women consider them to be intrinsically spiritual, including Lee Cullen Khanna, 'Women's Worlds: New Directions in Utopian Fiction', Alternative Futures, 4 (2–3) 1981; and Carol Pearson and Katherine Pope, *The*

Female Hero in British and American Fiction (New York, 1981)

15 Charlotte Perkins Gilman, *Moving the Mountain*, p. 6.

16 Sally Miller Gearhart, *The Wanderground* (London: Women's Press, 1979), p. 147.

17 Charlotte Perkins Gilman, *Moving the Mountain*, p. 131.

18 Ibid., p. 6.

19 Ibid., p. 199.

20 Ibid., p. 123

21 Quoted in Larry Ceplair, *Non-Fiction Reader*, p. 28; Carol Farley Kessler, *Her Progress*, p. 58.

22 Charlotte Perkins Gilman, *Moving the Mountain*, p. 22.

23 Ibid., p. 224 and p. 225.

24 Ibid., pp. 68–9.

25 François René de Chateaubriand, *Travels in America*, trans. Richard Switzer (Lexington: University of Kentucky Press, 1969), p. 14.

26 Ibid., p. 15.

27 Charlotte Perkins Gilman, *Moving the Mountain*, p. 66.

28 Ibid., p. 220.

29 Ibid., p. 222.

30 Ibid., p. 202.

31 Ibid., p. 281.

32 Ibid., p. 43.

33 As early as 1847, the travel writer D. F. Sarmiento was observing that '... everyone travels, [and] there is no impossible or unprofitable enterprise in the field of transportation... The great number of travellers makes for cheap rates, and cheap rates in turn tempt those who have no precise object in mind to go somewhere'; Steven Kagel, ed., *America: Exploration and Travel* (Bowling Green, OH: Bowling Green State University Press, 1979), pp. 58–59.

34 Charlotte Perkins Gilman, *Moving the Mountain*, p. 145.

35 Ibid., p. 144.

36 Ibid., p. 179.

37 Steven Kagel, *America*, p. 127.

38 Bill Brown, 'Science Fiction, the World's Fair, and the Prosthetics of Empire, 1900–1915', in Amy Kaplan and Donald Pease, eds, *Cultures of United States Imperialism* (Durham and London: Duke University Press, 1993), p. 145.

39 Charlotte Perkins Gilman, *Moving the Mountain*, p. 150; p. 96; p. 151; p. 151.

40 Ibid., p. 192.

41 Ibid., p. 125.

43 William V. Spanos, *The Errant Art of Moby Dick: The Canon, the Cold War and the Struggle for American Studies* (Durham, NC: Duke University Press, 1995), p. 11.

44 Charlotte Perkins Gilman, *Moving the Mountain*, p. 185.

45 Ibid., p. 130.

46 Ibid., p. 55.

47 Northrop Frye says: 'considered as a final or definitive social ideal, the utopia is a static society; and most utopias have built-in safeguards against radical alteration of the structure'; Northrop Frye, 'Varieties of Literary Utopias',in Frank E. Manuel, ed., *Utopias and Utopian Thought* (Boston: Houghton Mifflin, 1966), p. 31.

48 Mary Ann Caws, *The Art of Interference: Stressed Readings in Verbal and Visual Communication* (Princeton, NJ: Princeton University Press, 1989), p. 15.

49 See Victor Luftig, *Seeing Together: Friendship Between the Sexes in English Writing, from Mill to Woolf* (Stanford: Stanford University Press, 1993), p. 225.

50 Charlotte Perkins Gilman, *Moving the Mountain*, p. 171.

51 Ibid., pp. 188–89.

52 Quoted in Lynette Hunter, *Rhetorical Stance in Modern Literature: Allegories of Love and Death* (London: Macmillan, 1984), p. 62.

'Once There Was a Pig... Does not Interest': Gilman's Desire for Narrative Control

JILL RUDD

Reading *The Living of Charlotte Perkins Gilman* (1935) one encounters many assertions, convictions and rules, a number of which are self-imposed and several of which are clearly an integral part of pleasure. An instance of this is contained in the description of a favourite word game played with apparent zest by Gilman and Martha Luther, which contains the remarkable assertion that a story beginning 'Once there was a pig' would not interest. Typically for Gilman there is no explanation of, or defence for, this statement, yet it surely needs one. There are, after all, many stories at least ostensibly about pigs (e.g. Beatrix Potter's *The Tale of Pigling Bland*), pigs and wolves (as in the story of the *Three Little Pigs*), or George Orwell's more equal pigs of *Animal Farm*, whose endurance testifies that they have been found interesting; not to mention the more general, long-established and continuing tradition of animal fable. Yet all of this is blithely ignored in Gilman's assertion of the proper way to play the 'best-loved sport' of the One Word Game. The passage reads:

> Our best-loved sport was The One Word Game. This is not only such a delicious amusement, but such an unfailing rest and restorative for a weary and worried mind, that it is worth describing. The whole procedure is for each in turn to contribute one word (only one, save for proper names which may be given in full), to an unfolding story which no one composes, but which is most astonishingly produced by the successive additions. Any word which follows in grammatical sequence will do, no matter how sharply it disagrees with what the previous speaker had in mind.

> The game was taught me with no rule whatsoever, but I have made these three, from experience. First, you must not try to make the story go your way, with, 'Now you must say' this, or 'Why didn't you say' that; it must be allowed to unfold from the successive words, the whole charm is in the total unexpectedness. Second, it must be about persons. 'Once there was a pig', or the like, does not interest. Third, it should be a simple descriptive tale, like a child's fairy story, about persons and what they wore, said and did. (L p. 79)

Here, then, is Gilman's familiar desire to state rules simply as rules, in unambiguous terms and with the clear intention of adhering to them. Elsewhere in *Living* she records her desire to test regulations, or measure one kind of rule against another, but in every case there is a delight in the fact of the rule itself, matched only by her exasperation at rules which she regards as self-evidently unjust or foolish.[1] Yet it is perverse to add rules, however few, to a game whose acknowledged appeal lies in its simplicity, its capacity for legitimate waywardness and its very lack of rules. In its original form the One Word Game allows for flights of imagination triggered by a quickness of response to syntax and vocabulary, frequently expressed in puns and the like. It goes against this spirit to restrict such freedom in any way; particularly, one would have thought, for one who describes the game as 'massage for the brain' and who had, we know, a lively humour and imagination. Moreover, the rules themselves are contradictory. The first one seeks to preserve the free-flowing spirit of the game by prohibiting overt attempts to control, or create a plot, and preempting possible wrangles over a fellow-player's choice of word. This first rule could be described as embodying the etiquette of the game. In contrast, the two following regulations invented by Gilman not only undermine the first rule in dictating the kind of tale which must emerge, but also contradict each other in that 'Once there was a pig' sounds very much 'like a child's fairy story'. Thus to advocate following the form of a particular genre of story and then immediately exclude favoured material for that genre is paradoxical, if not simply provoking, and demands some kind of explanation.

Part of this explanation may be found, I suggest, in Gilman's own contrary impulses and views of herself, as promoted in *Living*, where she presents herself both as someone with a rich and vivid imaginative life and as someone who can impose and obey the most rigorous strictures. The imposition of rules upon a game which is otherwise almost entirely free can thus be seen as analogous to Gilman's own self-restraint in contexts of personal liberty, where those restraints then become ways of ensuring such liberty. Obedience to rules which have been either scrutinized and accepted or voluntarily imposed thus becomes a device for assuring a degree of latitude, without abandoning a sense of structure altogether. While such wariness is to be expected of a reformer (as opposed to a revolutionary), what is particularly marked in Gilman's case is the great store she set by obedience itself, even when the strictures being obeyed were not regarded as laudable. The well-known passage in which she makes a great point of giving up her internal, imaginary world is an example of just this pride in the virtue of obedience, coupled with disgust at the dictat she is required to obey:

> My dream world was no secret... Then, influenced by a friend with a pre-Freudian mind, alarmed at what she was led to suppose this inner life might become, mother called on me to give it up. This was a command. According to all the ethics I knew I must obey, and I did...
>
> Just thirteen... No one could tell if I did it or not, it was an inner fortress, open only to me...
>
> But obedience was Right, the thing had to be done, and I did it. (L pp. 23–24)

This absolute confidence in the rightness of obedience is reiterated when Gilman recounts her first act of considered rebellion at fifteen and its consequences. The incident is described by Gilman as 'one of the major events of a lifetime, making an indelible impression' (L p.33) and consists of refusing to apologize for something she has not done. Once again it is her mother's request she is denying, yet on this occasion Right and Obedience are opposed: to 'apologise for what I had not done was flatly dishonest, a lie, it was wrong' (L p. 34). So no apology is made, but the next chapter finds Gilman impelled to reconcile the desire to do right and the desire to obey authority as represented by her mother; a difficulty she resolves by recourse to the notion of duty:

> Out of much consideration I finally came to a definite decision as to my duty. The old condition of compelled obedience was gone forever. I was a free agent, but as such I decided that until I was twenty-one I would still obey. (L p. 36)

Both these incidents witness the formulation of a creed which allowed Gilman to override her own judgement and do things of which she herself did not approve, but would none the less do out of respect for, not her mother so much as the tradition of duty owed to parents by minors. Clearly she gains satisfaction from obeying the terms of that social contract and regards her ability to do so as a praiseworthy element of her personal development. It is worth remembering that although we, as literary critics, may be tempted to interpret the renunciation of her imaginative world as the act which permanently stunted her literary abilities, Gilman herself never recorded this view. Rather she preferred to promulgate a version of herself as being without a talent for, or real interest in, imaginative writing (fiction or poetry) which in terms of style could be regarded as anything other than functional and humdrum. Nor must it be forgotten that *The Living* is itself a carefully constructed and highly selective piece of autobiography, written at the end of her life, by which time she had had considerable experience in honing her rhetorical skills and projecting a public image. It is suggestive that both the obedience of the thirteen-year-old and the considered defiance of the fifteen-year-old are placed at the ends of chapters.

With this in mind it is worth returning to these passages and noting that in each case the emphasis is less on the fact of obedience and more on the pleasure that comes with proving herself able to obey rules. Thus, even if, as Ann J. Lane suggests,[2] Gilman did disobey various rules between the ages of thirteen and twenty-one and simply omits to tell us, what we are left with is a description of a mind which is most at ease when operating within recognized and codified limits. It may be from this that the compulsion to create systems and regulations arises; even when such regulations appear spurious, even (perhaps, now, particularly) in times of relaxation. Creating rules allows for the satisfaction of keeping them—they are secure bounds within which to work.

While all this may go some way towards accounting for the creation of extra rules for the One Word Game, the question of why one such rule should be the rejection of pigs (and all non-human subjects) as potential material remains to be answered. This seems especially odd in a writer who declared that words should have a purpose and that her own writing style had remained underdeveloped in the interest of devoting such time and energy as she had to communicating her views in the most direct and effective manner possible (see L pp. 284–5). One might have thought that for a writer of this ilk the fable genre, with its straightforward patterning and simple rules, would have provided an ideal form in which to work. Of course she did write fables, and several of them contain animals and several more have non-human subjects. It is to these we shall now turn to see how far they justify Gilman's claim that 'once there was a pig... does not interest'. Animals appear in Gilman's writing in a variety of ways, all of which are established literary uses and may be broadly distinguished into types. There are poems and fables which use animal protagonists, but are clearly stories about humans. The use of animals simply allows for the issues to be put clearly, without clouding them with considerations of human character or social pressures. Thus the animals are used almost symbolically in the manner of moral fables. Then there are stories in which the central character is human, but interacts with animals, or is explicitly compared to them, in some way. Again the use of the animals lends a clarity to the points under consideration, and also offers opportunities for humour, which may query the wisdom of the human course of action, but also leaves us in no doubt as to the actual superiority of homo sapiens. Finally there are stories which are about animals, or in which the animals are central to the plot, and where that plot invites or requires us to consider them as whole animals, not just emblematic of particular qualities or attitudes. Inevitably there is some blending of these types and in some texts several kinds of use of animals may co-exist. In the following discussions of some examples of her writing involving animals, I will show that Gilman use animals most freely when there is no question of them becoming the focus of attention, that is to say we automatically translate the tale out of the animal and into the human. The matter is somewhat different in the cases where we are able to read the texts without immediately regarding the animals as solely symbols or metaphors. In such cases reading with an eye to the animal adds to the possible interpretations, which in turn renders the use of the animals both more effective and less controlled. Gilman's assertion that stories taking animals as protagonists are not interesting is in fact a way of avoiding tales where this very interest in the animal overrides the sure and closed human application desired by Gilman. Hence, her censorship of certain material for writing links directly with her desire to ensure that her texts obey her intentions and are under her tutelage and control. By thus curbing her texts (and simultaneously attempting to direct her readers' responses into agreement with the views expressed in them) she also curbs her imagination, an effect she may well have been aware of and desirous of following her collapse and painstaking self-rehabilitation after her marriage to Walter Stetson and its consequences.

However, the purpose of this chapter is not to enter into the discussion of Gilman's life, a debate so ably carried on by other voices, but to focus on a particular aspect of her writing: the use of animals in her texts. To begin with, one story whose title declares its animal, or at least avian, protagonists, is 'Two Storks' (1910) (SS pp. 203–05). This could be described as a pure moral fable in which anthropomorphized storks illustrate an ideal of parenthood. The reader is not expected to think of the protagonists as actual storks, beyond the fact that they fly, which in turn allows for a simple metaphorical use of the ideas of flight and spreading one's wings. Within three sentences her terminology is endowing the storks with human spheres of reference, so that the pair are referred to as 'married', the young male's previous companions as 'striplings' and the females heretofore ignored by him are most explicitly humanized with the phrase 'ladies, either maid or matron', while his ideal mate is the 'All-Satisfying Wife' (SS p. 203). Our frequent use of such terms as 'nest' for 'home' and 'brood' for 'children' is the central strength of this tale, as it allows us to be carried along with the avian topos while yet always thinking in human terms. Yet this device, while familiar, is also important in that all is well as long as we use terms applied to birds for human conditions. The moment we apply human expectations to the birds, the folly of the human social expectations is revealed and the fable promptly makes its point. The irony of the male stork accusing the female of being unnatural, of forgetting 'the Order of Nature' when it is he himself who has overridden the order of nature in his eagerness to preserve his 'highest ideals' is reflected in the movement of the short story itself, as the reader is well aware that *all* storks must migrate in order to survive: it is not a male phenomenon. Thus our knowledge of what birds actually do is called upon here to make the point of what humans ought to do and we are aware that this is the case from the start. The birds in this short story serve entirely human purposes.

Likewise, in the poem 'Females' (OW p. 169), Gilman makes use of simple and direct comparison between human and animal worlds to hammer home the point that women are as much a part of the human race as men and ought therefore to be treated as being as capable and as strong as men. We know this is the point of the poem, not only because of what we know of Gilman's convictions on this matter, but also because the use of animals in this text direct us to this reading. The opening stanza is memorably clear in its direct assertion:

> The female fox she is a fox;
> The female whale a whale;
> The female eagle holds her place
> As representative of race
> As truly as the male. (OW p. 169)

There can be no doubt of the point being made here and sustained through the next three stanzas. The fact that there is a specific term for a female fox is ignored here, since regardless of terminology we accept that a vixen is 'representative of race/ As truly as the male'. The same is true of whale and eagle, where the argument is made all the more forcibly because everyday speech does not even contain a word for female whale or eagle; we think of these beasts in terms of species first and only secondly in terms of sex. The case alters rather when we shift our attention to humans, but, oddly, here the poem's force slackens also. The expectation is that women are able to do whatever men do, the offered analogy being the 'fleet-foot mare' of the third verse who, 'upon the course / Doth hold her own with the flying horse / Yea, and she beateth him'. There is even a possibility for arguing that the female of the species is more capable than the male, since the examples of hen and cow suggest that not only does she fend for herself with equal success as the male, but provides for the young as well; something neither cock nor bull does. Yet, with all these animal examples offering strong support for the refutation of the term 'parasite' for women, the poem itself wavers uneasily. The woman denies that she is a parasite since she earns her living as wife and mother, work which is as valuable as the planting, building and buying implicitly attributed to men. This is a different argument from that offered by the rest of the text, in which the females rear young in addition to doing what the males do, not instead of it. It seems the narrative voice of the poem is criticizing women on these grounds, and is then sharply taken to task and put right in the stanza given to the woman. When the original voice returns, though, the certainty of argument disappears. If we accept that the 'human race holds highest place / In all the world so wide', then it could be argued that the woman is right in declaring that she pulls her weight by doing her job and need not also do man's. Yet in spite of this, the textual voice refers to '*inferior* women' (my emphasis) who 'wive / And raise their little ones alive, / And feed themselves beside'. Are we to understand that the term 'inferior' is being rendered highly ironic by the context? If so, such irony is at odds with the next stanza's view that 'race is higher than the sex' and 'to be human is more great / Than even womanhood'. What began as a direct and inspiring assertion that females and males are to be regarded as equally valid, equally representative of species, is in danger of being lost by becoming embroiled in a complex argument about gender roles. Gilman retrieves her text and her original stance by returning wholly to the animal world in a repetition of the first stanza, which deflects the argument and reassures the audience. Once again we are safe and confident of the point being made. The animals here have not only served to define the argument, but also rescued it from the complications which arise as soon as a powerful and direct point is placed in a human context. By reasserting her animal subjects, Gilman has also reasserted her control of the text.

Gilman's use of animals is not always so direct. Focusing on the animals in 'When I Was a Witch' (1910) reveals an intriguing mis-match between the plot and the compulsion to obey rules of genre or caricature. The protagonist discovers her magic powers when feeling outrage at the treatment of horses and vehemently wishing retribution on those who use and abuse them: 'I wish... that every person who strikes or otherwise hurts a horse unnecessarily shall feel the pain intended—and the horse not feel it!' (R p. 22). On several occasions in the story she fulminates against the way animals are kept and takes steps to rectify matters. As well as humanitarian, reformist zeal, there is a powerful comic effect here, heightened in the case of the lap-dog she encounters, which she describes in terms that emphasize the abuses of overbreeding, abuses which she seeks to rectify by promptly wishing all unhappy dogs dead:

> A poor wretched, little artificial dog—alive, but only so by virtue of man's insolence—not a real creature that God made. And the dog had clothes on—and a bracelet! His fitted jacket had a pocket—and a pocket-handkerchief! He looked sick and unhappy.
>
> I meditated on his pitiful position, and that of all the other poor chained prisoners... 'I wish that all the unhappy dogs in cities would die at once!'
>
> I watched the sad-eyed little invalid across the car. He dropped his head and died. (R p. 25)

One can only hope that as it rolled its eyes the beast had time to register gratitude for its unexpected and unrequested release: a rather drastic solution to the problem of in-breeding and over-pampering. In each case the witch's disgust is directed at those who impose upon the animals, who maltreat horses and over-breed dogs, with the horror of the situation being highlighted by the fact that the animal in question is unable to control its circumstances and is forced out of its natural habits. Here again Gilman uses the animals in the text straightforwardly to prove a point. The focus is firmly on the way the animal is treated, whether in direct terms of abuse and starvation or the more hidden abuse of deliberately creating a breed which appeals to humans, but is far removed from any original notion of the species (in this case dog). Indeed, the dog in the car is placed almost entirely in the human sphere by being dressed in a jacket. More doll than dog, it travesties both canine and human beings and thereby also comments on our relations with animals as pets in a way which is easily comprehensible. The fleeting figure of the cat in this story is, however, more complex, as this animal is not restricted to the spheres of abused servant or over-pampered pet.

Every witch should have a cat, preferably a rather wild or malignant specimen, usually, of course, black. The power of this iconic beast is displayed in 'When I Was a Witch' by the fact that it is the cat who initiates the magical action. It elicits recognition and pity from the otherwise disgruntled potential witch. This pity is so passingly expressed as to be scarcely noticeable—'Poor thing, it had been scalded'—but is significant in being the first mention of the succession of acts of unthinking cruelty which provide the framework and impetus of this short story. The cat then moves from being heard at a distance to curling round the soon-to-be-witch's legs. Somewhere between half-noticing the cat as scalded and leaning over the parapet with unmitigated ill-will, the speaker has acquired magical powers. Her position is simultaneously assured and acknowledged by the cat's attention, as if in confirmation of her new status as a witch. Ironically, and with rather black humour, this recognition, which is tantamount to volunteering for the post of witch's cat and familiar, results not in a better life for the feline, but in prompt death. Inspired by being kept awake by caterwauling, the woman utters a rather more sweeping wish than that later employed for dogs, and heartily desires *all* urban cats 'comfortably dead'. The humour is preserved by the context and by the adjective (though it is unlikely that it is the cat's comfort that is being consulted here) which manage to prevent this incident being numbered among the acts of senseless cruelty, against which the protagonist fulminates throughout the tale.

The point here is that Gilman seems at first happy to use the established forms—where there's a witch, there's a cat—but then chokes off that particular avenue of thought, just as she had choked off the rich imaginative world of her 'inner fortress' in which she had been Princess, Prince and had inhabited a magical realm. Clearly Gilman is not writing a fairy or witch story; but equally the habit of obedience to rules was strong enough for her to include the necessary feline element. Then, however, and now in obedience to the implications of retaining the cat, Gilman removes it from the scene, thereby in effect removing the magical element. Although the speaker's wishes continue to come true, the excising of the cat removes the elusive suggestion of an external and therefore potentially uncontrollable source of this magical power, replacing it instead with the inherently weaker and more constrained (though perhaps politically more powerful) idea that the remaining wishes have the ability to come true only because they are fuelled by a spirit of revenge. Anger, here, replaces magic, which in turn hints that the social alterations and improvements posited in the tale are those of an active, strong-willed reformist, not those of a dreaming utopianist. The story thus slips sideways, away from the realms of fairy story where retribution may lie in wait for a witch, towards the less complex form of entertaining, reformist fable.

A conclusion to be drawn from this might be, not that stories about pigs do not interest, but that they carry the danger of interesting too much. As long as Gilman restricts her use of the animal kingdom to instances which rely on how humans regard them and the consequences that has for humanity, she is on safe ground. A case in point is her use of the milch cow in *Women and Economics* (1900), where she comments on the deliberate breeding of cows to produce milkers rather than roundly healthy cows and draws a direct comparison with the way women, like such cows, are encouraged to over-develop sex characteristics to the detriment of their general strength and the health of society as a whole. Another might be her poem 'A Brood Mare' (OW p. 161) in which she seizes upon the point that, where breeding is concerned, each sex is as important as the other, and so ridicules the way females have been overlooked even on stud farms. The horse-trader's claim that 'Mares do not need to have themselves / The points which they transmit' is rendered laughably hollow when he is finally forced to admit that the one colt the mare has produced died, despite his vaunted policy of mating her 'carefully / With horses fine and fit'. The short paragraph printed below the title of the poem in the 1899 edition is slightly ironic in tone as it makes the point of the poem itself explicit, while also hinting that what ought to have been a transparently obvious fact from the start has only the status of a 'growing conviction' in horse-breeding circles:

> It is a significant fact that the phenomenal improvement in horses during recent years is accompanied by the growing conviction that good points and a good record are as desirable in the dam as in the sire, if not more so.

Underlying this poem is Gilman's belief that women have a responsibility to select their partners with care and an eye to stock as well as character, and therefore a right to know all relevant facts about their potential spouse. This is the main burden of such stories as 'The Vintage' (1916) (SS pp. 104–11) or 'The Crux' (1910) (R pp. 116–22) in which Gilman is careful not to blame the women outright, presenting them as misled or uninformed. Nevertheless, a hint of opprobrium of the women as well as the men (though to a far lesser degree) hangs around these tales and is also fleetingly evident in the final verse of 'A Brood Mare':

> He looked a little dashed at this,
> And the poor mare hung her head.
> 'Fact is' said he, 'she's had but one,
> And that one—well, it's dead!' (OW p. 161)

The shame attributed to the mare as indicated by the hung head is a wash of human reaction over what has been simply an outline portrait of a brood mare. More than that, it suggests that the mare has something for which to be ashamed. Yet if we follow the invitation to attribute emotions and understanding of the previous argument to the mare, we must also absolve her of any guilt for producing a weakly colt. She, after all, has not been in a position to dictate her own physical health or well-being, so it seems a little hard to blame her for her own poor state and inability to produce strong foals. Such blame is suggested, however, by the mare's imputed consciousness of her own inability. If the stallions are all so carefully selected the fault must lie with her and, it appears, she must accept some portion of blame. This short line betrays an attitude which surfaces elsewhere in Gilman's writing, being something of a leitmotif in *Women and Economics* and also underpinning the moral of 'His Mother' (1914) (SS pp. 73–80) in which the mother of the seducer, Jack, admits her own responsibility for his character and sets about redressing some part of his wrongs. While realizing that the uninformed could not be held responsible for their upbringing, she yet felt that they could be expected to exercise their native intelligence and seek out information and strive to better themselves and their offspring. This may be an uneasy conclusion to reach, especially from such a simple poem, but 'A Brood Mare' is a text to be read both transparently as a comment on horse-breeding, and allegorically as a comment on how women are reared.

Clearly the use of animals in *Women and Economics* and 'A Brood Mare' are not instances of animals being regarded as characters, nor are they proto-ecofeminist protests; instead it is the way such animals are regarded and placed in the human system which is significant and the knock-on effects such usage has for humanity which is highlighted, as parallels are drawn between our treatment of animals and of each other, or contrasts are made between what the human world regards as obviously right and the behaviour observable in the 'natural' world.[3] Such use of animals as exempla is a hallmark of fables and parables, literary forms which seem to have suited both Gilman's didactic purposes and her humour. In such texts her control over the material seems absolute, as the form of the parable draws strict bounds around the texts, providing space for the freedom of caricature without raising expectations or possibilities of greater development.

Two texts are relevant here. 'The Lady Oyster' (1912) (SS pp. 210–12) is one of Gilman's funniest parables, where the joy of drawing ludicrous, but telling, comparisons between a well-provided-for wife and a variety of other female creatures allows for much fun and several sharp comments. If the successful achievement of the criteria which define a mother leads to true female fulfilment, then the Lady Oyster with her three million eggs is to be envied. This story is very much in the genre of animal parable as each species is allotted its generic trait—the mothers being given positive tags (which in retrospect become ironic), the more sceptical, but still female, creatures receiving wryer titles. Thus the Oyster is Happy, the Mud-Wasp Merry, the Sheep Satisfied, the Lady Lovely, whereas the Crab is Captious, the Bee Benevolent, the Skunk Skeptical and the Aunt Audacious. I suspect that the rather nice pun Aunt/Ant is not actually at work in the text, though it is strongly suggested, and, if perceived, allows for a move back down the ladder of species by having the human criticized by the insect, albeit one renowned for its strong social structure. Even if we resist the temptation of this possible pun, what we have here is the use of the animal world to illustrate the sharp difference between what we declare and what we know to be true. Out of the million oyster eggs created, perhaps one survives, the Mud-Wasp's careful preparations for the nourishment of its larvae are easily thwarted by a bird—this is the real world, of which our ideal of motherhood refuses to take account.

In similar vein 'Wedded Bliss' (1893) (OW p. 157) reveals the ludicrous nature of the romantic expectations associated with marriage. In this poem Gilman unites in matrimony those usually coupled in the relation of hunter and prey and then promptly separates them as each follows its own natural inclinations. An eagle marries a hen; it is a blissful union as the highly anthropomorphized eagle wishes to soar, but wants a wife who does not, while the hen wishes to sit, but likes to have a soaring spouse to admire. Likewise, lion marries sheep and salmon weds clam, in defiance of appetite, and thenceforth, we are assured, live in happiness, alone. With admirable skill, Gilman leaves us to notice that these are cross-species matings, doomed to failure, especially as the male of each couple is likely to feed, quite literally, on the female. Our knowledge of the natural world is thus subtly invoked in order for a point to be made through the combination of the poem's humour and our reaction. We know that such pairings are impossible in the real world and it is our knowledge of that reality which makes the poem's initial point and allows us to ponder the predatory aspects of marriage as an institution. Moreover, underpinning this use of impossible pairings is the cliché of 'opposites attract'. This combines with our habit of reading animals as types of people and so allows the poem to become a wry comment on romantic ideals as the females are left in sedentary admiration of their more active and assertive males. The fact that these females are as happy to continue to exist alone despite being married is one of the dryly under-emphasized aspects of a poem rich in laconic humour.

A slightly more whimsical use of the animal is evident in 'The Lion Path' (OW p. 12) in which the reader is presented with an epic world in which a path must be taken by some young hero across a lion-infested plain, via unmarked paths. These lions have the usual heritage of story-book lions and are assumed to be predatory and fierce, especially where humans are concerned. As such they are denizens of the fictional animal world rather than the real one. However, once the path has been struck, these same lions are revealed to be not the foes of myth and fable at all, but simple kittens spitting in the grass—if indeed they are there at all. This is clever: according to the stories lions are dangerous creatures and are also real (as opposed to dragons, say). Here we have such lions being created by the conviction of their presence as the text explicitly demands 'Who dares to go who sees / So perfectly the lions in the path?' We are not at this point allowed to be sceptical of their presence, which thus ensures that these half-perceived, but wholly believed-in lions are having the very effect that real lions are supposed to have in fiction. Yet, although they *are* real storybook lions, they are also not actually there. Instead there are kittens, or perhaps even these are merely figments of the collective imagination of the tradition, or the young hero's society. We know that we must read this poem allegorically, but the question is where does the allegory stop? Are the lions 'really' kittens, made so as a result of the hero's courage and the whole a moral on facing one's fears? If so it is the kittens who are real within the text, while the lions are simply figments of anxiety—overblown kittens. Or are the kittens just as much the result of collective imagination and tradition as the lions, in which case the poem becomes a text about the creative process, or indeed about the way we see the non-human world almost entirely in terms of how it affects us? Here, then, Gilman is using the rules of writing about animals in essentially human texts and also using the recognition that the representations found in literature are not true reflections of the creatures concerned, so much as true of the attitudes which imbue our associations with these beasts. Underpinning this poem are thus two real worlds: that of the animal kingdom as humans view and create it and that of the creative process. However, while Gilman may use these rules, she is not able to assert her desired understanding of the text to the exclusion of all other possible readings, as its very animal matter and the blurring of allegory with epic allow for interpretation beyond the bounds of simple moral lessons. We may choose to ignore the exhortation to moral courage and instead question the necessity of following the path at all, preferring to leave the kittens be and allowing them to be lions if they wish.

Another poem approaches this same double use of the animal world from the opposite angle. Happily, it, too, uses lions. The eponymous 'Little Lion' is probably not a lion at all. In a move which is so familiar as to be scarcely noticed we instantly recognize and perform the reading which regards the poem as pure parable and, while not declaring its precise referents, nevertheless invites a humanized interpretation. For ease the complete text follows.

THE LITTLE LION

It was a little lion lay —
In wait he lay—he lay in wait.
Came those who said, 'Pray come my way;
We joy to see a lion play,
    And laud his gait!'

The little lion mildly came—
In wait for prey—for prey in wait.
The people all adored his name,
And those who led him saw the same
With hearts elate.

The little lion grew that day,—
In glee he went—he went in glee.
Said he, 'I love to seek my prey,
But also love to see the way
My prey seek me!' (OW p. 114)

We recognize at once that the little lion is likely to be a young man who will be influential: we do not know for sure if that influence is benign or malign, nor if the people who lead the young lion in the second stanza are the same as those who rejoice in his play in the first. Nor is it clear if the lion is being led by one group of people in order to prey on another (those who 'adore' thus falling prey not only to the lion, but also to the machinations of those who 'led'). Unequivocally a poem about power, this apparently simple text is also about the equivocations surrounding power, equivocations that arc reflected in the very structure as we are left shifting uneasily between reading the term 'young lion' purely as metaphor and retaining in our minds the image of a wild beast being led by people who believe themselves masters of it, but could easily become its prey.

Finally, a poem most fully in the tradition of the animal fable which most nearly approaches the very kind of story so breezily dismissed in Gilman's elaboration of The One Word Game. This poem is 'The Fox Who Had Lost His Tail' (OW p. 104). Making use of the habits of parable, Gilman begins openly with the fact of the absent tail, providing no explanation for its loss. She deals entirely with foxes; no other animal intrudes, though human attitudes pervade. Clearly this is a text inviting interpretation, even exegesis, and one useful for all sorts of moments when one might feel inclined to indulge in a little moralizing. The 'tail' could represent many things in almost any given situation. Equally, the blackest scepticism about the tailless fox's recommendations is a transparently human reaction, which is instantly recognized, if not lauded or condoned. Yet when the fable is read as a reformist parable possible confusions arise, which themselves raise interesting points about the ungovernable quality of satire, even in its mildest, most reformist forms. A first reaction may be to castigate the general pack of foxes who refuse to believe that taillessness could be a preferable state. They are set in their ways, bigoted and incapable of believing that any recommendation for change could be made in a spirit of genuine benevolence and philanthropy (or more properly philalopy).

As such they epitomize the worst of automatic conservatism, whose reactionary tendencies need not arise from obvious narrow-mindedness or bigotry, but simply from over-caution and wariness, combined with a desire to avoid being conned or caught out. This reading brings us firmly into line behind the tailless fox and his sole advocate, encouraging us to recognize that radical change may look more unnatural and terrible than it actually is and that any long-term benefit will outlive the short-term pain. On the other hand we can understand their caution: there is something deliberately perverse about encouraging an animal, who is naturally possessed of a tail fine enough to merit the special term 'brush', to cut it off. Losing a tail and making the best of it might be one thing, deliberately lopping it off another. The perversity of such an action is particularly marked in the case of a fox, since the word 'fox' probably means 'the tailed one'. To remove that tail is thus literally to remove the animal's defining feature (though this very concept of definition is, of course, a human perception). How, then, are we to read this parable? Whom do we criticize? In the best tradition of the genre, the answers are not nearly as clear as they at first appear, and the fable is thus shown to be flexible and appropriate, if not in fact uncontrollable. Again, the text is here given in full:

THE FOX WHO HAD LOST ITS TAIL

The fox who had lost his tail found out
That now he could faster go;
He had less to cover when hid for prey,
He had less to carry on hunting day,
He had less to guard when he stood at bay;
He was really better so!

Now he was a fine altruistical fox
With the good of his race at heart,
So he ran to his people with tailless speed,
To tell of the change they all must need,
And recommend as a righteous deed
That they and their tails should part!

Plain was the gain as plain could be,
But his words did not avail;
For they all replied, 'We perceive your case;
You do not speak for the good of the race
But only to cover your own disgrace,
Because you have lost your tail!'

Then another fox, of a liberal mind,
With a tail of splendid size,
Became convinced that the tailless state
Was better for all of them soon or late
Said he, 'I will let my own tail wait,
And so I can open their eyes.'

Plain was the gain as plain could be,
But his words did not avail,
For they all made answer, 'My Plausible friend,
You talk wisely and well, but you talk to no end.
We know you're dishonest and only pretend,
For you have not lost your tail!' (OW p. 104)

Two things are of interest here—one is the way the poem uses the accepted character attributed to foxes. They are expected to be sly creatures who seek to trick other animals and so ought to be regarded with suspicion; here even the foxes regard another fox as a 'Plausible friend'. It is a nice touch. Second, the way the use of the animal is in conflict with the apparent point of the fable. One assumes the moral is two-fold:

a) that people are highly suspicious of suggestions for change, and will not act on them, however beneficial they are shown to be, and therefore lose the proffered benefit; and
b) that, recognizing this, one ought to become more open and amenable to such suggestions and not automatically suspect the intentions of those advocating change.

These two main conclusions are the result of reading the text with an eye to interpretation, which seeks to translate the story into human terms. However, if the foxes of the tale are allowed to remain as actual foxes, a third observation begins to overshadow these two apparently self-evident readings. No real fox would voluntarily remove its tail, nor would accidental loss *in fact* benefit a fox inhabiting the real world, though doubtless a fox which survived losing its brush would be able to fend for itself, especially in a semi-urban environment. So, if the foxes are allowed to become real in our minds as animals rather than metaphors, we can in fact draw the conclusion that it is not *in fact* beneficial to alter ourselves or our ways in the light of another's example or suggestion. Moreover, we may become suspicious not only of the first fox and even of the second, with his 'liberal mind', but of the tone of the poem itself. The repeated assertion that 'plain was the gain as plain could be' acts as a refrain and as such ought to convince, but once suspicion enters the very simplicity which makes it so effective as a refrain leaves it open to a sardonic tone. What may become plain is not the advantages of being tailless, but the folly of trying to proselytize the tailless state and the dubiousness of the proclaimed advantages. This is emphatically *not* the conclusion Gilman would wish us to draw, but it is a viable one precisely because of the operation of the animal within it. True to the rules of animal parable, Gilman has not curbed this tale/tail and the result is a better poem (to my mind) and inevitably a less limited one.

Here, then, in the independence of the text from even the most explicit authorial intent and its openness to several interpretations, may lie the answer to why 'once there was a pig' would not interest Gilman. It is because, once removed from the confines of naturalistic, realist writing, or even from those of overt reformist zeal, a story which begins thus could go in unexpected directions, following a scarcely controlled pig who, in becoming the focus of attention, may, in fact, interest too much.

Notes

1 Examples from early life include openly defying a rule of silence 'to see what would happen' (L p. 19) and proving a text book wrong by getting the right solution on her own to a long division sum and then seeing the teacher having to test the answer given in the book, thereby proving Gilman right (L p. 19). In each case she first challenges one rule and then puts another in its place. The first gives rise to the conclusion 'that things debarred may sometimes be done—in safety', the second 'science, law, was more to be trusted than authority'. These apparent acts of defiance thus become opportunities for reinstating the rule of law. It is the rules which need adjusting, not the habit of obedience. It is a pattern reflected in her fiction, and is indeed the underlying belief of *Herland*.

2 Ann J. Lane, *To 'Herland' and Beyond: The Life and Work of Charlotte Perkins Gilman* (New York: Meridian, 1991), p. 53.

3 Although Gilman took the management of the environment into account in her reformist ideas, as *Herland* witnesses, she was unwaveringly sure that humans were the superior species and that it was not only ethical, but also desirable, to order the natural environment and make use of other species in the ways which would produce the best results for humankind. It was the notion of 'best' that commanded her attention, as it did not mean breeding for weakness and short-term benefit, but with an eye to overall fitness and strength.

Spinster of Dreams, Weaver of Realities

ANNE CRANNY-FRANCIS

Charlotte Perkins Gilman remains one of the foremost Western feminist theorists and writers. She offered, and still offers, readers new ways of thinking about their society which deconstruct conservative views about femininity and masculinity, and about the nature of the work practices which defined Western socioeconomics in the early twentieth century. She also theorized the relationship between sex-role stereotyping and work, in the process reconstructing some of the fundamental concepts by which we think about our world. As a writer Gilman was acutely aware of the role played by texts in the constitution of the individual subject, and of society. Conservative texts worked to (re)produce a masculinist, capitalist society, by positioning readers to accept without question the validity of the causal relationships which define the capitalist 'Patriarchate'. In her writing Gilman utilizes the resources of the many different genres in which she writes to disrupt this conservative textual practice, and to (re)position readers as social critics.

I first worked on Gilman's novel *Herland* as part of a study of feminist writing, and I was intrigued by the way in which she reworked the conventions of the utopian romance to produce a feminist text.[1] For example, Gilman uses a male narrator in *Herland* which, on the one hand, was a conservative choice positioning readers to accept the authority of her text, but on the other hand, as she repeatedly deconstructs the objectivity and rationality of that voice, becomes a critique of assumptions of masculine authority. Science fiction writer, Alice Sheldon, writing as James Tiptree Jr, almost always uses a male narrator in her work, with the same result. Not only do these writers disrupt or denaturalize the authoritative male voice as a fictional convention and discursive reality, but they also deconstruct the androcentricity (to use Gilman's term) which assumes that authority in the first place. So a textual strategy used by Gilman which is sometimes disturbing for contemporary feminist readers can be seen to be a useful political/discursive practice, particularly when situated in its own space/time.

This exemplifies Gilman's textual practice which I explore further in this chapter, along with a consideration of her ideas and arguments about feminism and about socialism. To do this I have focused on one of the major repositories of Gilman's writing, her journal *The Forerunner. The Forerunner* was originally published by Gilman as a monthly journal, beginning in November 1909 and concluding in December 1916. All of the material was written by Gilman herself, even the advertisements which appeared in the first three issues. In the journal Gilman uses a wide variety of genres: poetry, short articles, serial articles, serial novels, short stories, commentary, review, even the sermon. Separately and together they constitute a compendium of Gilman's views on a range of issues, all of them fundamentally related to the nature of the individual and of society. They also demonstrate Gilman's textual practice: the way she uses familiar genres to construct a feminist polemic. I am going to begin by identifying some of the ideas which characterize Gilman's theoretical position, and then look closely at the first issue, which sets the stage for much of the writing which follows, to see how it works as an exercise in polemics.

Each volume of *The Forerunner*, except for Volume 2, features a serial article and a serial novel which runs for the entire volume (Volume 2 has two serial novels).

Volume	*Article*
1	'Our Androcentric Culture, or The Man-Made World'
3	'Our Brains and What Ails Them'
4	'Humanness'
5	'Social Ethics'
6	'The Dress of Women'
7	'Growth and Combat'

Each article details her reconceptualization of her own society, either directly theoretically or through a grounded analysis of a specific cultural practice (as in 'The Dress of Women'). The stories which are their fictional counterparts contextualize these views in some kind of narrative:

Volume	*Story*
1	'What Diantha Did'
2	'The Crux' *and* 'Moving the Mountain'
3	'Mag-Majorie'
4	'Won Over'
5	'Benigna Machiavelli'
6	'Herland'
7	'With Her in Our-Land'

Many of them are stories of strong women, acting out lives of social responsibility and integrity, as are many of the short stories. They are inspiring in providing a strong female main character who overcomes various adversities in her life—a female romance or quest narrative. In a characteristic, subversive move Gilman uses the conventions of the romance to reinforce the politics of her story. For example, in a number of these stories an unconventional woman—such as a woman who prefers a career to domesticity, or a woman who has lived and loved out of wedlock—maintains her integrity *and also* achieves a loving relationship with a partner (usually a man) who respects her. In a more conventional text such a woman would only achieve integrity at the expense of any kind of intimacy with a man. While some critics might suggest that it is more consistent, theoretically at least, for the female hero not to get a man, in terms of the genre Gilman is using, such a conclusion spells defeat: it says, bad women (that is, strong, decisive, independent) don't find love. Gilman's conclusion, her happy ending, confounds this view. In this way she presents not only a new kind of hero, but also a metatextual speculation on the more conventional use of the romance narrative to reinforce conservative values. I shall return to this aspect of Gilman's work when I look in detail at an issue of the journal. I want to return now to the articles, particularly those published in the early issues of the journal, which spell out Gilman's feminism and socialism.

The serial article in Volume 1, 'Our Androcentric Culture', is one of the clearest statements of Gilman's theoretical positioning. Gilman's analysis begins with an examination of the dualisms, male/female, and masculine/feminine. In a familiar move she begins with a kind of scientific (or scientistic) observation; that when we talk about other species—cows, sheep, goats—we don't specify their characteristics or behaviour according to whether they are male or female. Instead we say: goats do this... sheep are... But when we talk about masculinity and femininity, we tend to generalize across species: so that male humans/sheep/goats/swans are constructed as competitive and aggressive, while female humans/sheep/goats/swans are seen as nurturing and receptive. The problem with our constitution of human subjects, for Gilman, is that we have fetishized the male and female, and lost sight of the human.

This notion of a common 'humanity' is a cornerstone of Gilman's work. It features throughout her writing and is expanded further not only in this essay, but in others such as 'Humanness' (Volume 4) and 'The Humanity of Women' (Volume 1, issue iii [January 1910]). Effectively, what Gilman does is use this concept to disrupt the male/female duality, introducing the third term 'human'. The problem for women, she argues, is that they have been excluded from 'humanity' and defined solely in terms of their sex:

> Women we have sharply delimited. Women were a sex; 'the sex', according to chivalrous toasts; they were set apart for special services peculiar to femininity. As one English scientist put it, in 1888, 'Women are not only not the race—they are not even half the race, but a sub-species told off for reproduction only'. (Volume 1, issue i, p. 22)[2]

The misogyny of this view is traced by Gilman in the use of terms such as 'effeminate' as pejorative, in the notion that 'emasculate' is a term of reproach, and that a masculine-coded term such as 'virile' (derived from 'vir' meaning man) is opposed not to an equally powerful feminine term, but to 'puerile' which refers to children. Furthermore, she notes that women are customarily constructed in relation to men (as X's wife, Y's sister), but rarely does the reverse happen, and that one of the greatest ways of praising a woman's intelligence is to say that she has 'a masculine mind' (Volume 1, issue i, p. 23). This encoding of sexist and misogynist attitudes in language was again raised as a major issue in the Women's Movement of the 1960s and 1970s, with the work of writers such as Germaine Greer and later Deborah Cameron, Dale Spender, Cate Poynton.[3] Gilman's sensitivity to the way in which language constructs attitudes is part of the increasing awareness of the role of textuality—of discourse—in constructing reality, which characterized the early twentieth century and was later theorized by linguists, literary critics, philosophers and others. Contemporary feminist linguists and literary critics continue this investigation of the gendered encoding of language and texts.

Contemporary feminist theorists and writers also explore the notion that women are identified as a 'sex' rather than as 'human'. Gilman makes this point again in *Herland*:

> When we say *men, man, manly, manhood,* and all the other masculine derivatives, we have in the background of our minds a huge vague crowded picture of the world and all its activities...
>
> And when we say *women,* we think *female*—the sex. (H p. 137)

Joanna Russ makes the same point in *The Female Man*:

> Men succeed. Women get married.
> Men fail. Women get married.
> Men enter monasteries. Women get married.
> Men start wars. Women get married.
> Men stop them. Women get married.
> Dull, dull...[4]

The notion contained in the title to 'Our Androcentric Culture', that contemporary (Western) culture is man-made or androcentric, is also fundamental to her feminism. Gilman writes very explicitly about the elision of the feminine from social practice, again in ways that are reminiscent of contemporary feminist writing. For example, she writes that: 'We have taken it for granted, since the dawn of civilization, that "mankind" meant men-kind, and the world was theirs' (Volume 1, issue i, p. 22). Furthermore, she says, we are unlikely to hear anything different since 'history, such as it was, was made and written by men' (Volume 1, issue i, p. 22). Gilman reinforces this in her article on 'The Humanness of Women', published two issues later where she notes: 'human history so far is the history of a wholly masculine world... Theirs is the credit—and the shame—of the world behind us, the world around us...' (Volume 1, issue iii, p. 12). And Gilman relates to this her earlier point about the characterization of women as a sex, by noting that one result of this androcentricity is that the libraries are full of books by men *about* women ('volumes of... excuse and explanation... of abuse and condemnation'; Volume 1, issue i, p. 22) but none about men. Masculinity has been equated with humanity, against which women are measured and found lacking. This elision of the socially dominant (in this case, the masculine) is a common feature of many power relations. Other examples might include the elision of the specificity of the middle class in discussions of class; the elision of whiteness in discussions of race, or of Anglo in discussions of ethnicity in English-speaking societies. Instead middle class, white and Anglo are constituted as neutral or transparent and so become the invisible norm against which all other positions are measured:

> To the man, the whole world was his world; his because he was male; and the whole world of woman was the home; because she was female. She had her prescribed sphere, strictly limited to her feminine occupations and interests; he had all the rest of life; and not only so, but, having it, insisted on calling it male. (Volume 1, issue i, p. 23)

Among the results of this strategy, Gilman cites the denigration of activist women as 'unfeminine' (for daring to move out of their proper [domestic] sphere), and the undesirable masculinization of the public sphere. Gilman argues, in fact, that this construction of a wholly masculine public sphere is injurious to all, not only women. It produces 'a masculine culture in excess' which she later argues produces exaggerated notions of the 'masculine' and the 'feminine'. It also prevents women from participating in industry and in public affairs, which impoverishes the public sphere: 'This may be seen in the slow and painful development of industry and science [in her view, the domain of women] as compared to the easy dominance of warfare throughout history until our own times' (Volume 1, issue iii, p. 26). And it maintains women in a state of comparative ignorance which irreparably damages the private sphere, which is the training ground for citizens. It might be noted here that Gilman has no concept of tactical use or action which might have enabled a more complex understanding of women's positioning.

Gilman's interest in the family cannot be undervalued. It provides the grounding for her triad of male/female/human, since it is in the process of reproduction and child-raising that Gilman sees the need for sex-specific characteristics. Yet this family is not the limiting, neurosis-inducing nuclear family which is predicated on the public/private dualism she elsewhere deconstructs. Rather it is a strategic association of woman, man and child which is characterized by care and nurture, and also by an awareness of social responsibility. The graphic which features on the cover of Volume 1 of *The Forerunner* expresses the centrality of this concept in her work (see p. 168).

As I noted earlier, androcentrism is seen as having a number of disturbing consequences, some of which relate to the family as a unit, others to the stereotyping of masculinity and femininity. All of chapter 2 and much of chapter 3 of 'Our Androcentric Culture' deal with the kinds of femininity and masculinity demanded—which is to say, produced—by what she calls the Patriarchate. For example, she says in chapter 3 that 'what man calls beauty in woman is not human beauty at all, but gross overdevelopment of certain points which appeal to him as a male' (Volume 1, issue iii, p. 25). Gilman identifies some of these features as 'ultra littleness and ultra femaleness' (Volume 1, issue ii, p. 20), though she notes that this differs from culture to culture. Inevitably one is reminded of Marge Piercy's dystopian creation of Gildina in *Woman on the Edge of Time* (1979).

And just as Piercy gives the reader an equally appalling vision of the dystopian male (he's a partly cybernetic killer), to make the point that men too are affected—and deformed—by patriarchal expectations, so Gilman many years before had noted that 'the male idea of what is good looking is accentuated beyond reason' (Volume 1, issue iii, p. 26). One feature Gilman identifies is the projecting or prognathous jaw. Nevertheless, it is women who carry the major burden of these demands, delimited and confined as they are to roles which constitute them as incapable of autonomous existence.

Gilman argues that in the family androcentricity has a devastating effect:

> What man has done to the family, speaking broadly, is to change it from an institution for the best service of the child to one modified to his own service, the vehicle of his comfort, power and pride. (Volume 1, issue ii, p. 19)

The disastrous effect of this petty tyranny is not confined to the home but spreads out into the whole of society. In Gilman's philosophy, there can be no such thing as a tyrannical family and a democratic society, a despot at home and a democrat at work—a view she argues explicitly in her article 'Private Morality and Public Immorality' (Volume 1, issue iii, pp. 9–11). As the basis or grounding of her deconstructive triad, the family and family life are the key to social progress and the fullest possible development of 'humanity'. Early in her study of androcentric culture Gilman wrote that, 'Humanity... is not a thing made at once and unchangeable, but a stage of development' (Volume 1, issue i, p. 21), and she continued:

> Our humanness is seen to be not so much in what we are individually, as in our relations to one another; and even that individuality is but the result of our relations to one another. It is in what we do and how we do it, rather than in what we are. (Volume 1, issue i, p. 21)

In this sense, she predicts the negotiative model of individual subjectivity which underpins much contemporary feminist writing.

As the paradigm of social relations, the family is where the child learns how to behave; how to treat others, men and women; how to think about her or himself. For Gilman, then, the family is not a marginalized domestic space, of lesser importance than the greater public sphere, but rather the model for and producer of that public sphere. The family and the home have more than a personal or private significance in her writing; they are social constructions. In a sense, what Gilman has done in her writing about the family is to construct another triad—public/private/society—with society assuming the same importance as humanity in her model of subjectivity. She socializes the private, and privatizes the social: for her, 'the personal is political'.

In this light it is interesting to consider her view on desire, exemplified in her article, 'A Small God and a Large Goddess' (Volume 1, issue i, pp. 1–4). The small god Gilman writes about here is Cupid; the large goddess, Motherhood. For Gilman, Cupid symbolizes desire only, but love is a grander passion which encompasses all of society. Of mothering as a practice, she writes:

> Here is power and passion. Not the irritable, transient impulse, however mighty, but the staying power, the passion that endures, the spirit which masters weakness, slays selfishness, holds its ministrant to a life-long task. (Volume 1, issue i, p. 4)

If desire is the 'direct impulse of personal passion' (as she puts it), then love is the expression of personal passion which is also social. This theorization of the family and of the nature of love is fundamental to not only

Volume 1. No. 1. NOVEMBER 1909

THE FORERUNNER

BY

Charlotte Perkins Gilman.

CONTENTS

1.00 A YEAR THE CHARLTON COMPANY 67 WALL ST. NEW YORK .10 A COPY

Gilman's revaluation of femininity and masculinity, but also her socialism.

Gilman was one of the few writers at this time who combined socialism and feminism in a consistent and integrated way. She was able to do so because her theoretical framework, based on this notion of the family, of caring and of humanity, encompassed every aspect of social life. For Gilman, socialism was the social realization of humanity: the social practice of the care and nurture of family life. Earlier I mentioned her article, 'Private Morality and Public Immorality' (Volume 1, issue iii, pp. 9–11). In that article Gilman raises the issue of social morality. She writes: 'The racial mind, long accustomed to attach moral values to personal acts only, cannot, without definite effort, learn to attach them to collective acts' (Volume 1, issue iii, p.9). Because of this, terrible cruelty has been committed on the poor through bad housing, unsafe work practices, neglect of their needs, and since no one person can be held to blame, there is perceived to be no blame and no evil. The evil is social, systemic, but there is no recognition of systemic evil. Gilman concludes:

> From babyhood we should be taught that we are here dependent on one another, beautifully specialized that we may serve one another; owing to the State, our great centralised body, the whole service of our lives... our personal sin—the one sin against humanity is to let that miserable puny outgrown Ego—our exaggerated sense of personality—divert us from that service. (Volume 1, issue iii, p. 11)

Again it is the family in Gilman's view which paradigmatically constructs the society in which we live. If we learn to live interdependently in the family, with care and nurture, according to our special abilities and needs (that is, respecting our differences), then that same morality will operate in the public sphere.

As I noted earlier, Gilman's view of the individual subject predicts contemporary feminist notions of a negotiated materialist subjectivity. Gilman is forthright about the relationship between individual and social, refuting their dichotomization in conservative arguments. For example, in discussing her New Year Resolutions for 1910 she notes that: 'While we, socially, behave as badly as we do, we individually can accomplish little' (Volume 1, issue iii, p. 1). And to those who claim that perfecting the individual will create a perfect society, she says: 'You can amass any number of perfect parts of a mechanism—or organism—but if they do not *work together right* the thing is no good' (Volume 1, issue iii, p. 1). Nevertheless, this was a very major source of anxiety at the time; that socialism was anti-individualist and so would result in a society of clones. Gilman confronts many of these anxieties in an article titled, 'Why We Honestly Fear Socialism' (Volume 1, issue ii, pp. 7–10).

In this article she responds to the claims that an anti-individualist philosophy is necessarily anti-individual, by arguing that 'Our machine-like educational system, long hours of labor, specialized monotony of mill work, and "the iron law of wages" do tend to reduce us to a dead level. Socialism does not'. (Volume 1, issue ii, p. 8) She also responds to a number of familiar fears: that socialism will do away with private property; that everyone will be paid the same; that there will be no competition; that socialists are immoral; that they are all atheists; and that no one would work in a socialist society. On the subject of work, Gilman echoes the writings of many other socialists, such as William Morris, when she claims that people work because they enjoy it:

> The lazy old orientals called it a curse! Work, a curse! Work; which is *the essential* process of human life; man's natural function and means of growth!
>
> We have despised it because women did it. Glory to the women—without them we should have had no industry. We have despised it because slaves did it. Glory to the slaves! (Volume 1, issue ii, p. 9)

Apart from demonstrating Gilman's reproduction of racist attitudes, this statement affirms a view of work as essential and vital to human development—and it also illustrates the conjunction of feminism and socialism in Gilman's work.

This conjunction is obvious, of course, when her views of the family are considered. After all, one of her major stated reasons for arguing the emancipation of women is that they may then be better, more informed and intelligent mothers, who will produce more informed and intelligent citizens. Yet this argument may also be largely strategic: a way of arguing for women's rights which works with, rather than against, popular prejudice about the role of women. Her argument about work approaches the positioning of women from a different perspective, an economic one. And it aligns women, again strategically, with others whose work is appropriated without reward: slaves. The prejudice against work, Gilman argues, is a result of misogynistic and exploitative attitudes, not an intelligent evaluation of work as a practice. In her article on 'The Humanness of Women', Gilman aligns her feminist demands with her socialist vision:

> A socially conscious world, intelligent, courageous, earnest to improve itself, seeking to establish a custom of peaceful helpful interservice—such a world has no fear of woman, and no feeling that she is unfit to participate in its happy labors. The new social philosophy welcomes woman suffrage. (Volume 1, issue iii, p. 14)

Gilman consistently interrelates capitalism and the oppression of women, referring to the men who support conservative values as 'Male-Individualists'. She writes often about the consequences of male desire, not so often on the nature of male fear. However, in recognizing the social positioning of women to be a complex of both impulses—fear and desire—Gilman arrives at the definition of the stereotype later formulated by Homi Bhabha in relation to racism.[5] And again this is where Gilman's use of the term 'human' is valuable, since it confronts the stereotype with the sameness on which it is founded, but with which it elides. It is in the recognition of humanity as the common ground for individual subjects that their difference—in Gilman's work, as male and female—can be recognized and respected.

That feminists and socialists must both work for the betterment of society, and not fight each other, is perhaps most clearly expressed in one of the poems which break up the prose of *The Forerunner*, 'The Socialist and the Suffragist':

Said the Socialist to the Suffragist:
'My cause is greater than yours!
    You only work for a Special Class,
    We for the gain of the General Mass,
    Which every good ensures!'

Said the Suffragist to the Socialist:
    'You underrate my Cause!
    While women remain a Subject Class,
    You never can move the General Mass,
    With your Economic Laws!'

Said the Socialist to the Suffragist:
    'You misinterpret facts!
    There is no room for doubt or schism
    In Economic Determinism—
    It governs all our acts!'

Said the Suffragist to the Socialist:
    'You men will always find
    That this old world will never move
    More swiftly in its ancient groove
    While women stay behind!'

'A lifted world lifts women up,'
    The Socialist explained.
    'You cannot lift the world at all
    While half of it is kept so small,'
    The Suffragist maintained.

The world awoke, and tartly spoke:
'Your work is all the same;
Work together or work apart,
Work, each of you, with all your heart—
Just get into the game!' (Volume 1, issue xii, p. 25)

Gilman's writing brings socialism and feminism together in the figure of an egalitarian family: post-patriarchal, post-capitalist, respectful of differences, and working together out of care to build a peaceful society. *The Forerunner* is part of this work, and I am now going to look briefly at the first issue of the journal, to see how it acts as part of this political programme/struggle.

As I noted at the beginning of this chapter, the contents of *The Forerunner* include a wide variety of genres: poetry, articles, short stories, sermons, serialized novels and articles, book reviews, commentary, and for some issues, advertisements and a 'Problem Page' all written by Gilman. I have also mentioned briefly some of the ways in which Gilman's writing subverts the conventions of the genres she uses: for example, the use of the romantic story to construct a feminist heroine who achieves true love, thereby confronting the moralistic convention which would have the feminist heroine righteous, but alone. The issues which concern me in this intertextual study of the journal are: Why did Gilman use such an array of genres, rather than publishing a series of pamphlets containing her views? How do the different genres interact to construct a reading position for her audience? And is the intertextual positioning more or less powerful than a simple, single genre address?

My first question might be answered in part by a study of the opening pages of the very first issue of the journal (see Fig. 1). The cover graphic shows the family which, as I have argued, grounds Gilman's theory and argument.[6] This graphic might be expected to appeal to a primarily feminine audience, given that the family was constructed at this time as the domain of the feminine. Yet it also features a man, where it might have been a 'mother and child' image. This might be taken as a rejection of any kind of essentialism, a move which would make the journal more widely accessible. Around this central graphic are balanced: above the graphic—the title and the author's name, the well-known speaker, writer and activist, Charlotte Perkins Gilman; below the graphic—a table of contents which announces a variety of genres, 'verse', articles, 'serial', commentary and review, problem page. In terms of the principles of layout described by Kress and van Leeuwen, the graphic is the balancing point of the composition, 'the space of the central message'.[7] So it establishes a relationship between Gilman's writing and the notion of family which is subsequently confirmed by an analysis of her work. And note that the graphic image arranges this family in a triadic pose around the representation of a globe, which is the balancing point of the graphic composition. So the central message of this illustration is not motherhood or fatherhood or family life, but the contribution of all three to the world in which they live and which they constitute—their own society. Again this is an effective representation of Gilman's argument. So the cover suggests that the journal is a set of writings in different genres, some fictional, some not, all focusing in some way on the family, and on all those involved in the family; and further that this is not a sentimental fetishization of the family, but a view of the family situated in its society. The cover might be expected, therefore, to appeal to a number of different audiences—readers of women's journals, as well as those interested in social and political issues.

On the first page, inside the cover, is a poem, 'Then This:', which explains the purpose of the journal:

THEN THIS:

The news-stands bloom with magazines,
    They flame, they blaze indeed;
So bright the cover-colors glow,
So clear the startling stories show,
So vivid their pictorial scenes,
    That he who runs may read.

Then This: It strives in prose and verse
    Thought, fancy, fact and fun,
To tell the things we ought to know,
To point the way we ought to go,
So audibly to bless and curse,
    That he who reads may run. (Volume 1, issue i)

Gilman's poem rejects the sensationalism of the popular press, aimed at the commuter or the person in a hurry. Instead she claims for her journal an amalgam of fact and fancy, argument and fun, which will accelerate the development of the reader. Interestingly, she also specifies a male reader, though this may have been an ironic or a careless acknowledgement of the convention which characterized the reader as male. But why use verse?

Verse of this kind—a kind of doggerel—was not uncommon in popular journals, including explicitly politicized publications such as socialist journals and papers attached to political organizations (such as Keir

Hardie's paper, *Labour Leader* in Britain). Its most obvious characteristic, as verse, is that it appeals not only to the intellect via argument or explanation, but that it uses its sensuous or affective potential to transform an intellectual appeal into an ethical or moral one. As a kind of preface to the journal it positions the reader to anticipate not only argument and exposition, but also moral and ethical appeals based on appeals to emotion. And it might be argued that this was how verse generally worked in these journals and papers. It was not an attempt to elevate the standard of the writing to some kind of canonical form, but rather a way of foregrounding, and perhaps authorizing, the interpersonal or affective component of the social critique presented in the journal.

In the first issue of *The Forerunner* this poem is followed by the article 'A Small God and a Large Goddess', which begins on the facing page, immediately under the publication details and an epigram:

> Said the New Minister: 'I shall not give you a text this morning. If you listen closely, you will discover what the sermon is about by what I say.' (Volume 1, issue i, p. 1)

This epigram seems to acknowledge the active nature of the reader-text relation assumed by Gilman's practice: the meaning cannot be summarized in an accompanying text, but is constructed in the process of listening—or, in the case of *The Forerunner*, in the reading.

'A Small God and a Large Goddess' was referred to earlier for its analysis of Cupid. In it Gilman reconstructs desire as the minor prelude to a grander passion which sustains both the individual and society. As part of her argument, she describes the social consequences of the worship of Cupid, or individual desire; in the process revealing that desire is a social, not just individual category—though individualist ideologies would confine it to the individual subject.

In other words, Gilman deconstructs the concept of desire and its practice in the constitution of intimate heterosexual relationships and gendered identities. Apart from this explicitly textual reading, however, it is useful to contextualize the article in relation to the kinds of texts which often appeared in the women's magazines which are one obvious generic context for *The Forerunner*. These magazines were full of stories about relationships, mostly fetishizing the power of desire. Her opening article can also be read, then, as a metatextual comment on these journals. What this 'sermon' is about, then, may not only be the difference between desire and love, but also the fetishization of desire in writing and the social consequences of that for the positioning of readers—particularly women readers.

This article is followed by another short poem, 'Arrears', which deals with the debt owed to the common worker for the standard of living enjoyed by the many. The poem argues that rather than thanking God for their blessings, people should acknowledge this labour and direct their gratitude where it might do some good: 'we can now begin to pay / The starved and stunted heir' (Volume 1, issue i, p. 4). The appeal to emotion is evident throughout, with the worker constructed as a slave and the (implicitly, middle-class) reader held responsible for his pain and that of his children. Again, Gilman gives individual emotion a social dimension, uniting it with its source to constitute an ethical rather than solipsistic exercise; she doesn't focus on emotion for its own sake, but for the motivation it might provide to redress a social evil. The meaning is in the reading and that meaning is not only in the lesson about the appropriation of labour, but also in its positioning of the reader as recipient of the fruits of others' labour.

This poem is followed by the short story 'Three Thanksgivings' ,which describes the successful attempt of an elderly woman to pay off her mortgage and remain in her own home, rather than move in with either of her children or be forced to marry against her wishes. She earns the mortgage money by opening up part of her home as a club for women. The main character of this story might have operated as a point of identification for her readers. On the one hand, her story is a fairly conservative version of 'self-help' (even to its elision of the viewpoint of the woman's 'black servant')'; on the other hand, it illustrates the capacity of women to work in a 'public', financial capacity and their ability to work together and to enjoy being together—all of which were precluded by the stereotypical feminine.

Gilman's first narrative, then, is a kind of anti-romance. She reworks the conventions of narrative to produce a female hero who saves herself from the prince, and whose self-discovery (an implicit feature of most narratives) is of independence and self-reliance. Again this story cannot fail to have a metatextual function, implicitly commenting on the more usual romance narratives, which assume an emotionally (privately) manipulative, but publicly helpless and dependent femininity. One of the hall-marks of narrative is that it elides its causality, leaving the reader to assume that its description of events is a natural or obvious one. Politicized writers from a number of positions have found this structure useful in that it naturalizes a patently 'unnatural' point of view; patently unnatural, because it contradicts the natural/ized conservative position. In so doing it prompts readers to think about not only the ideas or values assumed in the story, but also the discursive function of a text as it produces or constructs a particular society through its positioning of the reader.

This same metatextual practice is evident in the serial novel of Volume

1, 'What Diantha Did', chapter 1 of which appears in this issue. Between the two stories Gilman places a satirical poem, 'How Doth the Hat'—a deconstructive analysis of the hat as fashion accessory—and a meditation, 'Introducing the World, The Flesh, and the Devil'. The point of the meditation is that they (the World, The Flesh, and the Devil) are all 'Just Us'; Gilman uses a religious genre to state her materialism. Her use of that genre is ironic, given the subject-matter, but further it taps into the means by which opinion, attitudes and values are constituted. Gilman's ironic use of this genre reveals its basis in the appeal to fear and/or desire, the emotional basis of ideology.

Following 'What Diantha Did' and preceding the first instalment of the serial article 'Our Androcentric Culture', Gilman again places two small texts which appeal to the reader emotively, in each case via a familiar, everyday concept or practice. The first is a meditation on the concept, 'Where the Heart Is', and the second a short poem about 'Thanksgiving', arguing that, instead of giving God thanks one day each year for our blessings, we should daily thank both God and the workers whose labour provides our living conditions. 'Thanksgiving' is not unlike 'Arrears', the earlier poem, in that it positions the (again implicitly, middle-class) reader as exploiter—and it unites this uncomfortable positioning with a reference to a shared cultural practice, Thanksgiving. 'Where the Heart Is', by contrast, is reminiscent of Olive Schreiner's writing, making a short, exotic narrative the site for meditation on an everyday idea. The exoticism of her stories (one is about a lost child from an ancient culture adopted by English travellers, who inherits their fortune; the other about space travellers returning to Earth) works, like any of the non-realist genres, to free the reader, metaphorically or imaginatively, from everyday constraints and permit the exploration of new ideas, new concepts, new ideologies. Gilman's stories seldom explicitly present a future vision; instead they re-evaluate the everyday and, perhaps most importantly, reveal its grounding in a particular kind of imaginary.

Like William Morris in the 1890s, and like the feminist science fiction and utopian fiction writers of the 1960s and 1970s, and the feminist critics of technology today, Gilman appreciates the power of the imaginary in the constitution of ideologies of all kinds, and on the discursive practices which characterize society at a particular time and place. While her major articles and stories argue explicitly and metatextually for a new kind of society—egalitarian, caring, just—these texts and the smaller texts among which they are embedded challenge the everyday imaginary, the commonsense of contemporary society and the texts which naturalize it. The middle verse of Gilman's final poem of the first issue, 'Thanksong', might serve as a gloss on her writing practice:

Thankful are we for light
    And the joy of seeing.
Stir of emotion strong,
    And the peace of being. (Volume 1, issue i, p. 27)

The connection between seeing/understanding, emotion, and being runs as a thread through the tapestry Gilman weaves. I don't really want to reconstruct her here as the Lady of Shalott, but in a sense her work is a de- and re-construction of the Lady's practice.

The Lady of Shalott could only weave what she saw already in a mirror, the surface/configuration of another's imaginary. When she looked directly at life, the ideologies which sustained her and which constituted her discursive practice, started to unravel. It drove her mad, because she did not have anything to put in the place of her mediatory mirror. So she ended as a victim to the ideologies which sustained her world, primarily the romance world of Camelot. Gilman looks directly at life, and while there are discourses she does not see, she does have sufficient grasp of her own positioning to deconstruct the mirror of the conservative imaginary. In its place she begins to construct another imaginary—partly mirror-like, partly transparent—in which we can find the traces of conservative practice (attitudes to race, for example), but we also find a materialist understanding of contemporary social practice along with a metatextual grasp of contemporary discursive practice.

Gilman's achievement in her public writing was a formulation of the relationship between discourse—as both textually constituted and materially embodied—and the production or negotiation of subjectivity. So perhaps it is not surprising that her final work should be an analysis of religion, one of the great institutional discourses. And it may be that this study, *His Religion and Hers* serves as Gilman's formal theorization of discursive practice.

Notes

1 Anne Cranny-Francis, *Feminist Fiction: Feminist Revisions of Generic Fiction* (Cambridge: Polity Press; New York: St Martin's Press, 1990).

2 The edition used is *The Forerunner*, intro. Madeline B. Stern (New York: Greenwood Reprint, 1968).

3 See Deborah Cameron, *Feminism and Linguistic Theory* (London: Macmillan, 1985); Cate Poynton, *Language and Gender: Making the Difference* (Geelong, Victoria: Deakin University Press, 1985); Dale Spender, *The Writing or the Sex? or Why you Don't have to Read Women's Writing to Know it's No Good* (New York: Pergamon, 1989).

4 Joanna Russ, *The Female Man* (London: Women's Press, 1985), p. 126.

5 Homi K. Bhabha, 'The Other Question: Difference, Discrimination and the Discourse of Colonialism' in Russell Ferguson, Martha Gever, Trinh T. Minh-ha and Cornel West, eds, Out There: Marginalization and Contemporary Cultures (New York: The New Museum of Contemporary Art, 1990).

6 Cover graphic designed by Katharine Beecher Stetson Chamberlin; Schlesinger Library. Gilman Collection, Box 19, Folder 239.

7 Gunther Kress and Theo van Leeuwen, *Reading Images* (Geelong, Victoria: Deakin University Press, 1990).

Bibliography

Allen, Polly Wynn, *Building Domestic Liberty* (Amherst: University of Massachusetts Press, 1988).

Bakhtin, Mikhail, *Problems of Dostoevsky's Poetics*, trans. and ed. Caryl Emerson (Minneapolis: University of Minnesota Press, 1984).

Bammer, Angelika, *Partial Visions: Feminism and Utopianism in the 1970s* (London: Routledge, 1991).

Barton, George A., 'Ashtoreth and her Influence in the Old Testament', *Journal of Biblical Literature*, Tenth Year, 1891, Part II, pp. 73–91.

Bebel, August, *Woman in the Past, Present and Future*, 1st pub. 1883 (London: Zwan, 1988).

Beer, Janet, *Kate Chopin, Charlotte Perkins Gilman and Edith Wharton: Studies in Short Fiction* (Basingstoke: Macmillan, 1996).

Belenky, Mary Field et al., *Women's Ways of Knowing: The Development of Self, Voice, and Mind* (New York: Basic Books, 1986).

Bellamy, Edward, *Equality* (London: Heinemann, 1897).

Bellamy, Edward, *Looking Backward 2000–1887*, 1st pub. 1888 (New York and Toronto: The New American Library, 1960; Harmondsworth: Penguin, 1982).

Bhabha, Homi K., 'The Other Question: Difference, Discrimination and the Discourse of Colonialism', in Russell Ferguson, Martha Gever, Trinh T. Minh-ha and Cornel West, eds, *Out There: Marginalization and Contemporary Cultures* (New York: The New Museum of Contemporary Art, 1990).

Bleich, David, *Utopia: The Psychology of a Cultural Fantasy* (Ann Arbor: UMI Research Press, 1968).

Bloch, Ernst, *The Principle of Hope*, trans. Neville Plaice, Stephen Plaice and Paul Knight (Oxford: Blackwell, 1985).

Brown, Bill, 'Science Fiction, the World's Fair, and the Prosthetics of Empire, 1900–1915' in Amy Kaplan and Donal Pease, eds, *Cultures of United States Imperialism* (Durham and London: Duke University Press, 1993).

Buege, Douglas J., 'Rethinking Again', in Karen Warren, ed., *Ecological Feminism*, (London: Routledge, 1994).

Butler, Judith, *Bodies that Matter* (London: Routledge, 1993).

Callenbach, Ernest, *Ecotopia: The Notebooks and Reports of Edward Weston* (Berkeley: Banyan Tree Books, 1975).

Cameron, Deborah, *Feminism and Linguistic Theory* (London: Macmillan, 1985).

Campanella, Tomasso, *The City of the Sun: A Poetical Dialogue*, trans. Daniel J. Donno (Berkeley: University of California Press, 1981).

Campbell, Joseph, *The Power of Myth*, with Bill Moyers and Betty Sue Flowers, eds. (New York: Anchor Doubleday, 1988).

Caws, Mary Ann, *The Art of Interference: Stressed Readings in Verbal and Visual Communication* (Princeton, NJ: Princeton University Press, 1989).

Ceplair, Larry, ed., *Charlotte Perkins Gilman: A Nonfiction Reader* (New York: Columbia University Press, 1991).

Chimielewski, Wendy, 'Heaven on Earth: The Woman's Commonwealth, 1867–1983', in Wendy E. Chemielewski, Louis J. Kern and Marlyn Klee-Martzell, eds, *Women in Spiritual and Communitarian Societies in the United States* (Syracuse: Syracuse University Press, 1993), pp. 52–67.

Christ, Carol, *Diving Deep and Surfacing: Women Writers on a Spiritual Quest* (Boston: Beacon, 1980).

Clymer, Floyd, *Those Wonderful Old Automobiles*, (New York: McGraw-Hill, 1953).

Columbus, Christopher, *The Four Voyages of Christopher Columbus*, trans. Cecil Jane (New York: Dover, 1988).

Cranny-Francis, Anne, *Feminist Fiction: Feminist Revisions of Generic Fiction* (Cambridge: Polity Press, 1990; New York: St Martin's Press, 1990).

Cuomo, Christine, 'Ecofeminism, Deep Ecology, and Human Population', in Karen Warren, ed., *Ecological Feminism*, (London: Routledge, 1994).

Daly, Mary, *Outercourse: The Be-Dazzling Voyage* (San Francisco: Harper, 1992).

D'Eubonne, Françoise, 'Feminism or Death', in Elaine Marks and Isabelle de Courtivron, eds., *New French Feminisms: An Anthology*, (Amherst: University of Massachussets Press, 1980).

de Chateaubriand, François René, *Travels in America*, trans. Richard Switzer (Lexington: University of Kentucky Press, 1969).

Degler, Carl N., 'Charlotte Perkins Gilman on the Theory and Practice of Feminism', in Sheryl L. Meyering, ed., *Charlotte Perkins Gilman: The Woman and her Work* (Ann Arbor: UMI Research Press, 1989).

Dell, Floyd, *Love in the Machine Age: A Psychological Study of the Transition from Patriarchal Society* (New York: Farrar & Rhinehart, 1930).

Delphy, Christine and Diana Leonard, *Familiar Exploitation* (Cambridge: Polity Press, 1992).

Donaldson, Laura E., 'The Eve of De-struction: Charlotte Perkins Gilman and the Feminist Re-creation of Paradise', *Women's Studies*, 16, 1989.

Donawerth, Jane L. and Carol A. Kolmerten, (eds.,) *Utopian and Science Fiction by Women* (Liverpool: Liverpool University Press, 1994).

Dunne, Linda, 'Mothers and Monsters in Sarah Robinson Scott's *Millenium Hall*', in Jane L. Donawerth and Carol A. Kolmerten, eds., *Utopian and Science Fiction by Women* (Syracuse: Syracuse University Press, 1994) pp.54–72.

DuPlessis, Rachel Blau, 'The Feminist Apologues of Lessing, Piercy, and Russ', *Frontiers*, 4, Spring 1979, pp. 1–8.

Ellis, Havelock, *Man and Woman: A Study of Human Secondary Sexual Characteristics* (London: Walter Scott, 1904; New York: Arno, 1974).

Estes, Clarissa Pinkola, *Women Who Run with the Wolves: Myths and Stories of the Wild Woman Archetype* (New York: Ballantine, 1992).

Ferguson, Mary Anne, *Images of Women in Literature* (Boston:Houghton Mifflin, 1973).

Frye, Marilyn, *Willfull Virgin: Essays in Feminism* (Freedom, CA: Crossing, 1992).

Frye, Northrop, 'Varieties of Literary Utopias', in Frank E. Manuel, eds., *Utopias and Utopian Thought*, (Boston: Houghton Mifflin, 1966).

Galland, China, *Longing for Darkness: Tara and the Black Madonna, A Ten-Year Journey* (New York: Viking, 1990).

Gearhart, Sally Miller, *The Wanderground* (London: Women's Press, 1979).

Gilman, Charlotte Perkins, *Charlotte Perkins Gilman: A Non-Fiction Reader*, ed. Larry Ceplair (New York and Oxford: Columbia University Press, 1991).

Gilman, Charlotte Perkins, *The Charlotte Perkins Gilman Reader*, ed. Ann J. Lane (London: Women's Press, 1987, 1st pub. 1981).

Gilman, Charlotte Perkins, *The Diaries of Charlotte Perkins Gilman*, ed. Denise D. Knight, 2 vols (Charlottesville and London: University Press of Virginia, 1994).

Gilman, Charlotte Perkins, *The Forerunner*, intro. Madeline B. Stern (New York: Greenwood Reprint, 1968).

Gilman, Charlotte Perkins, *Herland* (1st pub. 1915), intro. by Ann J. Lane (London: Women's Press, 1979).

Gilman, Charlotte Perkins, *Herland and Selected Stories by Charlotte Perkins Gilman*, ed. Barbara H., (New York: Signet, 1992).

Gilman, Charlotte Perkins, *The Home: Its Work and Influence* (1st pub. 1903) intro. by William O'Neill (Urbana: University of Illinois Press, 1972).

Gilman, Charlotte Perkins, (as Stetson) *In This Our World* (Boston: Small, Maynard & Co., 1899).

Gilman, Charlotte Perkins, *The Living of Charlotte Perkins Gilman: An Autobiography*, intro. by Ann J. Lane (Madison: University of Wisconsin Press, 1991).

Gilman, Charlotte Perkins, *The Man Made World; or, Our Androcentric Culture* (New York: Charlton, 1911).

Gilman, Charlotte Perkins, 'The Man-Made World' (1911), in Lynne Sharon Schwartz, ed., *The Yellow Wallpaper and Other Writings by Charlotte Perkins Gilman* (New York: Bantam, 1989).

Gilman, Charlotte Perkins, *Moving the Mountain* (New York: Charlton, 1911).

Gilman, Charlotte Perkins, 'Our Brains and What Ails Them' (1912), in Larry Ceplair, ed., *Charlotte Perkins Gilman: A Nonfiction Reader* (New York: Columbia University Press, 1991).

Gilman, Charlotte Perkins, *Unpunished* (New York: Feminist Press, 1997).

Gilman, Charlotte Perkins, *Women and Economics*, 1st pub. 1898 (New York: Harper and Row, 1966; Amherst, NY: Prometheus, 1994).

Gilman, Charlotte Perkins, *The Yellow Wallpaper*, 1st pub. 1892, ed. Thomas L. Erskine and Connie L. Richards (New Brunswick: Rutgers University Press, 1993).

Gilman, Charlotte Perkins, *The Yellow Wallpaper and Other Writings by Charlotte Perkins Gilman*, ed. Lynne Sharon Schwartz (New York: Bantam, 1989).

Gilman, Charlotte Perkins, *'The Yellow Wallpaper' and Selected Stories*, ed. Denise D. Knight (Newark: Delaware Press, 1994).

Gilman, Charlotte Perkins, *The Yellow Wallpaper*, 1st pub. 1892, afterword by Elaine R. Hedges (London: Virago Press, 1981; New York: Feminist Press, 1973).

Gimbutas, Marija, *The Goddesses and Gods of Old Europe, 6500–3500 B.C.: Myth and Cult Images* (London: Thames and Hudson, 1982).

Goldfarb, Russell M., *Sexual Repression and Victorian Literature* (Lewisburg: Bucknell University Press, 1970).

Gough, Val, 'Lesbians and Virgins: The New Motherhood in *Herland*' in David Seed. ed., *Anticipations: Essays on Early Science Fiction and its Precursors* (Liverpool: Liverpool University Press, 1995), pp. 195–215.

Griffith, Nancy Snell, *Edward Bellamy: A Bibliography* (Metchuen, NJ: Scarecrow, 1986).

Gubar, Susan, '*She* in *Herland*: Feminism as Fantasy', in Sheryl L. Meyering, ed., *Charlotte Perkins Gilman: The Woman and her Work*, with a foreword by Cathy N. Davidson (Ann Arbor and London: UMI Research Press, 1989), pp. 191–202.

Hayden, Dolores, *The Grand Domestic Revolution* (Cambridge: MIT Press, 1981).

Heilbrun, Carolyn, *Writing a Woman's Life* (New York: W. W. Norton, 1988).

Heller, Adelle, and Lois Rudnick, ed., *Nineteen Fifteen: The Cultural Moment* (New Brunswick: Rutgers University Press, 1991).

Heyward, Carter, *Touching our Strength: The Erotic as Power and the Love of God* (San Francisco: Harper and Row, 1989).

Hill, Mary A., ed., *A Journey from Within: The Love Letters of Charlotte Gilman, 1896–1900* (Lewisburg: Bucknell University Press, 1995).

Hill, Mary A., *Charlotte Perkins Gilman: The Making of a Radical Feminist, 1860–1896* (Philadelphia: Temple University Press, 1980).

Hoy II, Pat C., Esther H. Schor and Robert DiYanni, eds, *Women's Voices: Visions and Perspectives* (New York: McGraw-Hill, 1990).

Hunter, Lynette, *Rhetorical Stance in Modern Literature: Allegories of Love and Death* (London: Macmillan, 1984).

Huxley, Aldous, *Island* (Harmondsworth: Penguin, 1981).

Johnston, Georgia, 'Exploring Lack and Absence in the Body/Text: Charlotte Perkins Gilman Prewriting Irigaray', *Women's Studies*, 21, 1992.

Jones, Howard Mumford, 'The Comic Spirit and Victorian Sanity', in Joseph E. Baker, ed., *The Reinterpretation of Victorian Literature* (New York: Russell and Russell, 1962).

Kagel, Steven, ed., *America: Exploration and Travel* (Bowling Green, OH: Bowling Green State University Press, 1979).

Kantrowitz, Barbara, 'Teenagers and AIDS', *Newsweek*, 3 August 1992, p. 46.

Kelvin, Norman, *The Collected Letters of William Morris: Volume 2* (Princeton: Princeton University Press, 1987).

Kessler, Carol Farley, *Charlotte Perkins Gilman: Her Progress Toward Utopia with Selected Writings* (Liverpool: Liverpool University Press, 1995).

Kessler, Carol Farley, ed., *Daring to Dream: Utopian Stories by United States Women: 1836–1919* (Boston, MA: Pandora-Routledge and Kegan Paul, 1984); 2nd edition, subtitled *Utopian Fiction by United States Women before 1950* (New York: Syracuse University Press, 1995).

Khanna, Lee Cullen, 'Women's Worlds: New Directions in Utopian Fiction', *Alternative Futures* 4 (2–3) 1981.

Kolodny, Annette, *The Lay of the Land: Metaphor as Experience and History in American Life and Letters* (Chapel Hill: University of North Carolina Press, 1975).

Kress, Gunther and Theo van Leeuwen, *Reading Images* (Geelong: Deakin University Press, 1990).

Kropotkin, Peter, *Mutual Aid: A Factor of Evolution*, first published 1902 (London: Freedom Press, 1987).

Lane, Ann J., ed., *The Charlotte Perkins Gilman Reader* (London: Women's Press, 1981).

Lane, Ann J., *To Herland and Beyond: The Life and Work of Charlotte Perkins Gilman* (New York: Meridian, 1991).

Lefanu, Sarah, *In the Chinks of the World Machine: Feminism and Science Fiction* (London: Women's Press, 1988).

Lerner, Gerda, *The Creation of Patriarchy* (New York: Oxford University Press, 1986).

Loeffelholz, Mary, *Experimental Lives: Women and Literature, 1900–1945* (New York: Twayne, 1992).

Luftig, Victor, *Seeing Together: Friendship between the Sexes in English Writing, from Mill to Woolf* (Stanford: Stanford University Press, 1993).

Malos, Ellen, *The Politics of Housework* (London: Allison and Busby, 1980).

Manual, Frank P. and Fritzie Manuel, *Utopian Thought in the Western World* (Oxford: Blackwell, 1979).

Marks, Elaine and Isabelle de Courtivron, ed., *New French Feminisms: An Anthology* (Amherst: University of Massachussets Press, 1980).

Marsh, Jan, 'Concerning Love: *News from Nowhere* and Gender', in Stephen Coleman and Paddy O'Sullivan, eds, *William Morris and News from Nowhere: A Vision for Our Time* (Bideford: Green Books, 1990).

Meyering, Sheryl, ed., *Charlotte Perkins Gilman: The Woman and her Work* (Ann Arbor: UMI Research Press, 1989).

More, Sir Thomas, *Utopia*, trans. Robert M. Adams (New York: Norton, 1992).

Morgan, Arthur Ernest, *Edward Bellamy* (New York: Columbia University Press, 1944).

Morgan, M., 'Marital Status, Health and Illness', *Social Science and Medicine*, 14A, 1980, pp. 633–43.

Morris, William, 'Looking Backward', in A. L. Morton, ed., *Political Writings of William Morris* (London: Lawrence and Wishart, 1984).

Morris, William, *News from Nowhere*, 1st pub. 1890 (London: Longmans, Green, 1902; London and Boston: Routledge and Kegan Paul, 1970).

Morton, Nelle, *The Journey is Home* (Boston: Beacon, 1985).

Moylan, Tom, *Demand the Impossible: Science Fiction and the Utopian Imagination* (New York: Methuen, 1986).

Muncy, Raymond Lee, *Sex and Marriage in Utopian Communities in Nineteenth Century America* (Bloomington: Indiana University Press, 1973).

Norris, Frank, *The Octopus: A Story of California* (New York: Doubleday, Page, 1901).

Pearson, Carol and Katherine Pope, *The Female Hero in British and American Fiction* (New York, 1981).

Plumwood, Val, 'Feminism and Ecofeminism: Beyond the Dualistic Assumptions of Women, Men and Nature', *The Ecologist*, 22 (1), 1992.

Plumwood, Val, *Feminism and the Mastery of Nature* (London: Routledge, 1993).

Pointon, Marcia, 'The Case of the Dirty Beau: Symmetry, Disorder and the Politics of Masculinity' in Kathleen Adler and Marcia Pointon, eds, *The Body Imaged: The Human Form and Visual Culture since the Renaissanc*

(Cambridge: Cambridge University Press, 1993, rpt 1994), pp. 175–89.

Poynton, Cate, *Language and Gender: Making the Difference* (Geelong, Victoria: Deakin University Press, 1985).

Ritzer, George, *The McDonaldization of Society* (Thousand Oaks, CA: Pine Forge Press, 1993).

Roost, Mary, *The Female Grotesque: Risk, Excess and Modernity* (New York and London: Routledge, 1994).

Russ, Joanna, *The Female Man* (London: Women's Press, 1985).

Salmon, Nicholas, Introduction to *William Morris, Political Writings: Contributions to Justice and Commonweal 1883–1890* (Bristol: Thoemmes, 1994).

Shange, Ntozake, *For Colored Girls who have Considered Suicide when the Rainbow is Enough* (New York: Bantam, 1982).

Showalter, Elaine, *Sexual Anarchy: Gender and Culture at the Fin de Siècle* (London: Bloomsbury, 1991).

Silkp, Leslie, *Almanac of the Dead* (New York: Simon and Schuster, 1991); *Ceremony* (New York: Viking, 1971).

Spanos, William V., *The Errant Art of Moby Dick. The Canon, the Cold War and the Struggle for American Studies* (Durham, NC: Duke University Press, 1995).

Spender, Dale, *The Writing or the Sex? or Why you Don't Have to Read Women's Writing to Know it's No Good* (New York: Pergamon, 1989).

Spretnak, Charlene, 'The Myth of Demeter and Persephone', in Judith Plaskow and Carol Christ, eds, *Weaving the Visions: New Patterns in Feminist Spirituality* (San Francisco: Harper and Row, 1989), pp. 72–74.

Stanton, Elizabeth Cady, *The Woman's Bible*, intro. by Dale Spender (Edinburgh: Polygon, 1985).

Stowe, Harriet Beecher, *Uncle Tom's Cabin: or, Life Among the Lowly* ed. Elizabeth Ammons, A Norton Critical Edition (New York and London: W. W. Norton, 1994).

Stuart-Wortley, Lady Emmeline Charlotte Elizabeth, 'REFORM—LIBERTY—MARCH OF INTELLECT—EQUALITY', *Impressions of Italy and Other Poems* (London: Saunders and Otley, 1837), *English Poetry Full-Text Database*, rel. 5, CD-ROM (Cambridge: Chadwyck, 1993).

Thompson, Paul, *The Work of William Morris* (Oxford: Oxford University Press, 1991).

Thoreau, Henry David, *Walden or Life in the Woods*, 1st pub. 1854, (New York: New American Library, 1960).

Tiptree, James, 'Houston, Houston, Do You Read?', in Susan Anderson and Vonda McIntyre, eds, *Aurora: Beyond Equality* (New York: Fawcett, 1976).

Todorov, Tzvetan, *Genres in Discourse* (Cambridge: Cambridge University

Press, 1990).

Tong, Deborah, *Feminist Thought* (London: Routledge, 1992).

Tooley, Sarah, 'A Living Wage for Women', *The Women's Signal*, 19 April 1894, *The Journal of the William Morris Society* 10 (4) Spring 1994, pp. 5–9.

Walby, Sylvia, *Theorizing Patriarchy* (Oxford: Blackwell, 1990.

Warren, Karen, ed., *Ecological Feminism* (London: Routledge, 1994).

Wells, H. G., *In the Days of the Comet* (London: Macmillan, 1906).

Whitford, Margaret, *Luce Irigaray: Philosophy in the Feminine* (London: Routledge, 1991).

Index